DRAWING

A CONTEMPORARY APPROACH

Sixth Edition

Teel Sale
Claudia Betti

THO

D1510469

THOMSON
WADSWORTH

Drawing: A Contemporary Approach, **Sixth Edition**
Teel Sale and Claudia Betti

Publisher: Clark Baxter
Development Editor: Erikka Adams
Assistant Editor: Erikka Adams
Editorial Assistant: Nell Pepper
Development Project Manager: Julie Yardley
Executive Marketing Manager: Diane Wenckeback
Marketing Assistant: Kathleen Tosiello
Marketing Communications Manager: Brian Chaffee
Senior Project Manager, Editorial Production: Kimberly Adams
Creative Director: Rob Hugel
Executive Art Director: Maria Epes
Print Buyer: Doreen Suruki

Permissions Editor: Ron Montgomery
Production Service: Pre-Press Company, Inc.
Text Designer: Jerry Wilke
Photo Researcher: Sarah Schneider
Cover Designer: Jerry Wilke
Cover Image: Jane Hammond, *Still Life with Seal,* 1999, 35½" x 29½". Acrylic, gouache, graphite, crayon, solvent transfers, color Xerox, linoleum, block prints, and rubber stamps on collaged Japanese papers. Private Collection, NY, NY. Photo credit: Peter Muscato.
Cover Printer: Courier Corporation/Kendallville
Compositor: Pre-Press Company, Inc.
Printer: Courier Corporation/Kendallville

Printed in the United States of America
1 2 3 4 5 6 7 11 10 09 08 07

Library of Congress Control Number: 2006931532

ISBN-13: 978-0-495-09491-3
ISBN-10: 0-495-09491-9

Thomson Higher Education
10 Davis Drive
Belmont, CA 94002-3098
USA

For more information about our products, contact us at:
Thomson Learning Academic Resource Center
1-800-423-0563

For permission to use material from this text or product, submit a request online at **http://www.thomsonrights.com**.
Any additional questions about permissions can be submitted by e-mail to **thomsonrights@thomson.com**.

Preface

The word *contemporary* in this book's title has two implications: First, the drawing methods are up to date; and second, the artistic concepts considered in the selection of the illustrations are current. Contemporary drawing involves complex responses, innovative practices, and reassessment of definitions. I have emphasized art's multidimensional pursuit of significance, which frequently means going beyond the conventional rules of composition.

In *Drawing: A Contemporary Approach* the formal elements are presented through a study of spatial relationships. The text is built around a series of related problems, each of which is designed to develop fluency in drawing, offer experience in handling media, foster self-confidence, and promote an understanding of art elements and their role in the development of pictorial space. Further, the text introduces a vocabulary that reflects dynamic new concepts and concerns in art.

This book presents rationally determined problems in a logical sequence, and this edition contains updated problems that reflect today's art techniques and visions. All of the problems have been designed to stimulate students to make sensitive, intelligent, and emotive responses in solving them. Relevant to this goal is the addition of sketchbook and computer projects in each chapter.

In this new edition I have aimed for the full spectrum of drawing practices used by the present generation of artists. This book investigates the numerous means contemporary artists employ to re-envision the common perception of an image, and the many ways they extend the limits of conventional art space.

Diligence and commitment to the practice of drawing are hallmarks of this book. The broad range of art production featured in the illustrations demonstrates to the student the indispensable role of drawing in every aspect of art making.

In keeping with current art trends, this edition includes the work of international artists, ethnic artists, and self-taught artists. Engagement with another culture's art is like learning another language; it enriches our understanding and broadens our vision.

Readers can gain important insights into the complexity of the role of drawing by considering the topics highlighted in Chapter 11, "A Look at Drawing Today." This chapter features major trends in drawing over the last five years, focusing on the younger generation of artists and the expansive role drawing has staked out for itself in recent years.

I wish to thank those who have assisted and encouraged me in preparing this edition, especially my husband, Rick, a great art companion and editor, and my artist son, Tom, who prepared the computer projects and collaborated on designing new problems. I would like to express appreciation to the reviewers for this edition: Diane Banks, James Madison University; Thom Bohnert, Mott Community College; Michael Campbell, Shippensburg University; Dylan Collins, Kent State University; Robert Kelly Detweiler, Santa Clara University; Christina Fuentes, Texas Tech University; Dana Hargrove, Rollins College; Jan P. Johnson, Broward Community College; Craig Lloyd, College of Mount St. Joseph; Elizabeth F. Leeor, Old Dominion University; Lenore McKerlie, University of Colorado; Darlene L. Swaim, Mesa Community College at Red Mountain; and Ruth Trotter, University of La Verne. I would also like to express my appreciation to the Thomson/Wadsworth team for their hard work and support: Clark Baxter, Allison Roper, Anne Gittinger, Kim Adams, and Diane Wenckebach. I want to acknowledge especially the designer Jerry Wilke.

It remains my hope that this book not only helps prepare students for a career in art but for a life in art as well.

Teel Sale
Denton, Texas
July 2006

For my family, who practice and live their art.
T.S.

Contents

PART 2
Spatial Relationships of the Art Elements

PART 4
Practical Guides

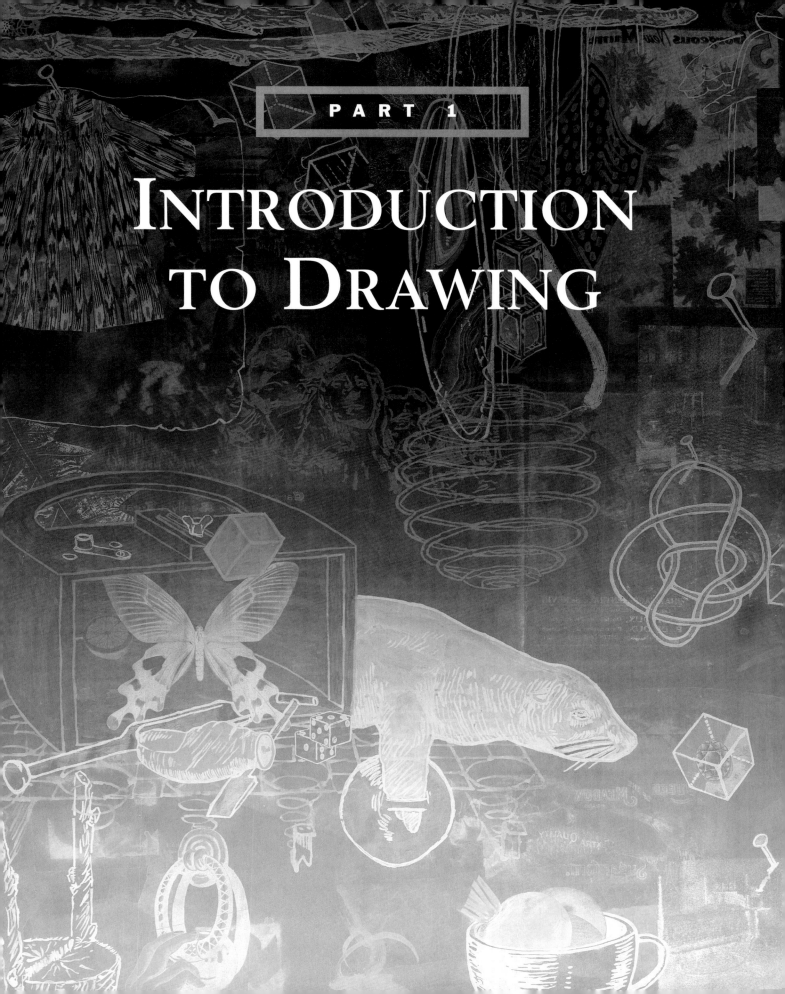

PART 1

INTRODUCTION TO DRAWING

CHAPTER 1

Drawing is all. —ALBERTO GIACOMETTI

Drawing: Definitions and Purposes

rawing is a complex, energetic, and ever-contemporary activity. It serves a variety of purposes: from accurate description to informal notation; from social commentary to playful, inventive meandering; from psychological revelation to dramatic impact. Art—especially the discipline of drawing—along with philosophy, history, and literature helps us interpret our experiences visually, emotionally, and aesthetically. For the visual artist, drawing is the very core of interpreting our experiences. It speaks in a voice like no other art form. Drawing provides a common ground for communication; it offers us a dialogue with ourselves and with others, the viewers. It engages us on vital emotional, intellectual, and spiritual levels. Drawing can turn fragile material into conceptual strength. It can record a fleeting movement with the sweep of the implement across the page, as is seen in the drawing by the Korean artist Yooah Park *(figure 1.1)*. It extends both mind and spirit by promoting a deep respect for looking and thinking. It is the most delectable of all the arts.

As an art form, drawings have a special appeal because of their immediacy and their ability to reveal how they were made. A drawing can be autobiographical, political,

1.1. YOOAH PARK. *Movement II.* Meok Oriental ink on paper, 1'1" x 4'7" (35 cm x 1.4 m). *Collection Park Ryu Sook Gallery, Seoul. Walker Art Center, Minneapolis, Minn.*

polemical, didactic, playful, dramatic, poetic, informative, or conceptual. It can be as quiet as a single mark or as busy as an anthill. It can be as small as a stamp or as monumental as a wall. The wall drawing by Julie Mehretu *(figure 1.2)* turns abstraction in a new direction. She draws complex action-packed maps that explore a fictional world.

DRAWING ACROSS TIME AND CULTURE

Drawing connects us directly to artists worldwide. The healing effect of expressing one's feelings through visual means is employed by people of all ages and from all parts of the globe. The act of drawing can evoke memories, call up feelings, or shed light on life's impulses—on death, love, power, play, intellectual pursuits, work, and on our dreams and emotions. The drawing in *figure 1.3* was made by Yasuko Yamagata, a 49-year-old Japanese survivor of the "unforgettable fire" caused by the atomic bomb dropped on Hiroshima in 1945. Alongside the drawing is a written description of that event. Although Yamagata is not a professional artist and, in fact, the drawing was made more than 30 years after the bombing, the impressions it conveys reverberate with the horror and immediacy of the moment. This drawing conveys a human response that speaks volumes more than mere media accounts.

1.2. JULIA MEHRETU. *Implosion/ Explosion* (detail). 2001. Ink and latex on wall, dimensions variable. *Courtesy The Project and The Studio Museum in Harlem, New York.*

1.3. **YASUKO YAMAGATA.** From *Unforgettable Fire, Pictures Drawn by Atomic Bomb Survivors.* *Hiroshima Peace Culture Foundation, Hiroshima.* © *By Permission of NHK (Japanese Broadcasting Corp.) and Hiroshima Peace Culture Foundation.*

The concentration required in looking at and questioning the appearance of objects and the sheer exuberance of making things has not changed since the earliest drawings were made. In some deeply satisfying way, mark making affirms our presence in the world. From cave paintings to the present, we find that directness and physicality are basic to drawing. Samia Halaby's drawing *(figure 1.4)* is made up of exuberant overlapping marks of varying weight and width to create an abstract landscape. The 18 foot drawing recalls the olive orchards of the artist's home in the West Bank of Palestine.

The African artist Michael Abyi deals with a mythic subject in *The Twins Who Killed Their Father Because of His Properties (figure 1.5)*. The artist's fertile imagination has conceived fantastic creatures made up of invented textures and shapes in a compact space.

1.4. **SAMIA HALABY.** *Olive Orchard in My Studio.* 2000. Acrylic on paper, 75" x 175" (1.9 m x 4.4 m). *Skoto Gallery.*

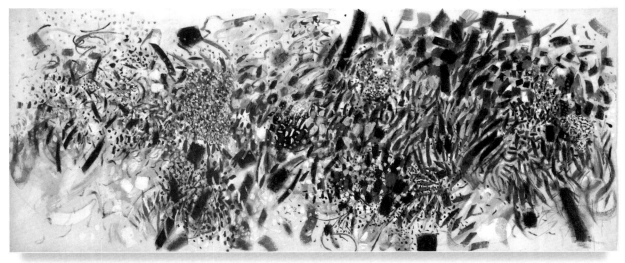

1.5. **MICHAEL ABYI.** *The Twins Who Killed Their Father Because of His Properties.* Ink on fabric, 2'9" x 1'10" (84 cm x 56 cm). *Collection Claudia Betti. Photo by Pramuan Burusphat.*

Masami Teraoka's watercolor *(figure 1.6)* combines a traditional Japanese style with contemporary Western materialistic ideas. The artist looks back to seventeenth-century Japanese art for technique, style, and image and invests it with a modern message. The Samurai Businessman is weighted down with accoutrements of the modern world—briefcase, watch, and calculator. His upward gaze, a convention in Japanese art, lends a note of insecurity, not a trait of a real samurai warrior.

Drawings such as Abyi's and Teraoka's are valued for their potential to work through ideas. This conceptual approach is called visual thinking; along with much practice at making and looking at drawings comes the more evolved stage of visual literacy and acceptance of different cultures, ideas, and people.

Drawings can be made with the most modest of means—look at the Zairian children drawing in the sand in *figure 1.7*. Not only artists make drawings, of course; people of all ages and from all walks of life participate joyfully in this activity.

SOME HISTORY OF DRAWING

Across time and cultures, drawing has always ranked high among the visual arts. From the Renaissance to the end of the nineteenth century, drawing was regarded as a conservative medium, seldom the subject of innovation. It was seen as a first step

1.6. **MASAMI TERAOKA.** *Samurai Businessman Going Home.* 1981. Watercolor on paper, 1'1¼" x 9¾" (34 cm x 25 cm). *Private collection*, New York. *Pamela Auchincloss Gallery.*

1.7. Photo of Zairian children. *AFP Photo/Christophe Simon.*

in the early idea of a work, a support to painting, sculpture, and architecture, and it still serves artists in this manner, as can be seen in *figure 1.8*. Arshile Gorky's preparatory drawing is derived from a photograph taken in Armenia. Using this image, a double portrait of himself and his mother, he painted two versions. Gorky drew and redrew many preliminary sketches and studies, confirming the conceptual effort that went into their making. The drawing has been overlaid by a grid to help the artist accurately transfer the image to the canvas in preparation for painting.

In the Renaissance, drawing was particularly suitable for visually describing the emerging disciplines of anatomy, perspective, and geometry. It was only in the seventeenth century that collectors began to display drawings in rooms called "cabinets," rooms with specially built storage drawers where drawings could be taken out, admired, and studied. Drawing—no longer a subsidiary to painting, sculpture, and architecture—was established as a major discipline in its own right. The assumption that drawing derives its imagery from objects in the real world has been undermined. An alternative tradition, the tradition of abstraction, was firmly established in the twentieth century. From the 1950s to the present, there has been a graphic explosion unlike any other period in art. The World Wide Web is itself a web of images.

1.8. **ARSHILE GORKY.** Sketch for ***Portrait of the Artist and His Mother.*** 1926–1936. Graphite on squared paper paper, 2' x 1'7" (61 cm x 48.3 cm). *Alisa Mellon Bruce Fund, Photograph © 2002 Board of Trustees, National Gallery of Art, Washington. © 2007 Artists Rights Society (ARS), New York.*

Drawings were traditionally classified into four types:

1. Those that investigate, study, and question the real, visible, tangible world.
2. Those that record objects and events.
3. Those that communicate ideas.
4. Those that are transcriptions from memory—a way of collecting and keeping impressions and ideas, a way of making visible the world of our imagination.

Contemporary drawings expand this classification. New graphic technologies are introduced daily, and because drawing has proven to be a flexible discipline for experimentation, it has gained strength and vitality from its newfound role. We can easily classify computer-generated images as drawings. They make use of graphic means, they employ the art elements of line, color, shape, texture, and value, and they are on paper *(figure 1.9)*. The series of drawings *(figure 1.10)* by Terry Winters illustrates his interest in digital, mechanical, and reproductive printing processes. His wall of drawings resembles a set of spinning helixes; the weblike lines could be forms seen under a microscope.

The definition of "drawing" has now expanded beyond pure graphic means (a more traditional definition), and the term "works on paper" emerged to designate a broader category to include printmaking, photography, book illustration, and posters. Even this expanded classification does not fully cover the contemporary role of drawing because mark making can be done on any surface—clay, glass, fabric, even on the earth itself.

Today drawing is a preeminent medium: It is economical—that is, ideas and images can be quickly sketched; it is flexible; it is open to experimentation. New technologies stretch its boundaries even further—the reaches of drawing have yet to be approached. Drawing has a physical allure; the various drawing media and surfaces are sensual and appealing.

Contemporary drawing has been redefined, reinvented, and reinvigorated. Expanded freedom in all art forms is a characteristic of our times and drawing has been in the forefront of innovation. Jane Hammond's work *(figure 1.11 and front cover)* is an example of the expanded and emancipated role of drawing in contemporary art. Hammond has been called the quintessential artist on paper of our time.

1.9. **JOSEPHA LOSADA-STEVENSON.** *Drawing Picasso 1.* 1989. Color thermal transfer and lithograph from computer-generated image, 1'5" x 1'8" (43.4 cm x 51 cm). *Courtesy of the artist.*

1.10. **TERRY WINTERS. *Black and White Examples*** (1–24). 1997. Ink on paper, 8½" x 11" (21.6 cm x 27.9 cm) each. *Courtesy of the artist and Matthew Marks Gallery, New York.*

TYPES OF DRAWINGS

Just as there are different uses for drawings (architectural design, scientific drawings, filmmaker storyboards), there are many types of drawings. In this section we look at the following types of drawings: subjective and objective drawing, informational drawing, and schematic drawing.

Subjective and Objective Drawing

In its broadest division, drawing can be classified as either subjective or objective. Subjective drawing emphasizes the artist's emotions; objective drawing, on the other hand, conveys information, not feelings. Subjective drawings can be expressive and intuitive; objective drawings are more rational and logical.

A drawing that combines both the subjective and objective approach can be seen in *figure 1.12* by the humorist Charles Addams. The left side of the drawing is an elevation of the facade of the Carnegie Mansion (now the Cooper-Hewitt National Design Museum); it is concerned with design information such as measurement, scale, and proportion between parts, and thus belongs to the objective category. The right half of the drawing, however, is subjective, ridiculous and playful in its embellishment of the building. Addams has ensconced his macabre cartoon characters in and under the mansion.

Another set of drawings that clearly contrasts the subjective and objective approach features skulls. For an anatomical illustration *(figure 1.13)* it is important that every part be clearly visible and descriptive. The illustrator has used shading to indicate receding spaces and has grouped lines to show the bulging features of the skull.

1.11. **JANE HAMMOND.** *Silver Rider.*
1999. Mixed media on Japanese paper,
3'6½" x 2'8½" (1.08 m x 82 cm).
Private collection, New York. Photo by
Peter Muscato.

1.12. **CHARLES ADDAMS** (United States,
1912–1988). ***Embellished Elevation of
the Carnegie Museum.*** 1975. Watercolor on Photostat, 16¹⁄₁₆" x 21⁷⁄₁₆"
(45 cm x 64.6 cm). *Cooper-Hewitt
National Design Museum, Smithsonian
Institution. Gift of Nino Luciano,
1975–87–1.* © Tee and Charles Addams
Foundation.

1.13. Anatomical drawing of a skull

The skull has always been a popular artistic and literary image because of its emotionally loaded content. Jean-Michel Basquiat depicted his mask-like animated skull using a crude technique that is characteristic of his work *(figure 1.14)*. He drew the images in a primitive style that supports the underlying content. Basquiat's cryptic imagery takes on the appearance of a secret, symbolic, hieroglyphic language. The play on the word *flea* and its homonym or sound twin *flee* gives us a clue to unravel the artist's coded message. The trailing lines suggest a pathway leading off the page; the gas pumps are a power source for movement, and together the images reinforce the idea of fleeing. The repeated phrase "All men return to dust" reiterates the idea of a journey. The dominant death's head leaves the viewer in no doubt that the journey Basquiat has in mind is the final one.

Basquiat's subjective style not only conveys the artist's heightened feelings but engenders a heightened response from the viewer as well. His handling of the media supports the raw and unwelcome message.

Informational Drawing

Informational drawing falls under the objective category and includes diagrammatic and architectural drawings (sometimes called mechanical drawings). Informational drawings present plans that allow measurements to be interpreted; they help to clarify concepts and ideas that are not actually visible. Many serious

1.14. **JEAN-MICHEL BASQUIAT.** *Untitled (Fleas).* 1986. Graphite, oilstick, and ink on paper, 3'6" x 2'5⅞" (1.07 m x 74 cm). © *2007 The Estate of Jean-Michel Basquiat/ADAGP, Paris/ARS, New York. Robert Miller Gallery, BASQ-1124.*

twentieth-century artists have used art as documentation and information. The
husband-and-wife art collaborators Christo and Jeanne-Claude wrap and curtain
landscape sites as well as urban structures such as bridges and buildings; dramatic
and unexpected sculptural forms result. They use Christo's drawings in their pre-
sentations requesting permission from authorities to execute their involved work.
Figure 1.15 is a drawing made for a project in Colorado, proposing the installation
of a series of horizontal fabric panels over the Arkansas River. Christo combines
photographs, collage, and drawing to create an accurate visual description of the
curtained river, as it will appear when installed. The viewer is presented with two
categories of visual information. The contour map at the top of the drawing gives
the exact location of the segment of the river to be covered. The schematic map
traces the contours of the adjacent mountains and highlights the path of the river.
In 2005 *The Gates* was a major Christo installation in New York's Central Park.
Christo's drawings are an invaluable means to communicate complex spatial and
structural solutions.

Diagrammatic drawings, a type of working drawing used by designers, architects,
and engineers, demonstrate a visual form of shorthand. These proposal drawings are
used widely in designs for buildings and city planning. ***Plan drawings*** make use of a
code or a key that relays essential data contained in the drawing, such as information concerning construction materials and scale.

1.16. **ZAHA HADID. *Site Plan, Grand
Buildings, Trafalgar Square London,
1985.*** *Zaha Hadid Architects.*

The architect Zaha Hadid, born in Baghdad and now working in London, has
achieved worldwide acclaim for the innovative nature of her architectural designs. To
convey her new visions, she has adopted radical methods of representation, departing
from traditional architectural drawings. In *figure 1.16* we see one of her dynamic site
plan drawings. Hadid combines the traditional flat, two-dimensional plan with an illusionistic three-dimensional segment that emerges from the center of the drawing.

Just as there is a key to reading a diagrammatic drawing, there is a key to reading
artists' drawings, and that key, as exhibited in Hadid's work, is to be open, alert, absorbed, and focused on the visual material at hand.

Schematic Drawing

Another type of objective drawing is the ***schematic*** or ***conceptual drawing***, a mental construct rather than an exact transcription of visual reality. A biologist's schematic drawing of a molecular structure is a model used for instructional purposes. Comic book characters and stick figures in instruction manuals are familiar examples of schematic drawings. These are visual conventions: We know what they stand for and how to read them. Schematic drawings are an economical way to give information visually.

In schematic drawing, the two broad categories of subjective and objective overlap. A schematic or conceptual drawing may be objective, such as those used in an instruction manual. Or it may also be subjective, like a child's drawing in which the proportions of the figure are exaggerated and scale is determined by importance rather than by actual visual reality.

Saul Steinberg uses the schematic, cartoon approach in a subjective manner to parody contemporary life. In *Main Street (figure 1.17)* he employs a number of conventions to indicate movement. The swirling lines used to depict the clouds suggest a turbulent sky; the cloud and ball, trailing long shadows, seem to be scurrying along at a quicker pace than the rather static figure, whose thrown-back arms and billowing skirt are indicators of a slower motion. The humorous intent is intensified by a shorthand style. In other words, "reading" the conventions is part of the enjoyment of the work; it is like recognizing an inside joke. Steinberg thought of drawing as a kind of writing. His work crosses the division between popular and fine art. It appears in galleries, on magazine and book covers, and is published in the form of cartoons and posters. A flourishing movement in contemporary art involves schematized drawings that employ apparently direct and simple means to carry sophisticated ideas and subjective expression.

SUBJECT AND TREATMENT

Broad categories of subjects for drawing (and art in general) include landscape, still life, and figure drawing. But how do artists treat these subjects? There are

innumerable modes of expression. Landscape, or nature, is a constant supplier of imagery, both for the ideas it offers and for the structural understanding of form it gives. Widely different treatments of the subject of landscape can be seen in the drawings by Halaby *(see figure 1.4)*, Christo *(see figure 1.15)*, and Ernesto Caivano *(figure 1.18)*.

Halaby treats landscape as an abstraction, whereas Christo proposes changes to an existing landscape and Caivano suggests a narrative or allegory. Caivano's work crosses the border between imagination and observation. His narrative drawings are not shown in a linear sequence; it is up to the viewer to create the story line—the viewer must creatively enter into the creative process. Caivano's seven-foot, scroll-like drawing refers to Oriental landscape paintings. His images span a broad range of sources, from John James Audubon's birds to Stealth bomber technology.

1.19. **SHIMON OKSHTEYN.** *Man's Shoe.*
1994. Pencil and graphite on canvas,
6' x 6'4" (1.83 m x 1.93 m). *Courtesy of
the artist and Stux Gallery, New York.*

Some artists treat an image with almost photographic realism and accuracy. There are several types of realism, such as naturalism, surrealism, photo-realism, and hyper-realism. Realistic artists are as interested in how an image is represented as they are in the subject depicted. Note the high degree of concentrated observation that went into Shimon Okshteyn's drawing of a man's shoe *(figure 1.19).* The monumental scale (over six feet by six feet) is also impressive. This pencil and graphite drawing can be classified as hyper-realistic.

Francesco Clemente presents himself in two states of being in his double portrait *(figure 1.20).* His self-portraits deal with introspection and mystical intimations. A drawing, then, may be slightly or highly expressionistic; there are as many degrees of subjectivity as there are artists.

1.20. **FRANCESCO CLEMENTE.** *Codice 1.*
1980. Pastel and tint, 2' x 1'6" (61 cm x 45.8 cm). *Collection of the artist, Rome and New York.*

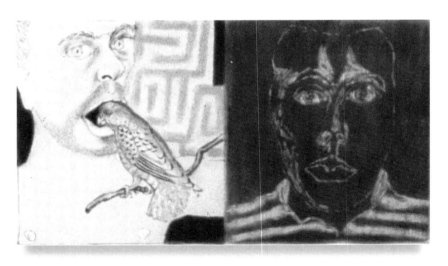

Some artists find significance in a commonplace subject, as in the Louise Bourgeois house *(figure 1.21)*. How does Bourgeois treat this subject? Bourgeois's image is reductive, abstracted, and symbolic. "This woman is in a state of semiconsciousness," Bourgeois says, "because, first of all, she believes she can hide, which is a foolishness; nobody can hide anything. And secondly, nobody would present herself naked the way she does. . . . She does not know that she is half naked, and she does not know that she is trying to hide. That is to say, she is totally self-defeating because she shows herself at the very moment that she thinks she's hiding" (Bourgeois, p. 45). Bourgeois's work (she is a preeminent sculptor) is fraught with trepidation, pain, anger, and guilt. Her work is full of tension between self-revelation and withdrawal. As the critic Lawrence Rinder said, "For Bourgeois, making drawings is as necessary as locking the door each night" (Bourgeois, p. 12). She says, "Drawings have a featherlike quality. Sometimes you think of something and it is so light, so slight, that you don't have time to make a note in your diary. Everything is fleeting, but your drawing will serve as a reminder; otherwise it is forgotten" (Bourgeois, p. 21).

Drawings not specifically intended for a viewing audience do not prevent our enjoyment of them. Jean Tinguely's quick sketch of a machine *(figure 1.22)* offers insight into his playful mind. The treatment is a mix of schematic drawing, verbal notation, and numerical calculations. Tinguely, a Swiss sculptor whose inventions were designed to incorporate unpredictable motions, makes a wry commentary on the role of machines in our technological society. His drawing style conveys the idea of a machine taking on a life of its own. This intimate sketch gives a glimpse into Tinguely's offbeat creative process.

Both the exotic and the commonplace are equally provocative subjects for the artist. An image can be treated symbolically, standing for something more than the literal image, as in Yolanda M. López's *Portrait of the Artist as the Virgin of Guadalupe (figure 1.23)*. The artist gives explicit directions for interpreting her drawing in its title. López is a Chicana artist who seeks to undermine the clichés of her culture. In this drawing, López casts the Mexican icon, the Virgin of Guadalupe, as a modern, athletic young woman grasping a serpent, a symbol of her nation, and

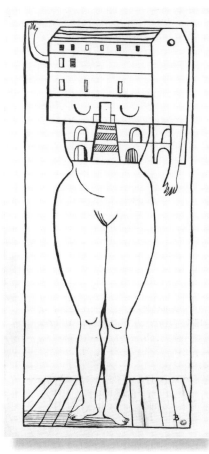

1.21. **LOUISE BOURGEOIS.** *Femme Maison.* 1947. Ink on paper, 9⁵⁄₁₆" x 7⅛" (25.2 cm x 18 cm). *Solomon R. Guggenheim Museum, New York 92.4008.* © *Louise Bourgeois/Licensed by VAGA, New York.*

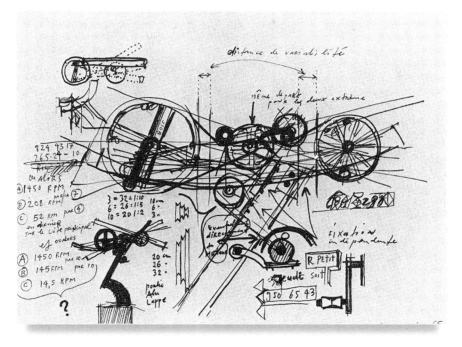

1.22. **JEAN TINGUELY.** *Study of Machine.* 1965. Ink, 1'5⅝" x 1'3⅞" (32 cm x 40 cm). *Courtesy Iolas-Jackson Gallery, New York.* © *2007 Artists Rights Society (ARS), New York/ADAGP, Paris. Photograph Ivan Dalla-Tana.*

1.23. YOLANDA M. LÓPEZ. *Portrait of the Artist as the Virgin of Guadalupe.* 1978. Oil pastel on paper, 2'8" x 2' (81 cm x 61 cm). *Collection of the artist. Photo: Bob Hsiang.*

1.24. PABLO PICASSO (1881–1973). © ARS, NY. ***The Judgment of Paris.*** March 31–April 7, 1951. Wash and Pen, 50.6 cm x 65.6 cm. *© 2007 Estate of Pablo Picasso/Artists Rights Society (ARS), New York. Photo: Thierry Le Mage. Photo Credit: Réunion des Musées Nationaux/Art Resource, NY. Musée Picasso, Paris, France.*

trailing a star-studded cape as she bursts out of the flame-shaped halo. Although the artist takes a humorous approach, she intends serious political implications.

Pablo Picasso's style or treatments of subjects are widely recognized. In *figure 1.24* we see several distinct styles, all hallmarks of Picasso's virtuosity as one of the premier draftsmen of the twentieth century. Not only is his style personal, his themes are stated in a highly personal way. In *The Judgment of Paris*, Picasso takes a surreal riff on a classical theme. The three goddesses become more armored and machinelike from left to right. The figure of Paris in the lower right-hand corner is diminished in scale and unequal to his task.

Some works are more meaningful when viewed in relation to art history or in the context of cultural differences. Art history is a never-ending source for subjects and treatments—for new ideas, or for old ideas reworked with fresh insight. Michael Hurson's sketch *(figure 1.25)*, an interpretation of Georges Seurat's famous painting, is one such example.

Creating a work of art about art is a favorite subject for artists. The image can be an object taken from the real world and then altered beyond recognition, as in the oversized comic book style work by the Pop artist Roy Lichtenstein *(figures 1.26, 1.27, and 1.28)*. Trained as a commercial artist, Lichtenstein worked in a stylized, abstract manner. His comic book style works on a double level as both fine art and commercial art. In these three works, we see an image of a bull abstracted through a number of stages. Lichtenstein selected his images from both popular and art-historical sources; here he makes a wry comment mirroring the style of the twentieth-century Dutch painter, Piet Mondrian. Lichtenstein was fond of images that are clichés, borrowed images that he invested with humor and irony.

1.25. **MICHAEL HURSON.** *Seurat Drawing #6.* February 24–26, 2001. Graphite, ink, pastel on paper, 1'2½" x 1'9¼" (36.83 cm x 53.95 cm). *Courtesy of the artist and Paula Cooper Gallery, New York.*

1.26. **ROY LICHTENSTEIN.** *Bull I* from *Bull Profile Series.* 1973. One-color linecut, 2'3" x 2'11" (69 cm x 89 cm). *© Estate of Roy Lichtenstein/ Gemini G.E.L.*

1.27. **ROY LICHTENSTEIN.** *Bull III* from *Bull Series.* 1973. Six-color lithograph, screenprint, linecut, 2'3" x 2'11" (69 cm x 89 cm). *© Estate of Roy Lichtenstein/ Gemini G.E.L.*

1.28. ROY LICHTENSTEIN. *Bull IV* from *Bull Series.* 1973. Five-color lithograph, screenprint, linecut, 2'3" x 2'11" (69 cm x 89 cm). © *Estate of Roy Lichtenstein/ Gemini G.E.L.*

1.29. LOUISA CHASE. *Untitled.* 1987. Oil on canvas, 6'6" x 7' (1.98 m x 2.13 m). *Courtesy Brooke Alexander, New York.*

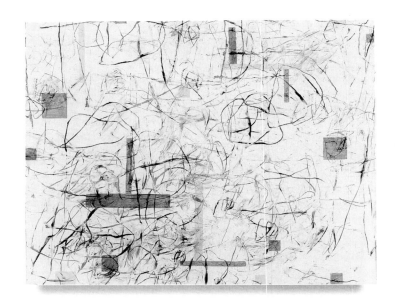

Mondrian's work is nonobjective; Lichtenstein's is abstract. (In the visual arts, work that intends no reference to objects or persons is called ***nonobjective. Abstraction*** is an alteration of forms derived from observation or experience in such a way as to present essential rather than particular qualities.)

A final note on subject and treatment: Louisa Chase's drawing on canvas *(figure 1.29)* is an example of how mark making can be the subject of art. The confined geometric shapes recede into a field of vigorously stated, layered marks. Try to imagine the work in its original size, over six feet by seven feet. The marks become sweeping gestures, tracing the physical motion of the artist as she worked. The drawing becomes a record of movement, time, and energy. Chase employs two modes—one using simple geometric shapes and the other asserting obviously handmade, random marks. She imposes diametrically opposed orders. It is as if something had gone awry in the Mondrian composition. Could we be witnessing a graffiti attack on an early modern work?

CONCLUSION

The process of drawing develops a heightened awareness of the visual world, an awareness that is both subjective (knowing how you feel about things) and objective (understanding how things actually operate). Perception, the faculty of gaining knowledge through insight or intuition by means of the senses, is molded by subjectivity as well as by the facts of the world. Art is a reflection of the culture in which it is made.

Drawing affords you an alternative use of experience. It provides a new format for stating what you know about the world. Through drawing you are trained to make fresh responses and are furnished with a new way of making meaning. Finally, drawing teaches you to observe, distinguish, and relate.

The therapeutic value of art is well accepted; the intellectual benefits are many. Art is a way of realizing one's individuality. Creativity and mental growth work in tandem. The making of art, the making of the self, and the development of one's own personal style are all a part of the same process.

We have looked at a few of the many reasons why artists draw and a few of the many means available to artists; now the exciting process of drawing begins.

CHAPTER 2

Drawing is a verb. —RICHARD SERRA

Learning to See: Gesture and Other Beginning Line Exercises

Artists learn to draw a subject by following its forms. The time it takes to map out these forms is an essential element in drawing. The mark that records the movement of the artist's implement, a two-dimensional movement in space, is the most basic feature of drawing. In addition to this spatial notation, drawings evoke a time response—the time required to make the movement that creates the mark. Auguste Rodin captures time and motion in his work *Cambodian Dancer (figure 2.1)*. Rodin's lines are rhythmic and energized. He projects the model's kinetics onto the paper; the rhythms of the marks fluctuate between fast and slow.

Scientist John Tchalenko considered the notion of time and motion by conducting a study on the interaction between the eye, hand, and brain of an artist while drawing a face. Sensors measured controlled and unconscious responses of an artist, Humphrey Ocean, and nonartists. The researchers compared the results and found that artists indeed see things differently from nonartists. Researchers noted that the artist explores the subject through a rapid series of "short fixations," as many as 140 per minute, lingering for as long as one second at least 12 times a minute *(figure 2.2)*. Another

2.1. **AUGUSTE RODIN.** *Cambodian Dancer.* 1906. Lead pencil and watercolor drawing, 1'1⁷⁄₁₀" x 10½" (34.8 cm x 26.7 cm). INV.M.R. 4455. © *Musée Rodin, Paris.*

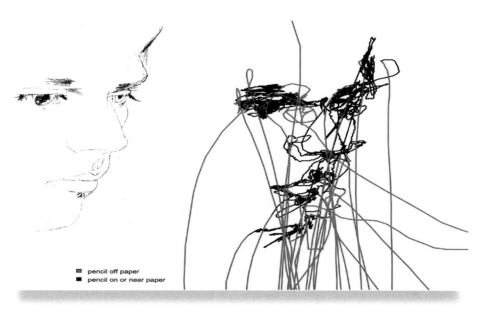

■ pencil off paper
■ pencil on or near paper

2.2. **HUMPHREY OCEAN.** *Computerized Version of Hand Movement and Finished Drawing.* 1999. Original reconstruction of pen movements by Professor Chris Miall, University of Oxford, 2'7³⁄₁₀" x 1'11³⁄₇" (79.5 cm x 59.5 cm). *National Portrait Gallery, London, England.* © *2007 Artist Rights Society (ARS), New York/DACS, London. © Photo by Chris Miall.*

sensor traced hand movements as they marked both on and off the page, recording the hand's movement in air, the markings on the page, and the amount of pressure exerted on the drawing implement. An imaging device scanned the brains of the subjects while they drew. The findings revealed that the seeing process for nonartists takes place in the visual cortex at the back of the brain, whereas the artist mainly engaged the frontal part of the brain, the site of emotion. It was here, too, that the artist stored previous information taken from his earlier drawing experiences. "In essence, the control subjects were simply trying to copy what they saw. But Humphrey was creating an abstracted representation of each photograph. He was *thinking* the subjects," explains Tchalenko (Alan Riding, "Hypothesis: The Artist Does See Things Differently," *New York Times*, May 4, 1999, Living Arts p. 2).

FACTURE, POCHADE, AND TIME

We are so accustomed to seeing reproductions of art, reduced in size and reproduced by mechanical means, that we often miss the handmade quality so valued in one-of-a-kind drawings. This handmade quality is called *facture*, a term that refers to the process or manner of making something. The kinds of marks artists make hold clues to unraveling the meaning of the drawing, which will be discussed later on in the chapter. For now, however, note what kinds of tools, media, and surfaces are being used. You will learn to build a descriptive vocabulary to discuss the quality and purpose of the marks, becoming aware of the speed or slowness with which they were made, registering their physical characteristics, and tracing the signs of facture in the drawing. For example, the crosshatched line, the scribble, the faint trailing line, the boldly stated ripping mark—all are signs of facture.

In the drawing by Joel Shapiro *(figure 2.3)*, facture is self-evident. The surface is built up of multiple overlaid marks that are scribbled across the entire surface. The

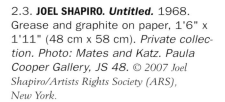

2.3. **JOEL SHAPIRO.** *Untitled.* 1968. Grease and graphite on paper, 1'6" x 1'11" (48 cm x 58 cm). *Private collection. Photo: Mates and Katz. Paula Cooper Gallery, JS 48.* © *2007 Joel Shapiro/Artists Rights Society (ARS), New York.*

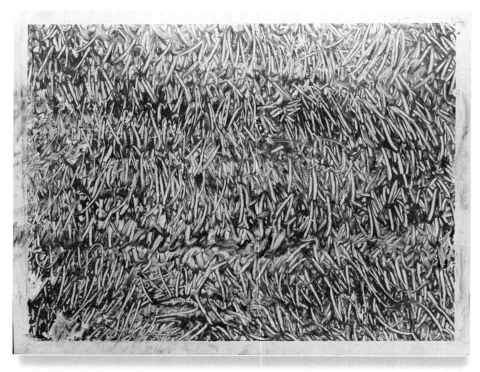

expressive, loosely controlled marks point out the properties of the media—grease and graphite. This greasy substance is pushed to the edge of each mark; the center of the mark remains clean and white, thus giving dimension to each line—every line appears outlined. Row after row of overlapping marks create a unified field. A grassy field, a scribbled-out letter, or a woven textile are some of the associations that come to mind when viewing Shapiro's work. The ambiguity of what the marks could refer to is an enticing part of this piece, but the real subject of the work is the act of mark making itself. The randomness and rapid gestural marks affirm the hand of the artist. Shapiro is classified as a Minimalist; *Minimalism* defines itself through the materials used, without allusions to subjects outside the work itself. Shapiro's drawing does not represent a subject or an object in the real world; it is a drawing made for drawing's sake.

Another descriptive term that is important to know is *pochade*, a French term meaning a rapidly made sketch, a shorthand notation, an abbreviated drawing. In a pochade, the speed of execution mirrors a burst of energy; it is a record of time, action, and medium. In Pierre Bonnard's pochade *(figure 2.4)*, the artist presents an emotional scene between two figures, a quarrel. The figures turn away from each other; the agitated marks mirror the tension between the couple. Line quality and composition reinforce the theme.

An important aspect of time as it relates to drawing is memory. Both making and looking at drawings develop memory. Your visual experience is enriched by learning to see through the practice of drawing. You should develop the habit of carrying a sketchbook with you to jot down quick notes and sketches as an aid to memory. Consciously be aware of trying to retain mental images. Whether an artist chooses to work abstractly or figuratively, learning to draw directly from life is essential.

2.4. **PIERRE BONNARD.** *La Querelle (The Quarrel).* 1900–1910. Pencil and black chalk with brush and ink, 7⅜" x 7⅞" (18.7 cm x 20 cm). *Private collection.* © 2007 Artists Rights Society (ARS), New York/ADAGP, Paris.

The two basic approaches to drawing involve time. The first approach, called gesture, is a quick, all-encompassing overview of forms in their wholeness. The second, called contour, is an intense, slow inspection of the subject, a careful examination of its parts. Offshoots of these two basic approaches are continuous-line drawing and organizational-line drawing.

GESTURAL LINE DRAWING

As we have learned from the description of the experiment recording an artist's eye and hand movements, eye-to-hand coordination lies at the very core of drawing. The formal definition of the word *gesture* amplifies its special meaning for the artist: the act of moving the limbs or body to show, to express, to direct thought. The gestural approach to drawing is actually an exercise in seeing. The hand duplicates the motion of the eyes, making a movement that quickly defines the general characteristics of the subject: placement, shape, proportion, relationship between the parts, and a definition of planes and volumes as well as their arrangement in space.

In *figure 2.5* we see how efficiently a gestural drawing by the contemporary architect Frank Gehry records his initial ideas for a proposed building in Cleveland. Because of the intricacies of his architectural designs, Gehry's gestural drawings are an essential first step in indicating spatial notations to describe the flowing curves and major planar segments of the yet-to-be-built structure. Spatial relationships between the swirls, blocks, and cubes jotted down in Gehry's energetic gestural shorthand are eventually translated into scale models, and then into a virtual model. "The dream, as you prepare the drawings and the models, . . . has to come out the other end with the passion and feeling you invested in it," explains Gehry in a *New York Times Magazine* article (Alex Marshall, "How to Make a Frank Gehry Building," April 8, 2001, p. 64).

Willem de Kooning is known as the modern master of gestural drawing. In his ink drawing *(figure 2.6)*, the highly active lines lend a kinetic effect to the drawing. The lines slash across the page; the marks are not contained within a form; they cross over, search out, and quickly describe the artist's eye and hand movements. It is not until we read the title of the drawing, *Folded Shirt on Laundry Paper*, that we begin to unravel the image, what the critic Klaus Kertess called "active, slipping semblances of form" (*Willem de Kooning: Drawing Seeing/Seeing Drawing* [New York: Drawing Center, 1998]). De Kooning frequently traced or glued portions of his gestural drawings directly onto the surface of his paintings to retain their energy and sense of immediacy.

More than seeing and organizing, gesture is the first step in establishing unity in a piece of art. Gesture is a metaphor for the energy and vitality of both the artist and the subject. In the energized work by Sean Scully *(figure 2.7)*, the marks pulsate across a loosely stated grid. The scribbled, gestural lines create rectilinear shapes that not only move across the various units but seem to vibrate from front to back. Scully establishes an early compositional layout with these quickly stated forms. As in *figure 2.3* facture is self-evident.

Another powerful example of gestural marks serving to communicate ideas is Mario Merz's crudely drawn beast *(figure 2.8)*. The ambitious scale of the drawing reinforces Merz's metaphor for brute nature. Merz asserts illogic, disorder, chance, and change in his work; the aggressively drawn, hulking animal carries a challenge, an anti-techno/scientific message. The marks used in building the powerful image are not only the result of loose wrist and hand movements, they are made with sweeping gestures involving shoulder rotations and physical movement across the 15-foot length of the drawing. The drawing becomes a backdrop against which the drawing performance takes place.

Contemporary artists continue to be attracted to gesture as an aid to seeing. In Beatrice Caracciolo's large work on paper, we see how suggestive gesture can be

2.6. **WILLEM DE KOONING.** *Folded Shirt on Laundry Paper.* 1958. Ink on paper. 1'4⅞" x 1'1⅞" (42.9 cm x 35.2 cm). Area Editions, Santa Fe, New Mexico. *© 2007 The Willem de Kooning Foundation/Artists Rights Society (ARS), New York.*

2.7. **SEAN SCULLY.** *Untitled.* 2000. Ink on paper. 6 x 5¾" (15.2 cm x 14.6 cm). *Copyright the artist; Courtesy, Timothy Taylor Gallery, London.*

of landscape *(figure 2.9)*. The division in the drawing between the marked area and the toned paper indicates a horizon. The heavier weighted lines in the lower right-hand corner offer a spatial interpretation because the mountainlike form is more diffused and lighter in value. The toned paper and smudges suggest a sense

2.8. **MARIO MERZ.** *Animale Terrible.* 1979. Mixed media on canvas, 7'5" x 15'6" (2.3 m x 4.75 m).

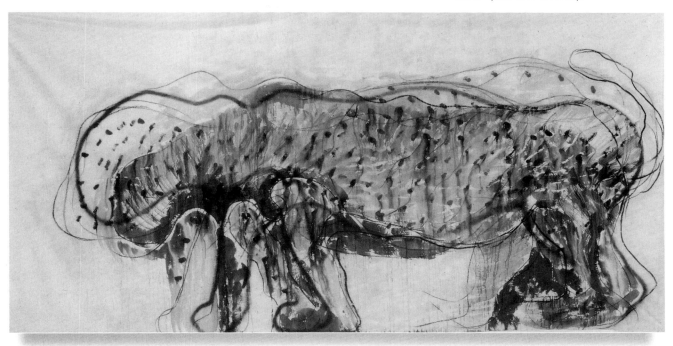

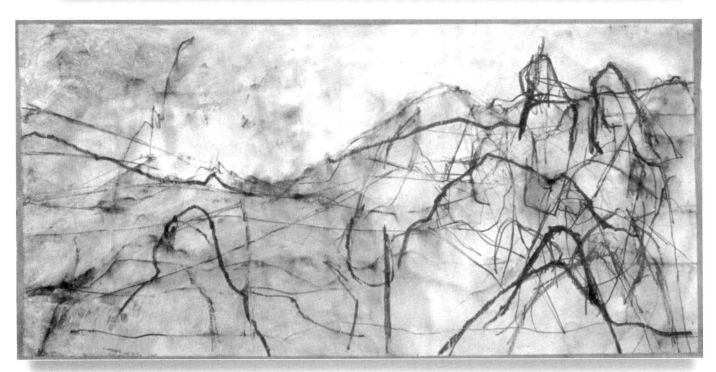

2.9. **BEATRICE CARACCIOLO.** *Untitled.* 1999. Mixed media on paper, mounted on board, 4'10¼" x 9'8" (1.48 m x 2.95 m). *Courtesy of the artist and Charles Cowles Gallery, New York.*

of light and shadow. The spontaneously weighted lines are created by changing pressure on the drawing implement to define the spatial relationships between near and far.

Artists use landscape as an internalization of the natural world. Gesture can convey an experience of vastness, of light and air. Gesture trains the eye and hand, and it opens the door to unexplored abilities.

Beginning to Draw

Some general instructions are in order before you begin to draw.

■ First, consult Guide A, "Materials," which contains a comprehensive list of materials for completing all the problems given in this book. Before beginning to draw from the figure or a still life, experiment with the media in your drawing kit: pencils, graphite sticks, pen and ink, brushes and ink, charcoal, crayons, and chalks. Remember the discussion on facture at the beginning of the chapter.

■ Fill several pages in your sketchbook with some media experiments, using the full range of implements. On each page group lines, changing the weight and pressure on your drawing implement. Vary the marks from long to short, from heavy to thin. Look at the drawing by Jasper Johns *(figure 2.10)*. Note how the lines range in weight from light to dark; some are tightly grouped, while others are more openly spaced.

■ When you have a feel for each medium, noting its inherent character, make a unified field drawing, one in which the marks continue from side to side and cover the page from bottom to top. Refer to *figures 1.4* (Halaby) and *2.3* (Shapiro) as examples of unified field drawings.

■ After you have made several pages of marks, lay out the drawings side by side and make a list of words that describe the various line qualities. Try to make marks that "look like" sounds; for example, percussive, soft, loud, and rolling crescendos with staccato accents. In fact, it is a good idea to make gesture drawings while

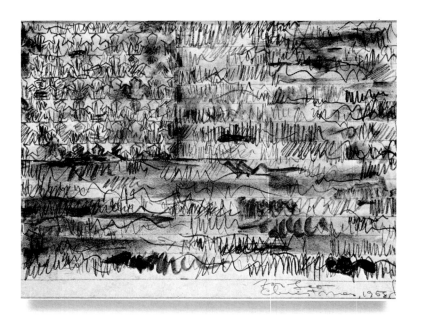

2.10. **JASPER JOHNS.** *Flag.* 1958. Pencil and graphite wash on paper, 7½" x 10⅜" (19 cm x 26 cm). *Private collection. © 2003 Jasper Johns/Licensed by VAGA, New York.*

listening to music. The music not only helps you relax, it encourages a rhythmic response.

■ Gesture drawing can be done in any medium. For now, however, in the initial stages of making figurative drawings (drawings of the model, still life, or landscape), use a compressed charcoal stick, vine charcoal, graphite stick, oil stick, or ink (with 1-inch or 2-inch [2.5-cm or 5-cm] varnish brush or a number 6 Japanese bamboo-handled brush). In the beginning of each drawing session, you can use vine charcoal on newsprint. Since vine charcoal is a very powdery substance, it does not adhere well to the paper and can be easily wiped off with a leather chamois skin, enabling you to layer several quick gestural drawings on the same sheet of paper. The draw-back to vine charcoal is that it breaks very easily and does not make a range of darker marks. However, the toned paper that results from rubbing out previous drawings makes an interesting surface to work on. Vine charcoal drawings can be sprayed with a fixative to make them more permanent.

■ Gesture drawing involves large arm movements, so the paper should be no smaller than 18 by 24 inches (46 by 61 cm). You can use a newsprint pad for dry media (it is too absorbent for wet media), and an inexpensive bond paper for wet media. Heavy brown wrapping paper that comes on rolls is ideal for both wet and dry media. Bond paper is smoother and allows a more flowing line. Later you can experiment with different papers. Pay attention to the surface you are working on; it determines the quality of the marks made on it.

■ Until you have fully mastered the technique of gesture, stand (do not sit) at an easel. Stand at arm's length from your paper, placing the easel so that you can keep your eyes on the still life or model at all times. Make continuous marks.

■ While you are becoming acquainted with the limits of the paper and with placement and other compositional options, you should fill the paper with a single pose or a single view of the still life or landscape. Later, several gesture drawings can be placed on a page. The drawings should be timed. At first, they should alternate between 15 and 30 seconds. Then gradually increase the time to three minutes. Spend no more than three minutes on each drawing; the value of quick gesture is lost if you take longer.

■ When you draw from a model, the model should change poses every 30 seconds for a new drawing. Later, the pose is increased to one minute, then to two minutes, then to three minutes. The poses should be energetic and active. Different poses should be related by a natural flow of the model's movement. The goal is to see quickly and with increasing comprehension. Immediacy is the key. Spend at least 15 minutes at the beginning of each drawing session on these exercises.

Types of Gestural Line Drawing

You will work with five types of gesture drawing in this chapter—line, mass, mass and line, scribbled line, and sustained. The distinctions among the five, along with a fuller discussion of each of the types, follow.

LINE GESTURE

Line gesture describes interior forms, following the movement of your eyes as you examine the subject. These lines should vary from thick to thin, from wide to nar-row, and from heavy to light. In line gesture, marks can be tangled and overlapped, and they are always spontaneously and energetically stated. They may resemble a scribble, but they are not aimless or meaningless.

Keep the following points in mind when considering line gesture exercises:

■ Keep the marks continuous, once you begin to draw. Do not lose contact with the paper. Look for the longest line in the subject. Is it a curve, a diagonal, a horizontal, or a vertical? Allow your eyes to move through the still life, connecting the forms. Do not simply follow the edge or outline of the forms. Coordinate the motion of your hand with the movement of your eyes. Remember, in gesture you are not concerned with copying what the subject looks like. You are describing the subject's location in space along with the relationships between the forms. Keep your eyes and hand working together. Your eyes should remain on the subject, only occasionally glancing at your paper. This procedure will be uncomfortable at first, but soon you will learn the limits of the page and the location of the marks on it without looking away from the subject. You will develop keener peripheral vision as you become more accustomed to this way of looking.

■ Avoid the stick-figure approach as you draw from the model. Begin your marks in the center of the forms, in the interior of the body, and move outward to the edges. Note the angles of the various body masses—upper and lower torso, upper and lower legs, angles of arms and head. Indicate the most obvious angles and general shapes first. Go from the large shapes to the small. Begin at the core of the subject rather than at its outer edge.

■ Take note of the amount of pressure you apply to the drawing implement; it is important—vary heavy, dark lines with lighter, looser ones. The darker lines might be used to emphasize areas where you feel tension, where the heaviest weight, the most pressure, the most exaggerated shape, or the most obvious change in line direction exists. By pressing harder on the drawing implement as you note objects farther from you, and by lightening the pressure for those nearer to you, you will have indicated the important spatial difference between background and foreground spaces. The ability to suggest spatial location is at the core of drawing from life.

■ Indicate height and width measurements of objects. It is easier to do this than it is to suggest depth, the third dimension. You are drawing on a surface that has height and width, so lateral and vertical indications—horizontals and verticals—are relatively simple. The paper has no depth, so you must find a way to indicate this crucial measurement. The use of diagonals, or angles penetrating space, is of prime importance.

■ Draw each object in its entirety, as if it were transparent, even though the objects overlap and block one another and you are unable to see the entire form. The same is true when drawing the figure; draw as if you were able to see through the form.

■ Capture the idea of movement. Gesture is particularly effective in capturing the idea of movement. Have the model rotate on the model stand, making a quarter turn every 30 seconds. Unify the four poses in one drawing. Walter Piehl Jr.'s rotating figure *(figure 2.11)* depicts a cowboy with his lasso. The indication of movement is especially pronounced in the areas of hat, hands, and boots, important focal areas.

■ Especially appropriate for gesture drawing is an exercise that has as its subject a linear movement, as seen in *figure 1.1*. The series of seven quick poses of a

2.11. **WALTER PIEHL JR.** *The Merry-Go-Round.* 1988. Pencil, 2' x 1'4" (61 cm x 41 cm). *Courtesy the artist.*

figure in motion could have been taken from an animated strip; each pose flows smoothly into the next. The artist has captured the time sequence in an economical way, using deft strokes related to Oriental calligraphy. Use ink and brush to record this cinematic movement. The format should be a narrow horizontal or a tall vertical.

■ Try to avoid centrally placed images in every drawing. Vary the placement by concentrating darks away from the center. Experiment with the activation of the entire surface of your paper by making the composition run off the page on several sides.

MASS GESTURE

In *mass gesture* the drawing medium is used to make broad marks, creating mass as opposed to line. In *figure 2.12*, a moving model is recorded with rapidity and ease using the mass gesture technique. The suggestion of mass and energy give a physicality to the drawing. The drips and splatters enhance the idea of motion.

To get the most out of mass gesture exercises, consider the following points:

■ Use the broad side of a piece of compressed charcoal broken to the length of 1–2 inches (2.5–5 cm), or use a wet medium applied with a brush. Remember to keep the marks broad.

■ Arrange objects in a spatial arrangement with intervals between them to provide areas of empty spaces. A tricycle, a tree branch, or a vase of flowers, for example, might serve the same purpose, affording intervals of negative spaces between the positive shapes. In some drawings, make marks in the blank, negative spaces first. When you are drawing from the figure, focus on the negative space surrounding the

2.12. **DAVID STERN.** *Moving Figure.*
1995. Coffee, ink on paper, 50" x 38"
(127 cm x 97 cm). *Arkansas Art Center.* ©
*2007 David Stern/Artists Rights Society
(ARS), New York.*

figure and on enclosed empty shapes—those formed between arms and body, for example.

■ As in line gesture, the pressure you apply to the drawing tool is important; vary heavy, dark marks with lighter shapes.

■ Differentiate between various levels of space: foreground, middle ground, background. This can be conveyed by controlling the darks and lights in your drawing. In addition to the spatial differentiation that mass gesture offers, it has the added bonus of indicating lights and darks at an early stage. Light and dark values can suggest atmosphere and space.

MASS AND LINE GESTURE

Mass and line gesture offers the benefits of both techniques previously discussed by combining the two approaches in one drawing. In the nine charcoal panels by Eugene Leroy *(figure 2.13),* darker values distinguish foreground from background. A sense of light and shadow is evoked along with a feeling of weight and volume.

Gestural mass and line may be stated with wet or dry media, or a combination of both. When using a charcoal stick, switch from the sharp edge to the broad side of the stick.

Here are some other guidelines to consider:

■ Begin with either broad shapes or lines and then alternate between the two. Define the more important areas with sharp, incisive lines or with darker shapes. Correct and amplify your initial image. You can change the position or placement of the forms, or enlarge or decrease the scale of certain parts. Keep the drawing flexible, capable of change.

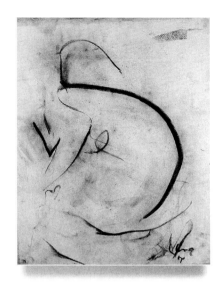

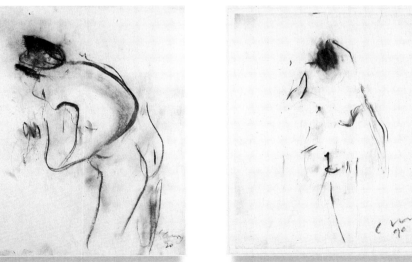

2.13. **EUGENE LEROY. *Untitled.*** 1990.
Charcoal on paper, nine panels 2'¼" x
1'7" (63 cm x 48 cm). *Michael Werner
Gallery.*

2.14. KARL UMLAUF. *Altered States V (detail).* 1990. Charcoal, paper, bone, and wood, 4'2" x 5' x 3" (1.27 m x 1.52 m x 7.6 cm). *Courtesy of the artist.*

■ In drawings using ink and brush, begin laying wash areas in the negative space. Let the washes cross over both positive and negative space. Karl Umlauf's piece *(figure 2.14)* crosses over the categories of sculpture and drawing by combining actual three-dimensional objects, such as shelves and bones, with a mass and line gestural drawing of the same subject. Darker marks offset the skeletal images, which are lighter than their enclosing spaces.

■ Overall, be attentive to unexpected events in your drawing. The British painter Francis Bacon says that for him accident always has to enter into his drawing; otherwise, he feels as if he is simply making an illustration of the image. Speed of execution is one means of creating such unexpected effects. A major part of aesthetic intelligence is the alertness and willingness to put accidents to creative effect.

Scribbled Line Gesture

The *scribbled line gesture* consists of a tight network of lines. The sculptor Alberto Giacometti's triple-head drawing *(figure 2.15)* is a good example of this technique. The free-flowing ballpoint pen builds volume; the multiple, overlapping lines create a dense mass that builds the volumetric heads. In Giacometti's drawings, we can see the same concerns that occupied him as a sculptor: the ideas of weight, weightlessness, spatial location, and penetration.

In order to achieve a tight network of lines in this type of drawing, remember the following:

■ Make your media choices wisely. Include felt-tip markers, pencils, ballpoint pens, and wax crayons.

■ Begin continuous overlapping lines at the imagined center of the subject. The lines build on one another, moving from the interior to the outside edge of the form. This technique has a parallel in sculpture: the use of an armature or framework to support a mass of clay or plaster the sculptor is modeling.

2.15. **ALBERTO GIACOMETTI.** *Diego's Head Three Times.* 1962. Ballpoint pen, 8⅛" x 6" (21 cm x 15 cm). *Private collection.* © 2007 Artists Rights Society (ARS), New York/ADAGP, Paris.

■ Keep in mind that in a scribbled line gesture, the outside edge of the form will be somewhat fuzzy, indefinitely stated. The darkest, most compact lines will be in the core of the form. The outer edges remain flexible, not pinned down to an exact line. The drawing tool remains in constant contact with the paper. Vary the amount of pressure to create lights and darks. The scribbles should vary between tight rotation and broader, more sweeping motions.

In addition to creating dense positive shapes, you can use scribbled line gesture to model negative space. In Mac Adams's *Study for Three-Part Poison (figure 2.16)*, the gestural marks at the bottom of the drawing are concentrated in the negative space surrounding the table and chairs. The activation of the negative space enlivens a static setting. The concentrated mass of lines surrounding the chandelier is in contrast to the delicacy of line and shape in the lamp itself. For Adams, the chandelier is a symbol of luxury and is, therefore, an ominous object. He uses this image frequently in his work as a metaphor for art—the danger that lies in seeing art as mere luxury.

SUSTAINED GESTURE

The use of *sustained gesture* combines a description of what the object is doing with what it actually looks like. Verisimilitude is not a primary concern in these beginning exercises; they are, however, a path to more accurate observation and drawing. Sustained gesture begins in the same spirit as before, with a quick notation of the entire subject. After this notation, however, an examination of both the subject and the drawing takes place. At this point you make corrections, establishing scale and more accurate proportion between the parts. Now you define precise edges. The result is that the sustained gesture drawing actually begins to look like the object being drawn.

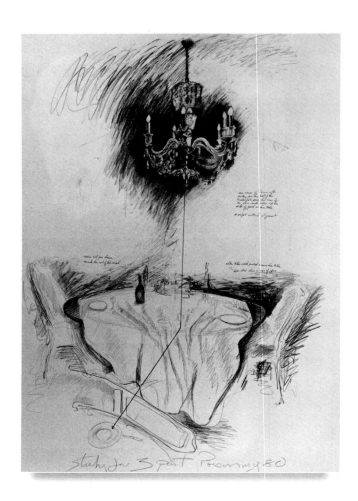

2.16. **MAC ADAMS. *Study for Three-Part Poison.*** 1980. Graphite on paper, 5'4" x 3'4" (1.63 m x 1.02 m). *Commodities Corporation, Princeton, N.J.*

In *Man Seated at Table (figure 2.17)* by the Italian artist Sandro Chia, the gestural underpinning of the drawing is apparent. The drawing offers insight into the artist's decision-making process. Faint traces of earlier figures, the altered scale of the head of the seated figure, a shift in the placement of the feet and table base—all are faint memories of various stages of the drawing. Revealing part of a work that has been drawn or covered over is called *pentimento* in Italian, meaning correction. While Chia has maintained the gestural approach throughout the drawing, in the final stage he has used more defined, darker contour lines. Chia's extended gestural approach reinforces the drawing's implied meaning; the shifting figure, the skull, and the spiral indicate that change is its primary subject. You can see that the *pentimenti* contribute to the meaning of the work. Consider this:

■ Before drawing a still life, think of a verbal description of what it is doing. If you speak of a drooping flower, an immediate visual image comes to mind. Look at the subject. Is the bottle *thrusting* upward into space? Is the cloth *languishing* on the table? Find descriptive terms for the subject and try to infuse your drawing with a feeling that is commensurate with the verbal description. It will bring life to your drawing.

■ If you are drawing from a model, take the pose yourself. Hold the pose for three minutes. Where do you feel the stress? Where is the most tension, the heaviest weight in the pose? Emphasize those areas in your drawing by using a darker line. Lighten the marks where there is less weight. Your memory of various poses will be

2.17. **SANDRO CHIA.** *Man Seated at Table.* 1984. Charcoal and pencil on paper, 3'2" x 2'6" (97 cm x 76 cm). *Arkansas Arts Center Foundation purchase, 1985. Acc. no. 85.62. © 2003 Sandro Chia/Licensed by VAGA, New York.*

enhanced so that when you are drawing without a model, you have your body memory to count on.

■ Draw quickly for the first two minutes; then stop and analyze your drawing in relation to the subject. Have you stated the correct proportion and scale among the parts? Is the drawing well related to the page?

■ Redraw, making corrections. Alternate drawing with careful observation of the subject. Avoid making slow, constricted marks. Give consideration to the placement of the subject on the page, to the distribution of lights and darks; look for repeating shapes. Avoid overcrowding at the bottom of the paper. By a more precise line or by a contrast between lights and darks in a particular area, create a focal point.

■ Rub out areas of the drawing with a chamois, a piece of paper, or your hand to create toned areas and to leave *pentimenti* in corrected areas.

■ Stand back from your drawing and assess it from time to time. A drawing changes with viewing distance; it will tell you what it needs when you look at it from a few feet away. Another way to assess the drawing is to see it as it is reflected in a mirror. The reversed mirror image frequently reveals glaring imbalances or mistakes.

A sustained gesture drawing can last 5, 10, 15 minutes or longer, as long as the gestural spontaneity can be maintained.

Of all the exercises discussed the sustained gesture is the most open-ended type. However, keep the following guidelines in mind as you work on different gesture exercise types.

1. Stand while drawing.
2. Use paper at least 18 by 24 inches (46 by 61 cm).
3. Use any medium.
4. Use large arm movements.
5. Scan the subject in its entirety before beginning to draw.
6. Be aware that the hand duplicates the motion of the eye.
7. Keep your drawing tool in contact with the paper throughout the drawing.
8. Keep your eye on the subject being drawn, only occasionally referring to your paper.
9. Avoid outlines. Draw through the forms.
10. Activate different areas of the paper by varying the placement of your subject.

OTHER BEGINNING APPROACHES

Other beginning drawing approaches are *continuous-line drawing, organizational-line drawing*, and *contour-line drawing* (including *blind* and *quick contour*). Like gesture, these techniques emphasize coordination between eye and hand. They help translate information about three-dimensional objects onto a two-dimensional surface.

CONTINUOUS-LINE DRAWING

In a *continuous-line drawing*, the line is unbroken from the beginning to the end. It is a single line, more slowly stated than a gestural line. The drawing implement stays in uninterrupted contact with the surface of the paper during the entire length of the drawing. Jasper Johns's charcoal drawing *0 through 9 (figure 2.18)* is a result of

2.18. **JASPER JOHNS. *0 through 9.*** 1960. Charcoal on paper, 2'5" x 1'11" (74 cm x 58 cm). *Collection of the artist.* © 2003 Jasper Johns/Licensed by VAGA, New York. Photograph by Rudolph Burkhardt, New York.

this technique. The numbers are layered, stacked one on top of the other, all confined within the same perimeter. The numbers are transparent and slightly unintelligible; the overlapping intersecting lines create shapes independent of the numbers themselves.

In continuous-line drawing:

■ Use graphite sticks, pencils, conté crayons, litho markers, felt-tip pens, brush, and pen and ink.

■ Once you make contact with the paper (you may begin anywhere: top, bottom, side), keep the line continuous. The completed drawing gives the effect that it could be unwound or unraveled. Use a single line to draw through the forms as if they were transparent. The line bridges spaces between objects. Outside edges as well as internal shapes are defined. A continuous-line drawing creates enclosed, repeated shapes.

■ Let the lines go off the page on at least three sides. Vary the weight of the line, pressing harder in areas where you perceive a heavier weight or a shadow, where you see the form turning into space, or in areas of abrupt change in line direction.

Many artists make use of this technique for finished drawings. In Brice Marden's art, the continuous overlapping line is a stylistic indicator *(figure 2.19)*. Although the lines are nonillusionistic, there is a suggestion of space due to the lines shadowing each other. The interlocking lines have an organic, fluid, scriptlike quality. The lines seem to hover above the surface; the background is a shallow plane in front of which the lines perform.

The following list highlights some important points to keep in mind when doing continuous-line drawing.

2.19. **BRICE MARDEN.** *Cold Mountain Addendum 1.* 1991–1992. Ink, ink wash, and gouache on paper. 2'2" x 2'10¼" (66 cm x 87 cm). *Collection of the artist.* © *2007 Brice Marden/Artists Rights Society (ARS), New York.*

GUIDELINES FOR CONTINUOUS-LINE DRAWING

1. Use an implement that permits a free-flowing line.
2. Use a single unbroken line for the entire drawing. A continuous overlapping line will create enclosed shapes.
3. Keep your drawing implement constantly in contact with the paper.
4. Draw through the objects as if they were transparent, defining both internal shapes and outer edges.
5. Fill the entire surface of your paper, encompassing positive and negative shapes.
6. Vary the weight of the line.

ORGANIZATIONAL-LINE DRAWING

Organizational line provides a structural, analytical framework for a drawing. This framework can be compared to the scaffolding of a building. Organizational lines take measure; they extend into space. Like gestural lines and continuous overlapping lines, they are not confined to the edges of objects. They, too, are transparent; they cut through forms, tying background shapes to objects. They organize the composition. They take measurement of height, width, and depth of the objects and the space they occupy. Organizational lines are grouped; they are stated multiple times, as in Giacometti's *Still Life (figure 2.20)*.

2.20. ALBERTO GIACOMETTI. *Still Life.* 1948. Pencil on paper, 1'7¼" x 1'½" (49 cm x 32 cm). *Collection of the Modern Art Museum of Fort Worth. Gift of B. Gerald Cantor, Beverly Hills, California. Copyright © 2007 Artists Rights Society (ARS), New York/ADAGP, Paris.*

When completing these types of drawing exercises:

- Use a pencil to make an organizational-line drawing of several objects in a room, including the architectural features—ceiling, juncture of walls, doors, and windows.

- Begin by drawing the horizontal and vertical lines of the room, establishing relative heights and widths of each object and of the background shapes. For example, extend the line of the tabletop to the edge of the page. These horizontals and verticals will create a gridlike surface. Note Giacometti's use of organizational line in *figure 2.20*. His searching lines extend beyond the confines of the objects to the edge of the picture plane. The objects are penetrated by groups of measurement lines. Multiple lines are clustered at the edges of forms, so the outer edge is never explicitly stated; the edge lies somewhere within the cluster. The drawing is structured around the spatial relationships between the table, the vase, and the architectural elements of the room.

- Establish relative heights and widths and locate the diagonals, stating the angles in relation to the corrected horizontal and vertical lines.

- Let the background lines cut through the still life, thus uniting background and foreground. By extending the lines through and beyond the objects, you will create organizational shapes.

- By closing one eye to diminish depth perception, hold a pencil at arm's length to measure the height and width of each object and make comparisons between sizes of objects. This is called *sighting* and is an important device in training yourself to register proper proportion. It is an indispensable aid for learning to translate three-dimensional objects onto a two-dimensional surface.

- Note how the buildup of lines creates a sense of volume, of weight, and of depth in your drawing. After you have accurately established proper proportion between the parts, darken some of the shapes to differentiate between foreground and background.

- Introduce the eraser as a drawing implement. Do not use the eraser to correct. Hold it as you would hold a drawing tool and make multiple "negative," white, erased marks. The result will be indefinite, blurred marks. Alternate using the original medium and eraser to finish the drawing. Erasure marks fasten the drawing to the page. The texture made by the eraser establishes a spatial and atmospheric feeling to the drawing. Experiment with different kinds of erasers. Kneaded erasers are suitable for use with powdery media; gummed erasers are less abrasive than most other erasers and will not destroy the paper's surface; Pink Pearl erasers with their gritty texture allow for more complete removal of graphite and pencil marks; white plastic erasers have a smooth texture that is not destructive to the paper and is suitable for working with graphite, pencil, or colored pencil. There are even erasers in the shape of pens that contain a chemical to remove ink marks.

Many artists use organizational line for its analytical approach in the beginning stages of a drawing. The structure this technique provides may be disguised under the completed work, or, as in Giacometti's drawings, it may be left as a record of how the drawing was built. Here are some important points to keep in mind when making organizational-line drawings.

GUIDELINES FOR ORGANIZATIONAL-LINE DRAWING

1. Begin with multiply stated horizontal and vertical lines; add diagonal lines.
2. Establish relative heights and widths of all objects and background shapes.
3. Allow lines to penetrate through objects, establishing relative scale between the objects and their location in space.
4. Extend lines to the edge of the paper.
5. When you have established proper proportions, differentiate between foreground and background by use of lights and darks.

CONTOUR-LINE DRAWING

In contrast to the immediacy of the gestural approach, which records forms in their wholeness, the contour approach is a slower, more intense inspection of the parts. A contour line is a single, clean, incisive line that defines edges. Unlike outline, which states only the outside edge of an object and differentiates between positive and negative edges, a contour line is more spatially descriptive. A contour line can define interior complex planes and shapes. Outline is flat; contour is *plastic;* that is, it emphasizes the three-dimensional appearance of the subject.

In the drawing by Benny Andrews *(figure 2.21)*, the artist has combined outline and contour in the same drawing. The figure of the musician is primarily outlined; the exceptions are the left hand and features of the face, which, along with the guitar, are delineated in contour line.

An effective way to distinguish between contour and outline is to imagine the difference between the simple outline of a hand and a drawing of a hand which relates information about its structure—wrinkles, joints, and fingernails. In addition to structural, or planar, edges, contour line can indicate the edge of value, or shadow, the edge of texture, and the edge of color.

There are a number of types of contour, several of which you will learn about in Chapter 5, "Line." The following general instructions, however, are applicable for all types of contour drawing.

GUIDELINES FOR CONTOUR-LINE DRAWING

1. Use a sharp-pointed implement (such as a 2B pencil, ballpoint pen, or pen and ink). Contour drawing requires a single, incisive, precisely made line.
2. Do not retrace already stated lines, and do not erase for correction.
3. Keep your eyes on the subject you are drawing. Eye and hand are one. Imagine that the point of your drawing tool is in actual contact with the subject. Do not let your eyes move more quickly than you can draw. Keep your implement in contact with the paper until you come to the end of a form. Keep eye and hand working in tandem. In a figure drawing, for example, this technique may lead you to draw the interior features and bone structure without completing the outside contour.
4. Vary the pressure on the drawing tool to indicate a shift in direction or to suggest a heavier weight.
5. Draw only where there is an actual, structural plane shift or where there is a change in value, texture, or color. Do not enter the interior form and aimlessly draw nonexistent planes or make meaningless, decorative lines. In this regard, contour drawing is unlike a continuous overlapping-line drawing.

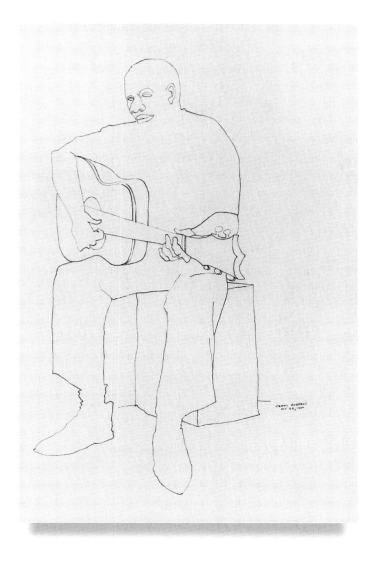

2.21. **BENNY ANDREWS.** *Yeah, Yeah.*
1970. Ink on paper, 1'6" x 1' (46 cm x
30 cm). *Arkansas Arts Center Foundation
Collection; the Museum Purchase Plan of the
NEA and the Barrett Hamilton Acquisition
Fund, 1981. 81.23.*

6. When you have drawn to the end of an interior shape, return to the outside
   edge. With only a glance for realignment, continue to draw, keeping your
   eyes on the subject. Do not worry about distortion or inaccurate
   proportions; proportions will improve after a number of sessions dedicated
   to contour.
7. Try to extend the length of time you spend on any one drawing; work with a
   spirit of careful, intense observation. In contour drawing, time is slowed down.
   A finished product is not the goal; the focus is on process. Contour drawing
   hones your visual acuity.

Contour drawing should be done frequently and with a wide range of subjects—
still life, landscape, figure, and room interiors.

BLIND CONTOUR-LINE DRAWING

Blind contour drawing is a variant of contour drawing and is especially helpful for
the beginning student. The previously stated guidelines for contour-line drawing are
also applicable for blind contour. The exception is that you cover your drawing
surface and drawing hand with a large piece of paper in order to hide your view of

2.22. **FAIRFIELD PORTER.** *Yellow Room.*
n.d. Pen and ink, 15½" x 10" (39.4 cm
x 25.4 cm). *Hirschl and Adler Gallery, NYC.*

the drawing. You are "drawing blind." Distortion and misalignment are a part of blind contour since you are not allowed to look at the drawing. Do not intentionally exaggerate or distort.

By comparing *figures 2.22* and *2.23* the difference in line quality between slow contour and blind contour will be apparent. Stephan Hirsh's double portrait is precise, accurately stated, and proportionate. In Fairfield Porter's blind contour drawing of a room, we see misalignments, a hesitant line, and dots, which indicate stopping and turning points.

SUMMARY

Gestural drawing is foundational; it is a record of the energy that goes into making marks. It makes a visual connection between the artist and the subject drawn,

2.23. **STEFAN HIRSCH.** American, 1899-1964. Papa Hirsch and Dorotheel, 1921. Pencil on paper. 9 x 7½". *Diane and Sandy Besser Collection.*

whether that subject is from the real world or from the world of the imagination. It can take place in the initial stages of a drawing and can serve as a means of early thinking about one's subject; it is an idea generator.

Gestural marks themselves can be the subject of the drawing. It is a fast, direct route to that part of us that has immediate recognition, that sees, composes, and organizes in a split second.

The basic approaches of gesture, continuous-line, and organizational-line drawing train the artist to search out underlying structure. They are quick means of noting planes and volumes and locating them in space. They help us digest the whole before going to the parts. These approaches furnish a blueprint for a more sustained drawing and provide a compositional unity early in the drawing.

Contour drawing, on the other hand, offers a means to a slow, intense inspection of the parts. It refines our seeing and leads us to a more detailed understanding of how the parts relate to the whole.

These comprehensive beginning approaches introduce ways of translating three-dimensional forms onto a two-dimensional surface. Through these techniques, we

2.24. ANDRÉ MASSON. *Automatic Drawing.* 1925. Ink, 1'3½" x 9½" (39.4 cm x 24.1 cm). *Musée National d'Art Moderne, Paris. Reunion des Musées Nationaux/Art Resource, New York.* © 2007 Artists Rights Society (ARS), New York/ADAGP, Paris.

are made aware of the limits of the page without our having to refer constantly to it. They offer a means to establish unity in the drawing, to place shapes and volumes in their proper scale and proportion. They introduce lights and darks as well as a sense of space into the drawing, suggest areas for focal development, and provide rhythm and movement.

Finally, these beginning approaches provide a flexible and correctable beginning for a more extended drawing. They give options for developing the work over a longer period of time. They point the route to a finished drawing.

SKETCHBOOK PROJECTS

At the conclusion of each chapter, you will find recommendations for sketchbook projects to be done in tandem with the studio problems. However, before you begin, read the first two Practical Guides, on "Materials" and "Keeping a Sketchbook."

Since the steps for each beginning technique have been thoroughly discussed in this chapter, it should be sufficient to offer you some ideas appropriate for each project.

Gestural Line Drawings

One major change from the instructions that were given previously in regard to gesture drawing involves scale. Since the sketchbook is so much smaller than your drawing pad, and since you will be drawing while seated rather than standing at an easel, remember that the gestural movement will be more limited. Your shoulder should still be relaxed and the wrist kept loose. Do not hold the drawing implement in the same way you hold it for writing; this produces a constricted line. You want the impetus for the movement to come from the arm and wrist even though the motions are scaled down, so experiment with handling the drawing tool loosely, holding it in the middle of the shaft or at the opposite end of the marker.

Here are some suggestions for subject matter:

- Animals, your own pet or animals in a zoo
- Crowds in a shopping mall
- Sports events or musical performances
- Children in parks or playgrounds
- Café scenes
- People dancing
- People waiting for buses or in buses, on planes, or on trains
- Landscapes (parks, waterscapes, city scenes, buildings)
- Family members or roommates performing daily chores
- Interior scenes (classrooms, dormitory rooms, rooms in your home)
- Clothing hung in closets, draped on chairs, thrown on the floor
- Draped fabric, unmade beds

Daily dedication to gesture will give a secure underpinning to your drawing skills.

PROJECT **2**

Continuous-Line and Organizational-Line Drawings

Continuous-line and organizational-line drawings can be done with more static subject matter than gesture drawings.

- Choose subjects that are arranged in spatial relationships, such as a group of objects on a table, a room setting that involves a grouping of furniture, or a landscape.
- Keep in mind the idea of transparency; make the lines cut through forms and through space. The relationship between the objects should be foremost in your mind.
- Practice sighting even when you are not drawing. Learn to visually take measure of objects and the space they occupy.

PROJECT **3**

Blind Contour Drawings

Literally anything and everything make appropriate subjects for contour drawings. Making contour drawings is a form of meditation. You can spend five minutes or an hour on a single drawing, depending on your time and mood. You probably have played the childhood game of repeating a word so many times that it loses its referential meaning and becomes pure sound. This could be an analogy for what happens in the process of a slow contour drawing. An ideal state comes when you are looking so intently at the object that you forget the name of the object being drawn. You become so absorbed in looking that the object becomes pure form.

Here is a starter list for blind contour subject matter:

- Hands, feet, and faces
- Articles of clothing such as gloves and shoes
- Fruits, vegetables, and plants
- Tools, drawing implements, and desktop articles
- Vehicles such as bicycles, motorcycles, automobiles, trucks
- Toys
- Friends—sleeping, reading, working, playing
- Animals
- Self-portraits
- Contents of a drawer, refrigerator, or cabinet

PROJECT 4

Automatic Drawing

Related to gestural technique is the Surrealist experiment with automatic drawing *(figure 2.23)*. The Surrealist André Masson characterized his response to the process as a "happy surprise or a strange malaise" (Doris A. Birmingham, "André Masson's Trance/Formations," *Art on Paper,* March–April 1999, p. 49). The technique is a form of self-hypnosis. The first condition is to free the mind and to enter into a trancelike state; second, to abandon oneself to "interior tumult"; and third, to begin rapid mark making or, as the Surrealists called it, "writing."

Automatic drawings are works made without prior planning, deliberation, or forethought. Despite certain similarities between them, they can be remarkably diverse. "When one goes very quickly, the drawing is mediumistic, as if dictated by the unconscious. The hand must move quite rapidly so that conscious thought cannot intervene and direct the gesture," Masson advised.

Automatic drawing can be done throughout your drawing career. It is an ideal relaxing technique, and you will learn how it can furnish you with fresh, new ideas. Think of it as an exercise that clears the mind, conditions the eye, and relaxes the hand.

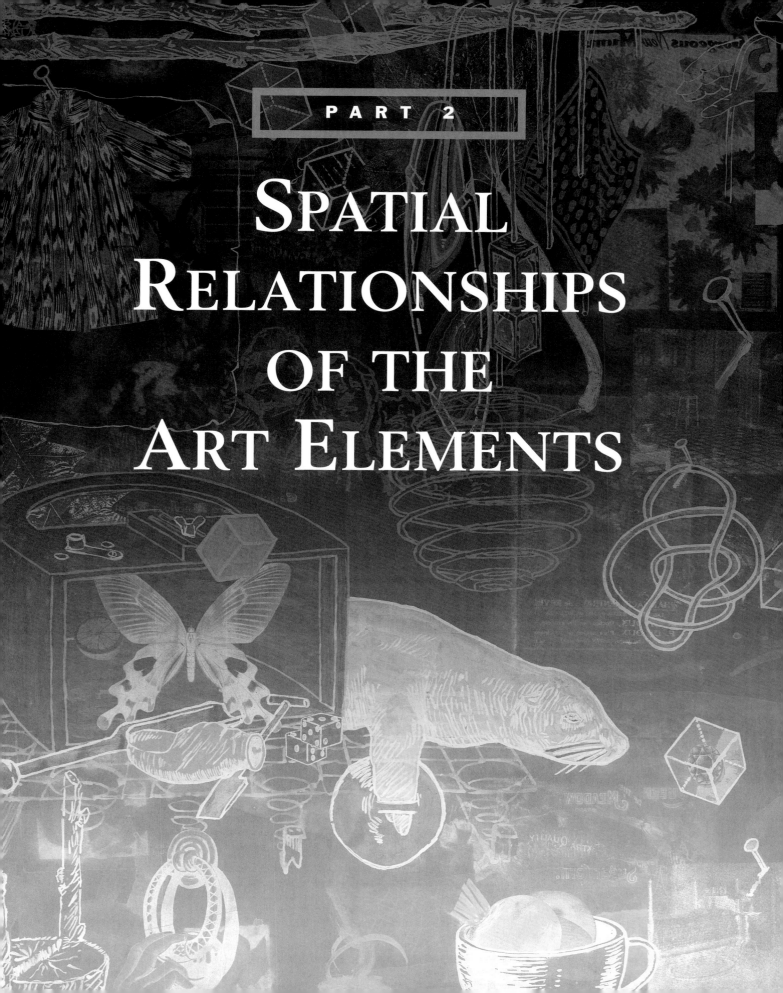

SPATIAL RELATIONSHIPS OF THE ART ELEMENTS

. . . ambiguity is the principal source of the inexhaustible richness of art. —ROGER N. SHEPARD

Spatial Relationships of the Art Elements

DEVELOPMENT OF SPATIAL RESPONSE

Octavio Paz writes that our senses are "capable of extending throughout the entire universe and touching it. Not seeing with one's hands but touching with one's eyes" (Paz, *Convergences*, p. 296). In Chapter 2, "Learning to See," we discovered how this is possible—to see with our hands and touch with our eyes—and we began to see how important space is to the artist. We readily interpret marks on a surface as spatial notations. This tendency stems from three main sources: first, the way we gather information from the world around us; second, the way we feel about things; and third, the culture we live in. We are fascinated with space and with *visual*, *perceptual*, and *spatial ambiguities*. An ambiguity presents two or more incompatible interpretations; both interpretations cannot be mutually held. Ambiguity can be illustrated with the famous image of the rabbit-duck, or of the vase made by two profiles of a person. The images switch back and forth as your eyes and brain make alternating interpretations. You are probably familiar with the drawings and prints of the Dutch artist M. C. Escher, whose work has been widely reproduced on posters and T-shirts *(figure II.1)*. Escher's popularity attests to our interest in spatial ambiguities.

Since the Modernist period began in the latter part of the nineteenth century, artists have favored spatial ambiguity in their work. Note with what simple means the Surrealist Oscar Domínguez has presented a complex spatial statement *(figure II.2)*. The head transforms from (or into?) a square plane, itself lying on top of (or behind?) the red border. The curved line at the top can be interpreted as the top of the head or as an eyebrow. Is the rectangle a window into space? Or is it the square-headed man's eye? Is the crescent the side view of his eye? Or are we looking through a window at a moon?

As Domínguez's work shows, marks are not simply two-dimensional lines on paper, they are spatial illusions. The predilection to perceive *pictorial space* is universal, but emotional responses to depicted space change over time with differing cultures. By *pictorial space*, we mean the kinds of space that are used on the *picture plane*, the surface on which the artist works, such as canvas or paper. The video artist Bill Viola has said that art deals with "how the world meets the mind, not the eye."

Many of our experiences are culture-based, so it is not a surprise that our art should reflect our culture. The drawing by Francis Yellow, a Lakota artist, is a striking example of the

role culture plays in art *(figure II.3)*. Employing a number of sophisticated spatial devices, the Native American artist recorded a battle between Plains Indians and U.S. soldiers. A nineteenth-century map of Nebraska provides the ground, both literally and figuratively, on which the encounter takes place. Familiar conventions of distance and scale are bypassed, and a powerful spatial code has been employed. The teepees are symbolic representations of the many Indian groups who took part in the battle; the abstracted horses and riders are contingent and overlap slightly, melding into one spinelike shape. The space used in this drawing is a *stacked space*, which indicates a progression moving from bottom to top, from near to far; however, there is no shift in scale to differentiate figures closer to the viewer from those farther away.

A difference in battle plan is relayed in the lineup of the two opposing forces; the straight line of the cavalry confronts the phalanx of the opposing fighters. The drawing resembles a game board in that it would seem logical to view this drawing as if it were on a table rather than hung on a wall. In the center of the "board," Yellow has depicted the first bloody encounter; the mythic red horse and rider rear violently into space while below them is a bloody blur

II.1. **M. C. ESCHER.** *Relativity.* 1953. Lithograph, 11" x 11²/₅" (28 cm x 29 cm).
© 2006 The M. C. Escher Company, Holland. *All rights reserved. www.mcescher.com*

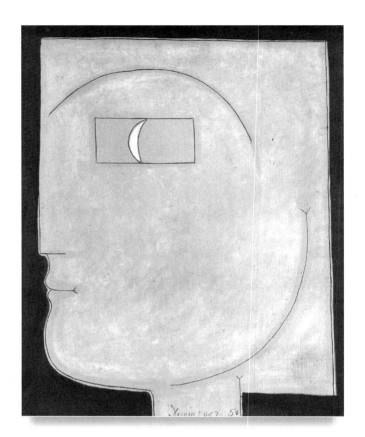

II.2. **OSCAR DOMÍNGUEZ.** *Tete.* 1950.
Oil on canvas, 1'9⅔" x 1'6" (55 cm x
46 cm). *Sotheby's catalog LN5173 #539.*
© 2007 Artist Rights Society (ARS), New
York/ADAGP, Paris.

II.3. **FRANCIS YELLOW.** *Wicoun Pinkte*
Maka Kin Ta Wicokunze Oyake Pelo
("They Said Treaties Shall Be the Law
of the Land"). Painting on a nineteenth-
century map.

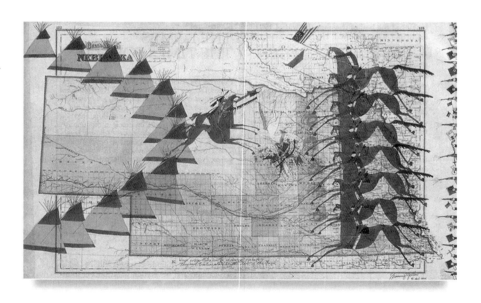

of the enemy. The negative spaces between the horses' chests and hindquarters echo the triangular patterns made by the teepees. In the frieze behind the soldiers, the artist has used *hierarchical space*, a spatial system that depicts persons or things according to rank, class, or status. From the sideline, tiny guns and treaties are waved in the air, giving rise to the title: *They Said Treaties Shall Be the Law of the Land.*

Each of us experiences and interprets space in an individual way. A child's idea of space differs from an adult's. In *figure II.4*, a Tunisian child has drawn a view of his hometown, an orderly, idealized place filled with

II.4. Drawing by a Tunisian child, from *Their Eyes Meeting the World* by Robert Coles, p. 77. *Copyright © 1992 by Robert Coles. Reprinted by permission of Houghton Mifflin Company. All rights reserved.*

people, places, and events important to him. Like other children's drawings, this one makes use of *conventionalized* or *symbolic space*, as opposed to *illusionistic, realistic,* or *naturalistic space*. Objects that are more important are larger, even though they occupy a more distant space, another example of hierarchical space. We recognize the conventions, the keys to interpreting the drawing. For example, the objects at the bottom of the page are meant to be closer whereas objects at the top of the page are to be seen as farther away. Fronts, sides, and roofs of buildings are depicted as if the viewer had an aerial view, but the mosque and the red building at the top of the page are drawn frontally. In other words, the child artist has shifted his viewpoint. Figures, plants, and animals are depicted schematically—note the stick figure at the upper left. A puzzling inset, a picture-within-a-picture, is placed off-center just below the road. Two children, their bodies cut off by the frame, appear to be looking out of the inset (a window superimposed on the otherwise logical space of the drawing). The child artist has invented a clever and personal device for showing us a view from his world. Spatially, this drawing carries the message that all is well in this teeming world of activity.

Pictorial space has been treated differently in different eras and cultures. A graphic example of this diversity can readily be seen in a 1994 drawing by Enrique Chagoya, *Uprising of the Spirit (figure II.5)*, whose subject is once again the clash between European and New World cultures. Conflicting icons represent three cultures, each occupying a

different space. Chagoya has recontextualized images from three different historical periods and geographical locations to signify the clash of three competing ideologies. The imposed popular culture of Mexico's North American neighbor is represented by Superman with his comic book spatial conventions. The flattened space used to depict the warrior comes from a Mixtec codex, or manuscript book, and contrasts with the illusionistic space of the insert. This sixteenth-century scene achieves its spatial effects through *linear perspective*, which literally means "to look through," as through a "window into space"—a convention unique to European art.

CATEGORIES OF SPACE

Art establishes a dialogue between the work of art and the viewer; it uses a language made up of the *formal elements:* color, line, shape, value, and texture. In art, form is created by the changing arrangements of the elements; a critical aspect of art is the way color, line, shape, value, and texture can be used to create pictorial space.

The chapters in Part II deal with the five art elements: shape, value, line, texture, and color, and the conventions used to create various spatial illusions. These elements will provide the building blocks for your own personal construction of space. Now let us categorize the different kinds of pictorial space and see how they contribute to the meaning of a work of art.

II.5. **ENRIQUE CHAGOYA.** *Uprising of the Spirit.* 1994. Acrylic and oil on paper, 4' x 6' (1.22 m x 1.83 m). *Los Angeles County Museum of Art (partial and promised gift of Ann and Aaron Nisenson). Gallery Paule Anglim.*

To help clarify some new terms with which to start building a vocabulary to discuss pictorial space, let's categorize some work according to spatial arrangements. In some drawings, artists translate objects as they exist in real space, which has height, width, and depth, onto a flat surface, which has only height and width. The space conveyed can be relatively *flat* or *shallow*, it can be *illusionistic* (that is, giving the impression of space and volume), or it can be *ambiguous*, neither clearly flat nor clearly three-dimensional.

In A. R. Penck's work *(figure II.6)*, the symbols and figures are stated as flat shapes to create a shallow space. (Of course, any mark on paper distinguishes between positive space and negative space.) Penck even dispenses with overlap, a common device for conveying the idea of arrangement of forms in space. The shapes resemble cutout forms with jagged edges. There is an illogical scale shift from the rather uniformly sized symbols to the taller figure on the right, which creates an ambiguity in scale. The work is abstract but highly personalized. Penck (a pseudonym; the original Penck was a geologist who studied the Ice Age) works in an autobiographical mode. His crossing (in 1980, during the time of the Berlin Wall) from East Germany to the West provided him with an archetypal theme of passage. The bleak images produce an impact of primitive and mythic import. We classify this artist's space as flat, two-dimensional space.

A second work that employs flat shapes while introducing overlap is the collage *Roots Odyssey* by the African-American artist Romare Bearden *(figure II.7)*. A more complex space than used in the Penck work is achieved by a division of the picture plane to indicate various levels of space: sky, water, ship, land, and figure. The looming foreground silhouette on the right claims the dominant conceptual space. The outline of Africa and the slave ship seem to spring from the figure's imagination. The rising sun and the abstracted birds provide a sense of implied movement and symbolically represent Bearden's hope for freedom. Each shape is clearly two-dimensional, yet overlap and scale shift contribute to a limited or shallow space. Penck and Bearden both deal with crossing over and dispersion.

The drawing of a room by Toba Khedoori *(figure II.8)* is a clear example of the category of illusionistic three-dimensional space. The viewer is led into deep space through a series of openings. By simple means of perspective (note the angles of the edges of floor and ceiling), overlap, modulated lights and darks, and a shift in scale from the front to the back openings, the artist suggests a deep penetration of space. Because the drawing is 12' by 12', even larger than the average room, the illusion is such that one feels one could literally walk into the drawing.

Another artist who exploits the spatial confines of the two-dimensional picture plane is Stephen Talasnik. His spatially illusionistic motifs *(figure II.9)* are large in scale, mirroring his interest in architectural structure. Talasnik conveys an illusion of volume by building a rich tactile surface created by abrasions and erasure. The result is a dramatic *chiaroscuro* effect; that is, using light and dark to create a sense of volume and dimension. Talasnik's monumental structural shapes look like scaffolds wheeling in a cosmic space; even the narrow dark shape at the bottom of the drawing suggests a vast horizontal plane on which the forms have been anchored. Lighter, faded-out structures seem to have been cut loose from their moorings and are

II.6. **A. R. PENCK.** *T.III.* 1981. Dispersion on canvas, 6'7" x 9'2½" (2.01 m x 2.81 m). *Collection Martin Sklar, New York.*

II.7. **ROMARE BEARDEN.** *Roots Odyssey.* 1976. Offset lithograph, printed in color, 2'4⁵⁄₁₆" x 1'9" (71.9 cm x 53.4 cm). *Collection Ben and Beatrice Goldstein, New York. © Romare Bearden Foundation/Licensed by VAGA, New York.*

II.8. **TOBA KHEDOORI.** *Untitled (Rooms).*
2001. Oil and wax on paper, 12' x 12'
(3.66 m x 3.66 m). *Courtesy the artist, Regen Projects, Los Angeles, and David Zwirner, New York.*

II.9. **STEPHEN TALASNIK.** *New Frontier.*
1993–1994. Graphite on paper, 1'2" x
4'8" (35.6 cm x 1.42 m). *Albertina Museum, Vienna. © Stephen Talasnik, Courtesy Marlborough Gallery, New York.*

floating off into space. Although this drawing makes use of illusionistic three-dimensional space, a spatial ambiguity pervades the work due to the illogical overlap of the structures and the tacked-on rectangle with its basketlike form at the right. So this drawing fits into a third category, *ambiguous space*.

Jim Nutt suggests a theatrical space for his metaphorical narratives *(figure II.10)*. Illogicality abounds in his quirky, ingenious, and wildly convoluted spatial innovations. The spaces conveyed in Nutt's explosive domestic scenes are *ambiguous*, neither clearly flat nor clearly three-dimensional. Dominating the work is the signature Jim Nutt frame, large pattern-painted frames that nearly overpower the scenes they enclose. Large quarter-circles that resemble heavy reinforcement tabs tack down the four corners of the enclosed central scene; they serve to "corner in" the participants in the drama. The shallow stagelike space is created by the receding wall and gridded ceiling. The arbitrary scale shift between hands, heads, and bodies (note the tiny figure on the lower right) creates an ambiguous space. The patterning of the frame, the tie, suit, dress, hair, and inner ears is a flattening device, and the overlap of arms and hands is a spatial indicator canceled by the arm and hand in front being smaller than the shape they cover. Spatial ambiguity is a foil for Nutt's psychologically ambiguous content.

TWENTIETH-CENTURY INNOVATIONS IN SPATIAL DEVELOPMENT

Artists' concepts of space have not only changed, but our ideas concerning real, physical space have also changed. Twentieth-century artists made many innovations in pictorial space. Five of importance to drawing will be considered, exemplified here by Pablo Picasso, Jackson Pollock, Robert Rauschenberg, Chuck Close, and Donald Baechler.

Cubists introduced reductive, abstracted forms, shattering the traditional idea of perspective by combining multiple views of the same object in a single composition, as seen in Picasso's drawing *(figure II.11)*. Traditional treatment of space was replaced by a discontinuity of space; the image was presented in multiple views—side, top, inside, outside, showing collapsed and simultaneous views of a single subject and of the space surrounding it. The resulting space is highly ambiguous. The Cubists described objects in a new way by depicting space itself as if it were made up of tangible planes and interlocking shapes. A new technique of the Cubists was the introduction of collage, which some critics have called the most notable innovation in drawing in the last 300 years.

A second innovation in pictorial space came with Jackson Pollock and the Abstract Expressionists. Pollock

II.10. **JIM NUTT.** *Not So Fast.* 1982.
Acrylic on Masonite, acrylic on wood
frame, 2'6¾" x 3'1½" (78 cm x 95 cm).
Private collection. Phyllis Kind Gallery.
AP1984.23.

II.11. **PABLO PICASSO.** *Bottle, Glass and*
Violin. 1912–1913. Paper collage and
charcoal, 1'6½" x 2'⅜" (47 cm x 62
cm). *Moderna Museet, Stockholm. © 2007*
Estate of Pablo Picasso/Artists Rights Society
(ARS), New York.

developed a unique method; by laying the canvas on the
floor, he was able to walk around it and paint from all sides
(figure II.12). He applied paint with rapid gestural movements, dripping, splattering, and pouring, allowing the liquid paint to weave rhythms over the surface. The shift
from the vertical to the horizontal had a surprising spatial
effect.

Abstract Expressionist images are not "images of"
anything; they are a result of action. This fundamental
change signals a real departure in the spatial orientation of
the work. The space in Franz Kline's black-and-white configurations *(figure II.13)* is ambiguous because the marks refer back to the flatness of the picture plane. The hallmark of
Modernist space is the *autonomy of the picture plane*.

II.12. **HANS NAMUTH.** *Jackson Pollock, 1950.* Photograph. *© 1991 Estate of Hans Namuth, courtesy Center for Creative Photography, University of Arizona.*

II.13. **FRANZ KLINE.** *Untitled.* 1954. Oil on paper, 11" x 8½" (28 cm x 22 cm). *Collection of the Modern Art Museum of Fort Worth, Museum Purchase, The Benjamin J. Tillar Memorial Trust. © 2007 Franz Kline Estate/Artists Rights Society (ARS), New York.*

In the aftermath of the Abstract Expressionist movement, which lasted well into the 1950s, Robert Rauschenberg, along with other Pop artists, brought further spatial innovations to art. Pop artists' aim was to reintroduce everyday life back into art. Rauschenberg realized that additive material could be whatever he chose, and his choices were extraordinary: chairs, tables, stuffed goats and roosters, and pillows and mattresses are among the actual objects he incorporated into his work. He called these hybrid composite works "Combines." Unlike other artists who incorporated found objects in their work, he did not reconfigure the objects; they were left as they were, lifted from real space to have a life on another surface. Rauschenberg took nonart material and turned it into compositionally intricate works; he "represented" photographs from newspapers, magazines, and advertisements by rubbing or transferring them onto the picture plane, as seen in *figure II.14*.

The critic Leo Steinberg characterized Rauschenberg's working surface as a "flatbed picture plane" (Steinberg, *Other Criteria*, p. 82). That is, it is like a flat, horizontal surface on which anything can be placed. Steinberg saw this new conception of the horizontal plane as a depository for "culture."

A third innovation of pictorial space was that of the Photo-Realists, who recorded the patterns that a camera sees—both its focus and distortion. For Photo-Realists the subject was the photograph itself. Duplicating what the camera sees and how a photograph looks results in a space that is three-dimensionally illusionistic and flat at the same time. It is a hybrid space. An example can be seen in Chuck Close's photo-realistic work created with fingerprints *(see figure II.15)*.

Postmodernism employs the full range of pictorial space: flat, ambiguous, and illusionistic, frequently including all in the same composition. One particularly interesting development has been the overlay of images; even more innovative is the fact that the images are unrelated by technique, as in the Baechler drawing *(figure II.16)*. This Postmodern work is a *pastiche* (a combination of several styles in one work) of several spatial conventions. Postmodern art is characterized by layered images appropriated from various sources, both from popular culture and from art. In Baechler's work, the abstracted black-and-white flower is flattened by a heavy outline. The background is an irregular grid of squares and rectangles made up of patterns of large and small dots. The regularity of pattern creates a shallow, pulsating space; the larger dots tend to come forward whereas the smaller ones recede. A variety of spatial treatments are used in the rectangular insets. In the lower left, a hooded head is treated traditionally with modeling and shading; a three-dimensional space is the result. The same is true for the lemons and lime in the adjoining square; however, their isolation from the background makes them appear to float, so here the spatial interpretation is ambiguous. Two small insets

II.14. **ROBERT RAUSCHENBERG.** *The Vain Convoy of Europe Out West (Kabal American Zephyr).* 1982. Solvent transfer, acrylic, fabric, and paper on wood, with wood table, wood chair back, metal wheel, plastic traffic cone, license plate, animal horns, and metal oar, 6'2" x 8'½" x 3'5½" (1.88 m x 2.451 m x 1.054 m). *Private collection. Photographer Glenn Steigelman. © Robert Rauschenberg/Licensed by VAGA, New York.*

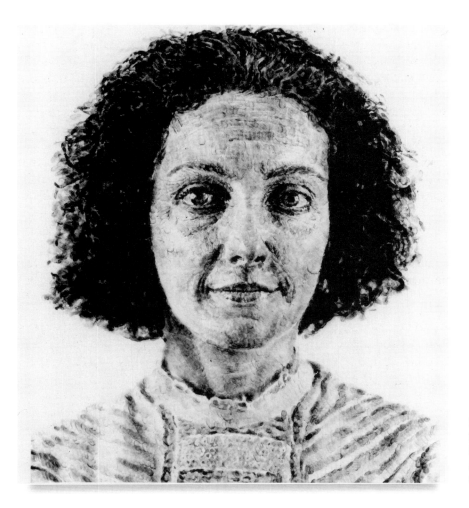

II.15. **CHUCK CLOSE.** *Emily/Fingerprint.* 1986. Carbon transfer etching, 3'10" x 3'½" (1.173 m x 93.1 cm). *Published by Pace Editions and Graphicstudio. © Chuck Close.*

taken from cartoon strips employ flat, conventional space; the pair of silhouetted figures in the lower right are flat, two-dimensional shapes; the two sets of concentric circles create a spatial tension owing to their shift in scale; and the pages of printed numbers invoke yet another kind of space. Baechler has established a tension between all the parts of a spatially complex work.

The Influence of Electronic Space

Production techniques, reproduction processes, digital tools, computer modification programs, and digital photography are only a few of the many technological advances that influence artists today. Video art is now a category in art like drawing or painting. Electronic space is decidedly different from the categories of space set forth in our earlier discussion.

Obviously, the computer and video screen have a different character and quality than paper or canvas. They are literally made up of particles of light and energy, yet in a sense they are more neutral than traditional art surfaces. The tactile difference is the defining one; there is an identifiable quality to a mark that has been electronically made. Because artists have always been attracted to new materials and new techniques, it is not surprising to find that technology influences contemporary art.

Howardena Pindell's "drawing" *(figure II.17)* is a photograph taken from a video screen. Light, energy, space, and movement go into its making. The drawing makes a sly comment on television sports shows with their instant-playback ability. It is as if a sports announcer had gone berserk with an analysis of a baseball play.

Machines will never replace the kind of critical thinking and informed making that is required in art. New technologies can help carry out artistic plans, but creative thinking remains indispensable.

Emotive Space

Before we conclude our discussion of space, let us look at an example of how space has been used to create an emotional effect. Martin Ramirez, a self-taught artist, was a mute and

II.16. **DONALD BAECHLER. *Black Flower #1.*** 1994. Gouache, gesso, and collage on paper, 4'11" x 3'11" (1.499 m x 1.194 m) overall. *Sperone Westwater.*

II.17. **HOWARDENA PINDELL. *Untitled (Video Drawing: Baseball Scenes).*** 1974. Color photograph, 11" x 1'2" (27.9 cm x 35.6 cm). *The High Museum, Atlanta. Courtesy of the artist.*

withdrawn psychotic. Institutionalized as a schizophrenic for the last 30 years of his life, he turned to drawing as a sympathetic companion. Meager supplies forced him to improvise materials. He glued together old scraps of papers, cups, candy wrappers—anything he could find to create a drawing surface. Often he made glue from mashed potatoes and water, even from bread and saliva. His working methods reflected his psychotic nature; he kept his drawings rolled up, working on only a small exposed area at a time.

The space in his drawings reveals his inner fears *(figure II.18)*. Entrapped animals occupy spaces too small to contain them. Walls close in on the frightened personal

II.18. **MARTIN RAMIREZ.** *Untitled (Horse and Rider).* ca. 1950. Pencil on paper, 2'1" x 2' (63.5 cm x 61 cm). *Phyllis Kind Gallery.*

stand-ins. In *Horse and Rider*, the horse has its head thrown back as if in anguish. The legs are peculiarly proportioned; the back legs are longer and nearer the viewer than is logical. The stereotypical *bandito* character has his head twisted backward. Both he and the horse are taut with tension; they seem ready to run. The tomblike space is psychologically loaded.

An inner world or a psychic reality can be created through pictorial space; it can alienate, distance, absorb, expand, or condense. *Emotive space* can refer to a dream space, a theatrical space, or a psychological space. It can be a void or it can be dynamic. Space can be mythic and symbolic. It can also be chaotic or orderly, or frightening or soothing.

CONCLUSION

Whether the emphasis is on flat, shallow, illusionistic, actual, or ambiguous space, the concept of space is a challenge of lasting interest to all who are dedicated to art, makers and viewers alike. It holds the key to unraveling the manifold meanings art can have.

The chapters in Part II deal with the spatial relationships of art elements, beginning with shape, value, line, texture, and color. In each chapter, we consider the way the elements can be used to create different kinds of space. At the end of each chapter, you will find a summary of the spatial characteristics of that element. Part II concludes with a chapter dealing with spatial illusion and perspective. Soon you will be well versed in the many uses of pictorial space.

SKETCHBOOK PROJECT

The sketchbook is flexible. It can be used as a drawing pad, as a notebook, and as a scrapbook. The following project encourages some informative collecting for spatial references to be used throughout your career as an artist.

Simple exercises like this will open your eyes to new possibilities in looking at and making art; they will be the means by which you build a solid critical vocabulary to use in art analysis and critiques, both of which are essential activities for the artist.

Making a Space Folder

- Find at least 10 examples each of three-dimensional, illusionistic space; two-dimensional or relatively flat space; and ambiguous space, a combination of both two- and three-dimensional space in the same work. From newspapers, magazines, postcards, and books on art, make a photocopy of each example.
- Place them in a folder and label each sample according to its spatial category.
- Jot a few notes that indicate the characteristics that determine your decision.
- As we complete each chapter, look at your samples once again and amplify your initial assessments. For example, after we have worked with some exercises in the following chapter on shape, you will have an expanded idea of how shape can be used to create various kinds of space.
- Throughout the course, as you find other examples of spatial treatment that appeal to you, clip them and add to your file. You will soon have a folder of material to assist with your own work.

CHAPTER 3

What I look for in the beginning are shapes, a subdivision
of the square. . . . go after the big shapes first, then make them
three-dimensional, from Matisse toward Vermeer. —**PHILIP PEARLSTEIN**

Shape/Plane and Volume

hilip Pearlstein's work, *Mickey Mouse Puppet Theater... (figure 3.1)*, illustrates the first element we will consider in creating pictorial spatial relationships—shape. A *shape* is a configuration that has height and width and is, therefore, two-dimensional. We will begin our study of pictorial space with shape; then we will learn how shape can be converted to plane; and, finally, we will consider how shape and plane can be made to appear as volume.

SHAPE

Geometric and Organic Shapes

Shapes can be divided into two basic categories: *geometric* and *organic*. Squares, rectangles, triangles, trapezoids, rhomboids, hexagons, and pentagons, as well as circles, ovals, and ellipses are only a few of many geometric shapes that are created by mathematical laws dealing with measurement and relationships of lines and angles.

Geometric principles have been used since prehistoric times. Cave paintings and petroglyphs make use of triangles, circles, squares, crosses, and other geometric forms, simple

3.1. **PHILIP PEARLSTEIN.** *Mickey Mouse Puppet Theater, Jumbo Jet and Kiddie Tractor with Two Models.* Early stages of an oil painting. *Betty Cunningham Gallery, New York.*

3.2. **KRISTINE SPINDLER-GUNNELL.** *People of the Raffia Palm.* 1993. Woodcut, 1'11" x 2'2" (58 cm x 66 cm). *Permanent Collection. Courtesy of Arrowmont School of Arts and Crafts, Gatlinburg, Tenn.*

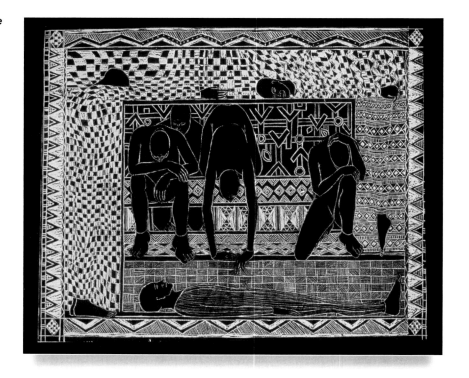

shapes to symbolize objects. Geometric shapes communicate in a universal language; simple signs can be read more quickly than words—think of signage in airports and on highways. Geometric forms lend themselves well to repetition and alteration and are favored for making patterns and decorations *(figure 3.2)*. Note how Kristine Spindler-Gunnell enhances a composition through repeating geometric shapes.

The geometric tradition is at work in contemporary art, as seen in Joel Shapiro's work *(figure 3.3)*. Shapiro's motifs are rectilinear forms overlaid onto an activated background. He uses slightly altered and repeated geometric shapes whose points of contact vary from shape to shape. It is this difference of placement that creates interesting tensions in the drawing.

Geometric forms are useful for analyzing and reducing objects to their basic fundamental shapes, as seen in the contour drawing by William Daley *(figure 3.4)*. His drawings are based on the interplay of geometric shapes suggestive of steps, fans, cylinders, lobes, and arcs. In large drawings made directly on the studio wall, he uses a compass and straightedge to achieve a mechanical effect. There is a slight suggestion of volume in Daley's drawing owing to the double outline of certain forms; here the shapes are seen as edges of planes.

A second category of shape is *organic shape*. Organic shape is less regular than geometric shape and is sometimes referred to as *biomorphic, amoeboid*, or *free form*. An example of organic shape can be seen in a drawing by Betty Woodman *(figure 3.5)*. Woodman isolates and recombines the component parts of vases. Using a two-part composition, she uses repeating organic shapes; the washes suggest transparent glazed surfaces used in ceramics. Just as Woodman deconstructs a vase to cancel its traditional uses, her drawing presents fragments in an expressive mode.

In Romare Bearden's collage, *Interior with Profiles (figure 3.6)*, the figures are built of organic shapes whereas the background is predominantly geometric—squares

3.3. **JOEL SHAPIRO.** *Untitled.* 1996. Silk screen, edition of 108, 3'9" x 3'3" (1.09 m x 99 cm). *© 2007 Joel Shapiro/Artists Rights Society (ARS), New York.*

3.4. **WILLIAM DALEY.** *Conic Loop Revisited.* 1994. Graphite, whiteout on Strathmore board, 2'6" x 3'4⅛" (76.8 cm x 1.019 m). *Arkansas Arts Center Foundation Collection: Purchase, Tabriz Fund. 1994.047.*

3.5. **BETTY WOODMAN.** *Drawing for Balustrade #81.* 1993–1994. Mixed media on paper, 7'11" x 4'5" (2.41 m x 1.35 m). *Arkansas Arts Center Foundation Collection: Purchase, Tabriz Fund. 1994.049.002.*

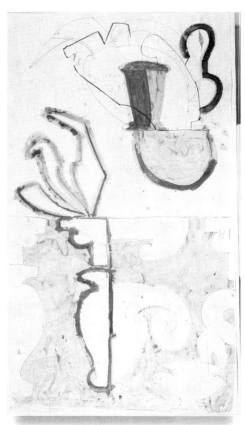

and rectangles. Shapes are created predominantly by textural patterns and by flat values. The collage is organized along horizontal and vertical axes, which both flatten and stabilize the composition. The figures remind us of an Egyptian frieze. Spatial ambiguity is reinforced by an illogical scale between the parts.

3.6. **ROMARE BEARDEN.** *Interior with Profiles.* 1969. Collage, 3'3¾" x 4'1⅞" (1.01 m x 1.27 m). *First National Bank of Chicago.* © *Romare Bearden Foundation/Licensed by VAGA, New York.*

Implied Shape

Shapes can be made by value, line, texture, or color. Alternatively, artists create shape through the use of implied shape. Implied shape forces a viewer to fill in the missing parts of a composition. In the drawing by Juliao Sarmento *(figure 3.7)*, the viewer fills in the missing parts of the body. Sarmento's drawing suggests an enigmatic narrative that is emphasized by the implied shapes. The figures dissolve into the paper itself, thereby encouraging the viewer to complete the shapes.

Our perception is such that we often fill in an omitted segment of a shape and perceive that shape as completed or closed *(figure 3.8)*. We tend to perceive the simplest structure that will complete the shape rather than a more complex one *(figure 3.9)*. We group smaller shapes into their larger organizations and see the parts as they make up the whole *(figure 3.10)*.

The open circular form made by a dragged-out brush in the work by Robert Motherwell conveys the artist's interest in stylistic gesture *(figure 3.11)*. The eye completes the circle in spite of the abrupt ending to the flow of the shape. The constricted opening leads the eye into an enclosed white shape. Many contemporary artists purposefully contradict accepted rules of composition and of perception; like Motherwell, they challenge the viewer visually to complete the circle.

Shapes can be further distinguished by the use of negative and positive shapes, which we explore in the following section.

3.7. **JULIAO SARMENTO. *They Pass in an Air of Perfumes (Dublin-Dublin, 1904).*** 1996. Mixed media on canvas, 51 x 35½ inches. *Courtesy Sean Kelly Gallery, New York. Used with permission, 2006. Photograph Orcutt and Van Der Patten, New York.*

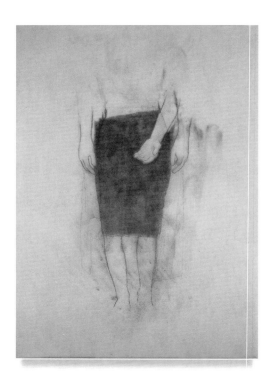

3.8. Incomplete shapes are perceived as completed or closed.

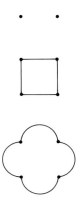

3.9. The four dots are perceived as forming a square rather than a more complex shape.

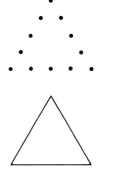

3.10. Smaller shapes are perceived as part of their larger organization.

POSITIVE AND NEGATIVE SHAPES

On the *picture plane*—the surface on which you are drawing—another distinction between shapes is that between positive and negative. *Positive shape* refers to the shape of the object drawn. In Robert Longo's drawing *(figure 3.12)*, the dark, static shape of the jacket overpowers the figure below. The image is isolated in an empty negative space.

Negative space describes the space surrounding the positive forms. Negative space is relative to positive shapes. In Jacob Lawrence's contour drawing *(figure 3.13)*, a family is gathered around a table. The floor forms a ground for the chair, for the child in the foreground, for the baby, and for the table. The chair is negative to the father, as is the table top; the plane of the table is also negative to the child and the book, to the objects on the table, and to the mother's hand. The wall is negative to the mother and child but positive to the rectangular opening. The tree, in turn, is positive to the space behind it. The mother is negative to the child in front of her but positive to the wall behind her. This convoluted description unravels the way shape is used to create space.

Although the space in Lawrence's drawing suggests a movement from near to far, it is a compressed progression from bottom to top of the picture plane. The idea of a progressive space lies more in the viewer's mind than in the drawing itself. The objects on the table are placed as if the table were horizontal, when, in fact, it is sharply tilted. Because of overlap, we have no difficulty deciphering the spatial layout of the drawing, but it is unrelated to the way space functions in the real world. The two elements of line and shape are the carriers of the drawing's meaning—unified shapes for Lawrence in this work symbolize a unified family.

In real life we are conditioned to search out positive shapes, but this habit must be broken in making art. On the picture plane all shapes, both positive and negative, are equally important. Combined, they give a composition unity. As we have seen in Lawrence's drawing, the integration of positive and negative shapes is so complete that it is nearly impossible to classify each shape as either positive or

3.11. **ROBERT MOTHERWELL.** *Untitled (Black Gesture).* 1982. Acrylic on rag board, 2'5" x 1'11" (74 cm x 58 cm). *Collection of the Modern Art Museum of Fort Worth, Museum Purchase; gift of the artist.* © Dedalus Foundation, Inc./Licensed by VAGA, New York.

3.12. **ROBERT LONGO.** *Untitled.* 1978. Charcoal on paper, 2'6" x 3'4" (76 cm x 1.02 m). *Collection Robert Halff. Metro Pictures.* © University Art Museum, University of California, Santa Barbara.

negative. The progression of space in the work does not follow the logical recession seen in real life.

Positive/Negative Interchange

The terms *positive/negative* and *figure/ground* are interchangeable. In the Kurt Schwitters drawing *(figure 3.14)*, the shapes switch from positive to negative. The

3.13. **JACOB LAWRENCE.** *The Family.*
1957. Pencil on paper, 2'3¾" x 1'11"
(70 cm x 58 cm). *The Arkansas Arts Center Foundation Purchase: Museum Purchase
Plan of the NEA and the Tabriz Fund, 1974.
1974.011.00b. © 2007 The Jacob and Gwen-
dolyn Lawrence Foundation, Seattle/Artists
Rights Society (ARS), New York.*

3.14. **KURT SCHWITTERS** (1887–1948).
Pencil Drawing, 1938. Pencil on paper,
410 mm x 308 mm. *Lent by Philip
Granville, 1999. © 2007 Artists Rights Society
(ARS), New York/VG Bild-Kunst, Bonn.
Photo Credit: Tate Gallery, London, Great
Britain.*

circle can be seen as either a positive shape or a negative void. This switching from solid to void creates an ambiguous space.

Other terms commonly used to describe positive and negative shapes include *foreground/background*, *figure/field*, and *solid/void*. Negative space is also called *empty space*; the spaces between objects or shapes are called *interspaces* or *interstices*.

Composite Shape

A *composite* shape is best defined as two or more combined objects that create a unified, single shape. Donald Sultan purposely creates an image *(figure 3.15)* that can be interpreted as either abstract or concrete. A tulip with its head turned inward to the leaves converts into a composite shape. Sultan reduces elements to shape and value, and he further reduces value to black and white. Since Sultan works with such simple subject matter, it is surprising to learn that he works from photographs. Using a Polaroid camera with an extremely limited depth of field, he shoots an extreme close-up of the objects. The composite shapes depend on the negative shapes to define them. This "flip-flopping" between figure and ground relates to film, where positive and negative are reversed.

Silhouette

We should not conclude our discussion of shape without looking at silhouettes. *Silhouettes*, or shadow portraits, were developed at the end of the eighteenth century as a way to produce inexpensive likenesses to a famous piece of art. By the middle of the nineteenth century, however, silhouettes were replaced by the invention of

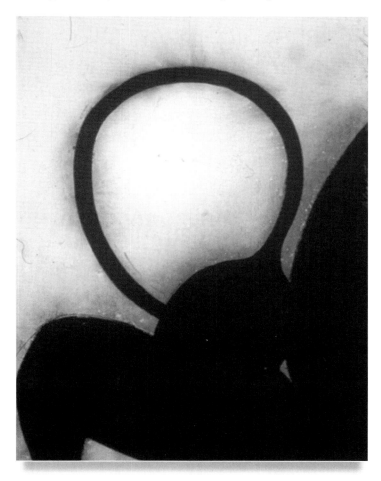

3.15. **DONALD SULTAN.** *Black Tulip Feb. 28, 1983.* Charcoal and graphite on paper, 4'2" x 3'2" (1.27 m x 96.5 cm). *Courtesy of the artist.*

3.16. **RUSSELL CROTTY.** *Untitled.* 1999.
Ink on paper in linen bound book, 32 x
83 inches open: 3 foldouts. *Courtesy of
CRG Gallery from the collection of Geoff Tuck
and Dave Richards.*

the camera. Recently, the silhouette has experienced a rebirth of sorts, which is exemplified in the work of artist Russell Crotty.

Crotty uses silhouette in his folded frieze, actually pages of a book *(figure 3.16)*. He depicts a tree or flame shape outlined against a darkened sky. The two silhouettes—the circle and the jagged triangular form—suggest a reduction of a landscape, troubling in its horizontal orientation.

PROBLEM 3.1

Geometric Shapes Used to Create Pattern

For this drawing, invent a subject taken from your memory. Use geometric shapes, outline, flat values, and invented texture to create patterns. Fill the entire page with enclosed shapes.

The print by Kristine Spindler-Gunnell is a good response to this problem (see *figure 3.2*). A composition within a composition using simplified figures is enhanced by the addition of the enclosing frame. Repeating geometric shapes weave a pattern of secondary shapes. Consider using a complex textile in your drawing as well.

PROBLEM 3.2

Geometric and Organic Shapes

Using gray charcoal paper and a black conté crayon stick, make a line drawing of a still life. With a white conté crayon stick, superimpose on the shapes in the still life positive and negative shapes of rectangles, triangles, and squares.

In a second still life drawing, impose circular forms. You will, of course, have to force the geometric shapes to fit the actual still life forms.

Look carefully at the subject. Which shapes are actually there? Which shapes are implied? Which types of shapes predominate? Invent shapes in the background that echo the positive ones.

In a third drawing, make a contour drawing of a figure in a room. Impose organic, amoeboid shapes on both the positive and negative forms. Ensure that negative spaces form enclosed shapes by making the composition go off the page on all four sides. An illustration of this exercise is seen in Jean-Pierre Larocque's drawing *(figure 3.17)*. The artist takes a playful approach in his exaggerated overlays.

PROBLEM 3.3

Interchangeable Positive and Negative Shapes

Make an arrangement of several objects in an environment. In this drawing, emphasize the negative spaces between the objects by making them equal in importance to the positive shapes. Make the positive and negative shapes switch off with one another; that is, make the positive forms seem empty and the negative shapes positive.

Robert Birmelin, in his oddly titled drawing, *The City Crowd, the Ear (figure 3.18)*, places emphasis on negative space. The centralized figure is a featureless shape. Dark values and grouped lines define the interstices between the figures. The foreground figure is cropped by the edge of the picture plane; this figure is massive and is swiftly moving out of the picture plane to the right. Negative shapes play a major role in defining not only space, but the positive figures as well. The empty white

3.17. **JEAN-PIERRE LAROCQUE.** *Untitled,*
1993. Gouache, graphite on paper,
30¼" x 44" (77 cm x 112 cm).
Arkansas Arts Center Foundation Collection:
Purchase, Tabriz Fund. 1994.050.001.

3.18. **ROBERT BIRMELIN.** *The City Crowd,*
the Ear. 1978. Conté crayon on paper,
1'10" x 2'5¾" (56 cm x 76 cm).
Arkansas Arts Center Foundation Collection:
Purchase. 1984.049.

figures are set in relief against their adjoining dark shapes. The agitated marks indicate the bustle of the crowd.

PROBLEM 3.4

Invented Negative Shapes

Make a drawing in which you invent negative shapes to relate to the positive shapes of your subject. A chair, bicycle, or tree limbs would be appropriate subjects.

Ada Sadler structures her drawing of a lawn chair around the ready-made patterns found in the chair's webbing *(figure 3.19)*. Cast shadows echo the woven seat; they form an undulating grid that anchors the chair. Triangles formed by the chair's tubular construction offer a secondary geometric theme. The consistency in the direction of the pastel strokes flattens the background shapes. Form and variation are the keys to this work.

PROBLEM 3.5

Composite Shape

Make a silhouette comprised of two overlapping objects to create a composite shape. We have seen an example of this merging of forms in the Sultan drawing (see *figure 3.15*), in which the tulip shape combines with the leaf and vase shapes to create a unified, single, composite shape. Ink or acrylic will produce a crisp

3.19. **ADA LIU SADLER.** *Taliesin West #2.* 1992. Pastel, 1'6" x 1'6" (46 cm x 46 cm). *Joseph Chowning Gallery, San Francisco.*

shape; charcoal creates a more dense mass and a more indefinite edge. Observe the edges of Sultan's image; pay attention to the leftover negative shapes. Place the composite shape tangent to the edge on at least two sides. Do not use a centralized shape completely surrounded by negative space.

A more complex handling of composite shape can be found in Mary Dryburgh's *Large Crow (figure 3.20)*. The bird is clearly defined; however, the remaining shapes are not immediately recognizable as objects from the real world. One can detect references to the crow's beak, head, wing, and tail in the surrounding positive and negative shapes. The negative white spaces are activated by smudges and powdery deposits from the charcoal. The crow is backlit, but otherwise the various positive and negative shapes occupy different levels of space.

The artist explains how she arrived at the composite shape: "A papier-mâché decoy sitting in my studio window amid assorted treasures. I like to start my drawings with an observed reality and explore other possibilities from that point."

THE SHAPE OF THE PICTURE PLANE

The shape of the picture plane is a major determinant of the layout of a drawing. Irving Tepper centralizes his subject in a square format *(figure 3.21)*. A centralized image can present the artist with a problem of how to handle the corners, but Tepper has resolved this problem by using circular shapes and abstract lines that reverberate outward from the saucer. The view is directly down into the cup, and this unusual point of view has the effect of transforming it into an abstract interplay of spherical forms.

3.20. **MARY DRYBURGH.** *Large Crow.* 1993. Charcoal on paper, 2' x 1'7" (61 cm x 48 cm). Collection of the artist. *Photograph by Photosmith.*

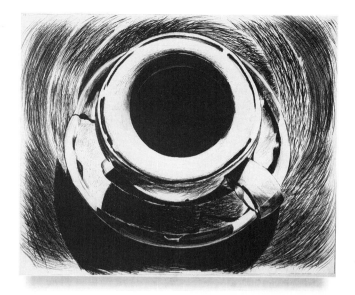

3.21. **IRVING TEPPER.** *Third Cup of Coffee.* 1983. Charcoal on paper, 3'7¾" x 4'3½" (1.111 m x 1.308 m). *Arkansas Arts Center Foundation Purchase, 1984.043.*

3.22. **NEIL JENNEY.** *Window #6.* 1971–1976. Oil on panel, 1'3¾" x 4'9½" (1.01 m x 1.46 m). *Thomas Ammann, Switzerland.*

The tree limbs in Neil Jenney's work *(figure 3.22)* conform to an eccentrically shaped frame. The branches are particularly suited to the chopped-off format; the angle of the limbs points to the lopsided structure. Jenney has updated the traditional window into space through the use of a nontraditional picture plane.

In both Tepper's and Jenney's works, we see how the shape of the picture plane is a major determinant in composition.

PROBLEM 3.6

Shape of the Picture Plane

Choose a subject from nature. On three different picture planes—a 12" square, a 9" by 18" rectangle, and an 18" circle—draw the selected image. Your goal is to fit the image into the confines of the three different planes. Distortion, exaggeration, and cropping will help determine your compositional choices.

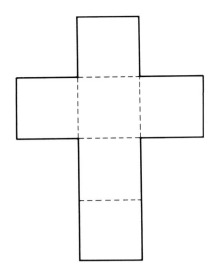

3.23. Cross-shaped form made from an opened box.

3.24. Diagram of a cube.

3.25. Cube diagram with interior lines erased.

SHAPE AS PLANE AND VOLUME

Volume is the three-dimensional equivalent of two-dimensional shape. Connected shapes become volumetric when they are read as *planes*. In art, volume is the illusion of three-dimensional space; volume defines *mass*, which deals with the weight or density of an object.

If you take a cube apart so that its six sides, or planes, lie flat, you have changed the cube from a three-dimensional form into a two-dimensional shape *(figure 3.23)*. This new cross shape is made up of the six planes of the original box and is now a flat shape. If you reassemble the cube, the reconnected planes (the sides, top, and bottom) once again suggest volume. If you make a representation of the box seen from below eye level with one of its corners turned toward you, it will be composed of only three visible planes. Even if you draw only these three planes, the illusion of three-dimensionality remains *(figure 3.24)*. If you erase the interior lines, leaving the outer outline only, you have again changed volume into a flat shape *(figure 3.25)*.

The key word here is *plane*. By connecting the sides, or planes, of the cube, you make a *planar analysis* of the box. Shape now functions as plane, as a component of volume.

In Joel Shapiro's diptych, or two-part drawing *(figure 3.26)*, shape is perceived spatially in two different ways. Shapiro is a minimalist sculptor whose work is concerned primarily with perceptual differences. The flatness of the black shape contrasts with the three-dimensional shape on the left, which has been broken up into planes. The blurred lines that extend outside the object's enclosed planes confound our perception of the figure as a box; the perspective produces an ambiguous space.

Using a more traditional presentation of shape as plane, Clarence Holbrook Carter creates an illusion of volume by connecting planes to create volumes *(figure 3.27)*. A monumental effect is achieved by seemingly simple means; the smaller, connected planes of the stairs lead to the middle ground occupied by buildings set at an angle. Carter achieves architectural unity by interlocking planes, by a consistent progression of small to larger shapes, and by the distribution of lights and darks.

Modeling is another way to transform shape into volume. *Modeling* is the change from light to dark across a surface to make a shape look volumetric. A drawing that uses both connected planes and modeling is *Stele (figure 3.28)* by Dorothea Rockburne.

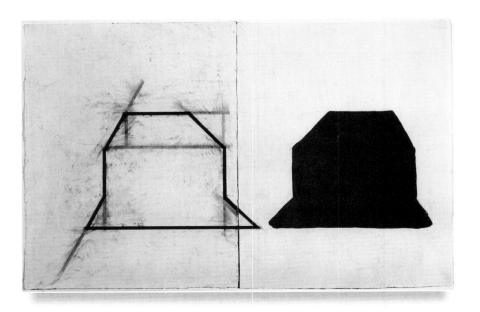

3.26. **JOEL SHAPIRO. *Untitled.*** 1979. Two parts: Charcoal and gouache on paper, 1'11¹⁄₁₆" x 3'½" (58 cm x 93 cm). *Paula Cooper Gallery. © 2007 Joel Shapiro/Artists Rights Society (ARS), New York. Photo by eeva-inkeri. JS 243.*

3.27. **CLARENCE CARTER.** *Siena.* 1981.
Acrylic on canvas, 6'6" x 5' (1.98 m x
1.52 m). *Courtesy Gimpel/Weitzenhoffer*
Gallery, New York. By permission of the artist.

Rockburne uses two modular units—triangles and squares of the same size. Modeling is employed at the edges of the triangles, suggesting folded paper, but these volumes are contradicted by the rigid black outline on the right. This heavier line converts to the centerfold of the origami-like shapes in the rest of the drawing. (*Origami* is the Japanese technique of folding paper to create three-dimensional shapes.) In Rockburne's drawing, the forms seem to project out of the picture plane rather than recede into it, thus giving the image a volumetric appearance.

You can clearly see the modeling technique in Fernand Léger's pencil drawing (*figure 3.29*). *Figure 3.30* reduces the Léger composition to shape. By comparing the two images, you can see how modeling transforms shapes into volume. The shading from light to dark is more pronounced on the women's forms. A spatial contradiction is the result of the combination of flat, cut-out shapes with illusionistically rounded forms. Léger has also used contradictory eye levels; for example, we see the women from one vantage point, the rug and floor from another—as if we were floating above the scene—and the tabletops from yet another. The composition is structured by means of repetition of volumes and shapes.

3.28. DOROTHEA ROCKBURNE. *Stele.*
1980. Conté crayon, pencil, oil, and
gesso on linen, 7'7¼" x 4'3¼" (2.32 m
x 1.30 m). *Emmerich Gallery.* © 2007
*Dorothea Rockburne/Artists Rights Society
(ARS), New York. Photograph by Rick
Gardner, Texas Gallery, Houston.*

3.29. FERNAND LÉGER. *Three Women.*
1920. Pencil, 1'2½" x 1'8" (37 cm x
51 cm). *Rijksmuseum Kroller-Muller,
Otterlo, Netherlands.* © 2007 Artists
*Rights Society (ARS), New York/
ADAGP, Paris.*

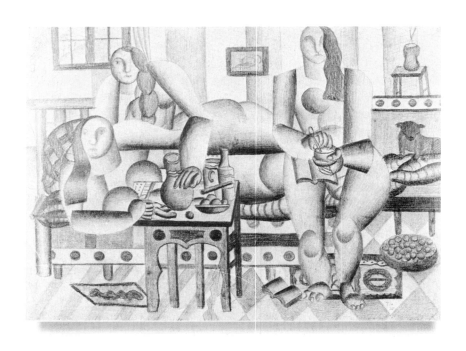

3.30. Shape analysis of Fernand Léger's *Three Women*.

3.31. **DIEGO RIVERA. *Study of a Sleeping Woman.*** Black crayon on off-white laid paper; actual: 62.7 cm x 46.9 cm (24¹¹⁄₁₆ x 18⁷⁄₁₆ in.). *Bequest of Meta and Paul J. Sachs. © President and Fellows of Harvard College.*

A third means used to create a sense of volume is overlapping. Léger uses overlapping shapes, but the use of contradictory eye levels creates an illogical space. For example, the women are presented from a frontal view, while the table is seen from above. In Diego Rivera's *Study of a Sleeping Woman (figure 3.31)*, the figure is constructed by a progression of forms, one overlapping the other from the feet to the

3.32. **LOS CARPINTEROS** (20th c).
© *Proyecto de Acumulacion de Materiales (Project of Accumulation of Materials)* 1999. Watercolor and pencil on paper, 46¼" x 138⅛".
Purchased with funds provided by Sylvia de Cuevas, Leila and Melville Straus, and The Contemporary Arts Council. (1608.2000). Digital Image © The Museum of Modern Art/Licensed by SCALA/Art Resource, NY. The Museum of Modern Art, New York, NY, U.S.A.

dark shape of the hair. The viewer's eye level is low; we look up to the figure. The organic shapes are given volume by use of modeling concentrated at those points of maximum weight and gravity. The compressed figure completely fills the picture plane. The simple overlapping volumes are the primary means by which a feeling of monumentality is achieved.

The following problems will offer some new ways to think about shape and volume. Remember to change the size and shape of the format to challenge your compositional abilities.

PROBLEM 3.7

Shape as Plane and Volume

Using paper bags, a stack of boxes, or bricks as the subject of your drawing, concentrate on the volumetric aspect of the objects; that is, on how planes connect to create volume. Use watercolor or acrylic to create a drawing that is primarily tonal. Indicate planar change by use of adjacent white, gray, and black shapes, as in

the drawing by the Cuban art team called *Los Carpinteros (figure 3.32)*, whose subjects include demolished architectural sites.

PROBLEM 3.8

Planar Analysis

Read through *all* the instructions for this problem carefully before beginning to draw. Spend at least an hour on this drawing and draw from a model. Use white charcoal paper and a 6B pencil that is kept sharp at all times. You will need a stack of 6"-square sheets of newsprint.

Using vine charcoal, make several drawings to acquaint yourself with the pose. With a chamois skin, rub out sections of the drawing that need to be corrected and then redraw, establishing proper proportion.

Now you are ready to begin drawing with the pencil. Use a light touch to establish proportions and organizational lines. Analyze the figure according to its planar structure. First, draw the largest planes of the torso and limbs. Work from

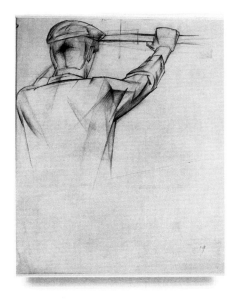

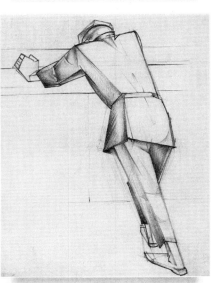

3.33. **ALEXANDER BOGOMAZOV.** *Figure Studies I–VI.* Pencil on paper, I: 1928, 1'1" x 10" (33 cm x 25 cm). II: ca. 1926–1928, 1'1½" x 11¼" (34 cm x 28 cm). III: ca. 1926–1928, 1'2¾" x 11½" (37 cm x 29 cm). IV: ca. 1926–1928, 1'1½" x 11½" (34 cm x 29 cm). V: 1926, 1'4⅜" x 1'3⅜" (42 cm x 31 cm). VI: 1926, 1'4⅜" x 1'3⅜" (42 cm x 31 cm). *Arkansas Arts Center Foundation Collection: Bequest of Andre Simon. 1995. 026.001–006.*

the general to the specific; determine where the figure turns at a 90-degree angle and enclose that plane. Reduce the figure to two planes, front and side for each segment of the figure. Look for multiple interconnecting planes and establish those edges.

After you have drawn for three or four minutes, rub the drawing with a clean piece of newsprint. Replenish the newsprint squares often. Rub inward toward the figure. Two warnings: Do not rub the drawing with your fingers, because the oil from your hands will transfer to the paper and make splotchy marks. And do not rub the drawing with a chamois skin because it removes too much of the drawing. Redraw the model, but do not simply trace the same planes, be sure to correct the groupings. You should alternate between drawing and rubbing.

This drawing will begin to resemble a jigsaw puzzle with planes sharing common edges. The rubbing and redrawing give the planes a volume and depth.

Analyze the group of figure studies by the Russian artist Alexander Bogomazov *(figure 3.33).* Bogomazov has employed a technique similar to the one described

above. The third and fourth drawings indicate the beginning stages, and the last two
drawings of the seated and leaning man show how the planes are converted to volumes through modeling.

PROBLEM 3.9

Modeling and Overlapping

Compose a drawing using as your subject furniture in a studio—chairs, easels,
tables. Concentrate on the space between the objects. Use overlap and establish different baselines for each object. In your drawing, distinguish between foreground,
middle ground, and background. Use charcoal, white chalk, chamois skin, and a
kneaded eraser.

Think in terms of the different levels of negative space—horizontal space between the objects, vertical space above them, and diagonal space between them as
they recede into the background. Imagine that between the first object and the last
are rows of panes of glass. Because of the cloudy effect of the glass, the last object is
more indistinct than the first. Its edges are blurred, its color and value less intense,
its texture less defined. A haze creates a different kind of atmosphere between the
first and last object. The illusion of depth through atmospheric effects such as those
just described is called *aerial perspective*.

Model both positive and negative space; different lights and darks will indicate
varying levels. Allow the marks to cross over both positive forms and negative
space. Vary the direction of the marks by erasure and rubbing. Use the eraser as a
drawing tool; imagine that the eraser can actually model space; use it to "reach
inside" the picture plane to the various levels of space.

Note how Ronald Milhoan has used overlapping and modeling to create an
illusion of three-dimensional space *(figure 3.34)*.

SUMMARY: SPATIAL CHARACTERISTICS OF SHAPE

Shape

A shape is two-dimensional if it has an unchanged or unmodulated value, color, or texture over its entire surface. Uniformity in color, value, or texture will make an otherwise volumetric form appear flatter. A form outlined by an unvarying line creates a two-dimensional effect.

Shapes of similar size, color, value, texture, or like form attract each other. It is by this means that the artist organizes the picture plane. Like attracts like. Normally small shapes tend to recede and large ones advance. Overlap suggests spatial positioning.

Shapes functioning as planes, as the sides of a volume, give an illusion of three-dimensionality. Shapes can be given dimension by tilting them, truncating them, or making them move diagonally into the picture plane.

When both flat, two-dimensional shapes and three-dimensional volumes are used in the same drawing, the result is ambiguous space. If a shape cannot be clearly located in relation to other shapes in the drawing, ambiguous space results.

If a line delineating a shape varies in darkness or thickness, or if the line breaks—that is, if it is an implied line—the shape appears less flat. Imprecise edges, blurred texture, and modeling make a shape appear volumetric.

SKETCHBOOK PROJECT

PROJECT **1**

Shaping the Composition to the Format

In your sketchbook, draw five or more different formats to be used as picture planes—a long horizontal, a square, a narrow vertical, a circle, and an oval. Using the same subject for each of the formats, change the composition according to the demands of the framing shape. Each different outside shape demands a different arrangement of the internal forms. The arrangement of the formal elements inside the picture plane must undergo change.

COMPUTER PROJECT

Today, most art departments offer access to computers and most art students own a personal computer, so problems using the computer as an aid to drawing will be offered, when appropriate, after the sketchbook problems at the end of each chapter. The computer projects given in this text were designed by Tom Sale. They were created in Adobe Illustrator, but could be modified for other programs such as Adobe Photoshop, Microsoft Paint, MacPaint, and others.

A digital camera is a useful tool for collecting images; in addition, a camera can provide a quick and entertaining way to visually document ideas. Sketchbook projects using a digital camera might include such subjects as "My Route to Class," "Things I Found on the Ground within a Fifteen-foot Radius of My Front Door," or "Ten Interestingly Shaped Trees."

Using a Computer to Determine and Modify Shapes/Experimenting with the Relationship between Positive and Negative Space

1. Using the pen tool, create an interesting organic shape. Fill in the shape with solid black. With the convert anchor point tool (or with other tools such as reflect, rotate, transform, and filter), create several variations of the original shape. Manipulate the shape by stretching, reversing, and resizing; these new shapes will be visually related because they have all been based on the original shape.

2. Draw a rectangle to serve as the picture plane. This plane should be slightly smaller than your maximum printable size (typically 8½" by 11"). Arrange the shapes on the picture plane so they are all tangent (touching one another) and spilling over the edges of the picture plane on at least three sides. You have now created a composite shape.

3. Using the pen and convert anchor point tools, trace the leftover, or negative spaces, created between the composite shape and the edge of the picture plane. Fill these negative shapes with solid black and arrange them in a new composition.

4. Using some of the original positive shapes and some of the negative shapes, experiment with a series of compositions. (In making the composition, you may need to rescale some of the pieces.) After you have made a dozen or more compositions, convert some shapes to white. By layering shapes and having areas of crossover value, you will have created varying levels of space as well as additional new shapes.

This technique is similar to cutting out shapes with scissors. The computer, however, allows you to make multiples and to manipulate the shapes more quickly and cleanly, leaving you more time to experiment with more variations than is possible using manual techniques *(figure 3.35)*.

You could make an *homage* to Joel Shapiro by creating a similar work on the computer (see *figure 3.3*). In art terms, an *homage* is a derivative work of art in the style of another artist to show respect to the creator of the original work.

Make a file to store selected compositions; these will serve you in good stead when you are stuck for an idea or when you are looking for a solution to problems in other compositions. You may even decide to convert one of the more successful arrangements into a finished drawing using cut paper, acrylic paint, or brush and ink. You can revise this problem, and instead of using black and white you could use colored or textured shapes. Expand your repertory of computer drawings by applying information you have learned in class.

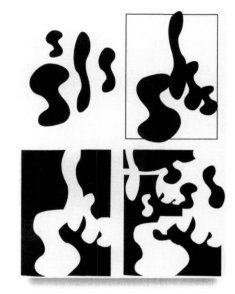

3.35. Computer drawings dealing with composite shapes and negative space. *Courtesy of Tom Sale.*

CHAPTER 4

To use black . . . is comparable to forging. . . . A black shape can hold its space and place in relation to a larger volume and alter the mass of that volume readily. —RICHARD SERRA

Value

imply defined, *value* is the gradation from light to dark across a form; it is determined by both the lightness and darkness of the object, by its natural color—its *local color*—and by the amount and direction of light that strikes it. Wayne Thiebaud's *Rabbit (figure 4.1)* presents a visual definition of value. In Thiebaud's drawing, value is modulated from white to gray over the surface of the rabbit's body. It seems to be sitting in a pool of light. Repeating shapes ripple across the rabbit's fur. The shadow cast by the ear can be read as a value scale like the one in *figure 4.2*.

DEFINITIONS AND FUNCTIONS

Value describes *achromatic color*; that is, color devoid of hue. An object can be red or blue and still have the same value. What is important in determining value is the lightness or darkness of the color. This approach is achromatic. Learning to separate color from value is an essential task in art. A good example of this separation in everyday life is black-and-white photography.

4.1. **WAYNE THIEBAUD.** *Rabbit (from Seven Still Lives and a Rabbit).* 1971. Lithography in color, 1'10¼" x 2'6" (57 cm x 76 cm). *Brooklyn Museum, National Endowment for the Arts and Bristol Myers Fund. Acc. 72.121.1.* © *Wayne Thiebaud/Licensed by VAGA, New York.*

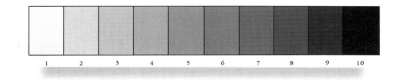

| 1 | 2 | 3 | 4 | 5 | 6 | 7 | 8 | 9 | 10 |

4.2. Value scale, from 100 percent white to 100 percent black.

Three different ways of using value for emotive and expressive content can be seen by the way deer are treated in the works of Rick Bartow, a Native American Yurok; José Bedia, an Afro-Cuban; and Kiki Smith *(figures 4.3, 4.4, and 4.5)*. Bartow's wounded animal is a stand-in for the artist himself, who uses Yurok myths and motifs for self-examination. An intensity of feeling is achieved by the vigorously scumbled, gestural application of values crossing over both positive and negative shapes.

In Bedia's treatment of the iconic face-to-face figures, sparks seem to fly between the silhouetted pair. Bedia is a member of an Afro-Cuban religious group that recognizes the kinship between the human and animal worlds. The electric sparks that each figure emits are conveyed by the paint splotches. Bedia limits his values to black and white.

Kiki Smith's gentle, life-sized deer are in a different mode. The deer are drawn in reversed values on panels made of saturated red and maroon papers. Smith uses a close range of values that might be seen on a real animal. These three artists use value in different ways but all three evoke an emotive or expressive response.

Value is a helpful tool of artists whose subjects are themes of social injustice. Ed Paschke presents the archetypal military strongman in his political print, *Kontato (figure 4.6)*. His use of value creates an eerie light that surrounds the image. Blurred value throws the figure out of focus. The work resembles a photographic negative. This sharp contrast of light and dark within the work is called *tenebrism*.

In addition to its expressive and emotive functions, value can be used to describe objects, the light striking them, and their weight, structure, and spatial arrangement. So value has two functions: It is objectively as well as subjectively descriptive. Susan Hauptman's drawing *(figure 4.7)* is a study in representational clarity. The composition is built with a full range of values, all visually accurate, from the wrinkled,

4.3. RICK BARTOW. *Deer Hunt II.* 1993.
Pastel, charcoal, and graphite on
paper, 2'2" x 3'4" (66 cm x 102 cm).
Francine Seders Gallery Ltd., Seattle.
Photograph by David Browne.

4.4. JOSÉ BEDIA. *Adquiere Cualidades.*
1994. Acrylic on paper, 2'7¼" x
4'7¼" (79.4 cm x 1.403 m). *Private
Collection. Courtesy of George Adams Gallery,
New York.*

4.5. KIKI SMITH. *Two Deer.* 1996. Ink on
paper, 4'6¾" x 7'7¾" (1.34 m x
2.33 m). *Photo by Ellen Page Wilson. Courtesy of Pace Wildenstein.* © 2004 Kiki Smith.

4.6. **ED PASCHKE.** *Kontato.* 1984.
Lithograph printed by Landfall Press,
Chicago. Printed in color, 34¼ x 24"
(87 cm x 61 cm). *Lent by the Publisher,*
Chicago.

4.7. **SUSAN HAUPTMAN.** *Still Life.* 1985.
Charcoal and pastel on paper, 2'7½" x
3'7¾" (80 cm x 1.11 m). *Private*
collection. Courtesy Allan Stone Gallery, New
York.

lightweight scarf to the shell-shaped vase. Values cross over positive shapes and
empty space in the upper third of the drawing; the white tabletop disappears, reap-
pears, and disappears again in the background space. The illusionistic textures in the
drawing are a result of a masterly handling of values. Although Hauptman's drawing is representational, it is highly subjective; an atmosphere of mystery pervades
the work.

4.8. **DIETER HACKER.** *Die Fremden-führerin (The Guide)*. 1985. Charcoal and watercolor on paper, 3'3⅜" x 3'11¼" (1 m x 1.2 m). *Arkansas Arts Center Foundation Purchase, 1986. 1986.047.*

Like Hauptman, the German artist Dieter Hacker presents a scene of mystery—theatrical and ominous in his drawing *The Guide (figure 4.8)*. Hacker uses value to create a room harshly lit by a single lightbulb. Drama is conveyed by contrast of the dark, threatening room, the glaring flash of light, and the expressionistic quality of the marks.

WAYS OF CREATING VALUE

There are two basic ways to define a *form*—by line or by value. Most drawings are a combination of line and value, as seen in Rico Lebrun's *Portrait of a Man (figure 4.9)*. Lebrun defines the subject's face by use of value, and the bulging shape of the body is relayed by quickly stated lines. The darker, heavier lines convey a sense of gravity and weight; Lebrun makes the head the focal point by carefully modeled values.

A drawing may be exclusively tonal, as in Robert Kogge's compact still life *(figure 4.10)*, in which the objects' actual values are carefully observed and translated onto the picture plane. A light source (from left front and slightly above the still life) creates minimal shadows, and, while suggesting the curvature of the rounded containers, the ultimate effect of the even lighting is to flatten the objects. The still life is held together by interlocking values; this spatial tension results in a contemporary look.

Tonal quality can also be made by smudging, rubbing, and erasing, as in Michael Mazur's realist charcoal drawing *(figure 4.11)*. The tropical landscape lends itself to a layered technique. The whites in the sky and the mottled highlights on the trees and on the ground have been created by erasure; the moss hanging from the trees is suggested by rubbing and smudging. The powdery medium of charcoal is ideal for these techniques since it lies on the surface of the paper rather than soaking in like a wet medium. Mazur's technique results in a dense, congested, illusionistic space.

4.9. **RICO LEBRUN.** *Portrait of a Man.*
1939. Ink and chalk. *Private collection.*
Constance Lebrun Crown, Santa Babara, Calif.

4.10. **ROBERT KOGGE.** *Untitled.* 1989.
Graphite on canvas, 2' x 3' (60.9 cm x
91.4 cm). *O. K. Harris Works of Art,*
New York.

4.11. **MICHAEL MAZUR.** *Landscape—Ossabow.* 1975. Charcoal with smudging and erasing on ivory weave paper, 5'11½" x 3'5" (1.816 m x 1.041 m). *Jalane and Richard Davidson Collection, Art Institute of Chicago.*

4.12. **DAVID MCMURRAY.** *Evidence* **(detail).** 1993–1994. India ink on paper, 4'2" x 5'7" (1.27 m x 1.7 m). *Courtesy of the artist. Photo by Richard Nicol.*

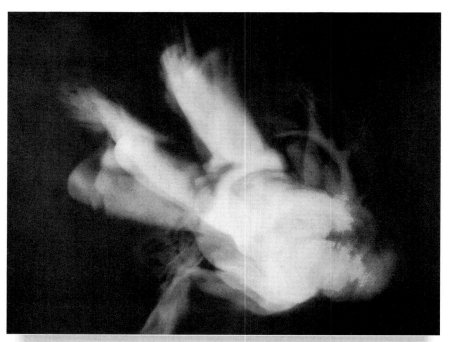

In the life-sized ink drawing by David McMurray, a close range of blurred values captures the notion of movement *(figure 4.12)*. The negative space is read conceptually as three-dimensional, but actually it is an unmodulated black.

The scene appears to be illuminated by a strobe light, producing the blurred values surrounding the prone figure. McMurray works from photographic double exposures. The X-ray values within the figure are a means of relaying disturbing content.

Value can be created by closeness of dots and short strokes and by pressure exerted on the drawing tool; this technique is called *stippling*. In Gregory Masurovsky's drawing *(figure 4.13)*, the pale, translucent surface is activated by nearly indiscernible marks, short squiggly lines and dots that congregate as if attracted by the magnetic force of the moon. The shapes created by a light range of values surge and dissolve like waves washing over the forms. The repetitive action requires a control of the drawing implement to create a subtle range of values.

Crosshatching, grouping parallel sets of crossing lines, is another means of creating value. In a lifelong occupation with still life *(figure 4.14)*, the Italian artist Giorgio Morandi constructs a calm classical composition using grouped parallel

4.13. **GREGORY MASUROVSKY.** *Les Phases de la Lune.* 1991. Pen and ink on paper, 2'2" x 3'3⅜" (66 cm x 1 m). *Lent by the artist. Arkansas Arts Center. © 2007 Artists Rights Society (ARS), New York/ADAGP, Paris.*

4.14. **GIORGIO MORANDI.** *Nature Morte au Gros Traits.* 1931. Etching, 9⅝" x 1'¼" (24 cm x 34 cm). *Harriet Griffin Gallery. © 2007 Artists Rights Society (ARS), New York/SIAE, Rome.*

lines and crosshatching. Background and foreground are uniformly textured, flattening the space. Stated in a close value range, the bottles are defined by groups of angled lines, which indicate planar change; the still life contours are strengthened, and thereby flattened, by outline. Morandi's value patterns create an otherworldly effect. Although the objects are drawn from real life, they seem strangely isolated.

ARBITRARY USE OF VALUE

Artists can ignore natural laws of perception, such as the way light falls across a form, to use value arbitrarily—to create a focal point, to establish balance between parts, to call attention to a particular shape, or otherwise to organize the composition. These uses of value are based on both the artist's intuitive responses and the need to comply with the demands of the design. In other words, *arbitrarily stated values* are light and dark patterns that differ from local values, the actual values one sees in real life.

Andy Warhol, in one of his many iconic portraits of Marilyn Monroe *(figure 4.15)*, has used an arbitrary arrangement of values. Values cross over both positive and negative space. Some segments of the face are left blank and other areas are defined in a value reversal. The black band that crosses the face joins the negative shape behind the head. If you block out the eye and mouth, the composition becomes an abstract arrangement of blacks, whites, and mottled grays. Arbitrary value patterns both integrate the work and confound a logical spatial analysis.

4.15. ANDY WARHOL. *Marilyn.*
1978–1979. Ink silkscreen on paper, 1'10½" x 1'5½" (57.1 cm x 44.4 cm). *Vrej Baghoomian Gallery, New York. © 2007 Andy Warhol Foundation for the Visual Arts/Artists Rights Society (ARS), New York.*

PROBLEM 4.1

Using Value Arbitrarily

Choose a still life or model as your subject, from which you are to make two drawings.

Using black, white, and two shades of gray, arbitrarily distribute values. Keep the values flat and unmodulated. Base your decisions according to compositional demands, not on the actual appearance of the subject.

In a second drawing of the same subject, model some of the shapes for a more volumetric appearance. You should have a major focal point and minor focal areas. A combination of flat shapes and modeled volumes in the same drawing results in ambiguous space.

DESCRIPTIVE USES OF VALUE

Value can be used to describe objects in physical terms of structure, weight, light, and space.

Value Used to Describe Structure

Value can describe the structure, or planar makeup, of an object. Value describing structure need not depend on the natural laws of light. A structural analysis is a type of abstraction; it is not related to imitation. It is a means of seeing the whole by separating the parts. In addition, a planar analysis gives us a better understanding of how to build volumes in space.

In the drawing of his mother, the Italian artist Umberto Boccioni has drawn a structural analysis of the head *(figure 4.16)*. Volume is indicated in terms of interconnecting planes. Planes indicated by darker values and closely grouped lines signify the planes turning from our view, into space. A planar drawing is a sort of diagram that plots the most essential planes and their junctures. Planar analysis is a step toward abstraction; it does not imitate, it analyzes. An analytical drawing takes things apart to discover basic structures.

PROBLEM 4.2

Using Value to Describe Planes

Using Boccioni's technique, with a skull as subject, make a drawing that analyzes its planar aspects. In order to create value, group lines within the planes. Recall that a change of line direction indicates a change of plane. Make your marks change directions just as the planes change. Make the strokes run vertically for those that are parallel to you and diagonally for planes that turn into space. This change in direction will emphasize the juncture of planes and will appear dimensional.

Value Used to Describe Weight

The weight, or density, of an object can be defined by value. We sense the pressure of gravity in all objects in real life. The artist frequently enforces this sense by placing darker values at points of greatest pressure or weight, or at places where the greatest tension occurs. Artists use weight or density even when they are not drawing

4.16. UMBERTO BOCCIONI. *The Artist's Mother.* 1915. Pencil and watercolor washes on paper, 25⅝" x 20⅞" (65.1 cm x 53 cm). *The Metropolitain Museum of Art, bequest of Lydia Winston Malbin, 1989 (1990.38.31). Image © The Metropolitain Museum of Art.*

objects in the real world. A completely nonrepresentational drawing can convey the idea of weight and mass.

The quote by the artist Richard Serra at the beginning of this chapter comments on the importance of black. Serra says "shapes refer to their internal masses. . . . Objects have weight because of the character of their geometries." This is well illustrated in a series of works that he calls *out-of-round* drawings *(figure 4.17)*, in which he uses a metal screen to force a compacted oil stick onto handmade paper. He doesn't see the finished drawing until he removes the screen. He adds that he is interested "in the compactness of the spread" as well as in how the drawings "cover the field as they are being made from the inside out" (R. Eric Davis, "Extend Vision: Richard Serra Talks about Drawing," *Art on Paper*, May–June 2000, p. 63).

In *Female Model on Ladder (figure 4.18)*, Philip Pearlstein gives weight to the shapes by depicting the effects of light and shadow. Key areas in which a heavy, darker-value line creates the illusion of weight are where the hand presses into the leg, where the thigh spreads on the ladder step, and in the folds of the stomach and the sag of the breast. Figure and ladder are analogous forms; the ladder becomes a

4.17. RICHARD SERRA. *out-of-round VI.* 1999. Paintstick on Hiromi paper, 6'7" x 6'7¼" (2 m x 2.01 m). *Courtesy Gagosian Gallery, New York. © 2007 Richard Serra/Artists Rights Society (ARS), New York.*

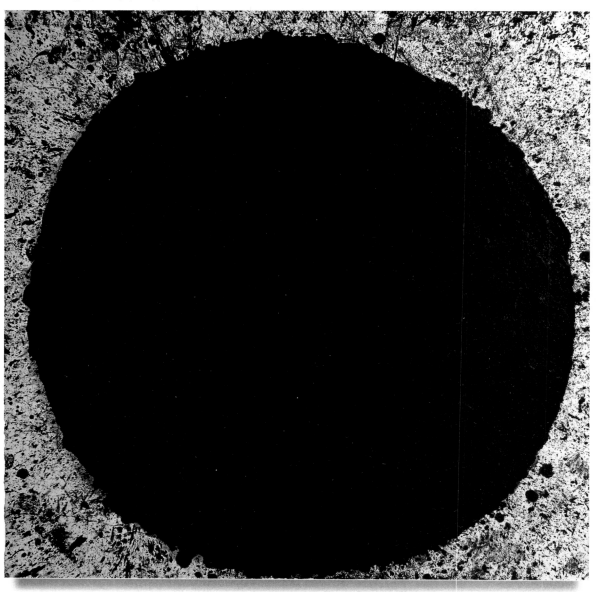

4.18. **PHILIP PEARLSTEIN.** *Female Model on Ladder.* 1976. Sepia wash on paper, 2'5½" x 3'5" (75 cm x 1.04 m). *Robert Miller Gallery. Courtesy Robert Miller Gallery, New York.*

visual metaphor for the framework of the figure. The expressive quality of the work is conveyed primarily by means of value—a cool, detached, analytical approach to a figure in an environment. The headless figure reinforces the impersonal theme of model in a studio.

Sometimes one can draw things as they appear, but if the light, the arrangement of objects, or the point of view, are not properly handled, the drawing will look wrong. Sometimes the artist has to adjust values in a drawing for it to appear visually coherent. This license to rearrange and alter is an important lesson for the beginning student to learn.

PROBLEM 4.3

Using Value to Describe Weight

Taking Heidi Fasnacht's drawing as an example *(figure 4.19)*, invent a single volumetric form using value to describe its mass and weight. With an oil stick, create a tangled, weighted line. Move outward from the center, leaving the outer edge blurred. As you draw, imagine that your marks are circumscribing a volume in space. Concentrate on the idea of density and gravity. In Fasnacht's drawing, the powerful motion of the conic form reminds us of a force in nature. Note how the smudged fingerprints convey her physical involvement in the drawing. Pay attention to pressure applied to the tool.

4.19. **HEIDI FASNACHT.** *Untitled.* 1984. Charcoal, pastel, and oil on paper, 5' x 4' (1.52 m x 1.22 m). *Tabriz Fund, 1988 (88.2). Arkansas Art Center, Little Rock.*

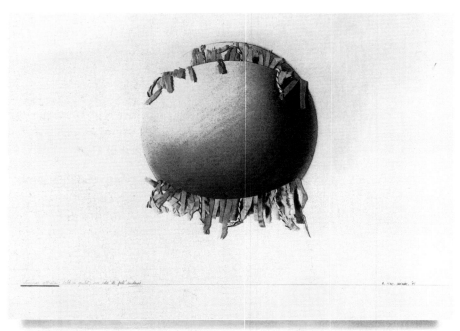

4.20. **GÉRARD TITUS-CARMEL.** *17 Exemples d'Alteration d'une Sphere. 12eme Alteration.* 1971. Pencil, 1'7½" x 2'4" (52 cm x 74.7 cm). *Private collection.* © 2007 Artists Rights Society (ARS), New York/ADAGP, Paris. Photo by Andrew Morain.

Value Used to Describe Light

Light falling on an object creates value patterns that obey certain rules. If light falls from one direction onto the object, the value created can reveal the structure of the object as well as its volumetric and planar aspects; for example, a sphere under a single light source will have an even change in value over its surface. The use of modeling to create a gradual transition from light to dark is called *chiaroscuro*. This technique can be seen in Gérard Titus-Carmel's alteration of a sphere *(figure 4.20)*.

Light falling on cylinders, cones, and organic volumes creates a gradual change from light to dark over their surfaces, whereas cubes, pyramids, and other angular forms change abruptly from light to dark at the intersections of their planes *(figure 4.21)*.

Generally, light as it falls over a form can be reduced to six categories: highlight, light, shadow, core of shadow, reflected light, and cast shadow *(figure 4.22)*. Within a single form or volume, we may see parts of it as light against dark and other areas as dark against light. Some areas may seem to disappear into the background; that is, if a light-valued object is set against a light background, the edge of the object will disappear. Values can cross over both objects and negative space, causing the edge of the object to seem to disappear.

Susan Grossman's charcoal drawing *Lexington Avenue (figure 4.23)* illustrates these effects. Buildings, cars, and people meld into their background values. The darker values in the middle ground absorb the objects, leaving only highlights to indicate individual forms. The light source comes from the left front of the picture plane; the progression of light is from front to back, light/dark/light. The edges of the running figure are dissolved into the lighter values of the pavement. The upper

4.21. Light on rounded and angular forms.

4.22. Six categories of light as it falls over a form.

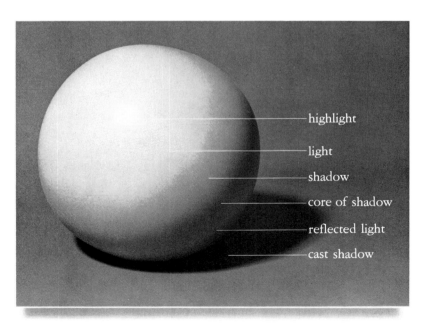

highlight

light

shadow

core of shadow

reflected light

cast shadow

torso of the striding figure on the right disappears into the darker values surrounding him. An intriguing aspect of Grossman's depiction of space is that the most blurred and imprecise contours appear in the foreground.

Multiple light sources can result in ambiguous space because the form revealed by one light may be canceled by another. Manipulation of light sources can produce striking effects that result in a very different mood from that produced by natural light. In a self-portrait *(figure 4.24)*, Alfred Leslie employs a stark underlighting to achieve a tense, apprehensive effect. The stylized hair and shirt contrast with the

4.23. **SUSAN GROSSMAN.** *Lexington Avenue.* 2000. Charcoal on paper, 5' x 7'6" (1.52 m x 2.29 m). *DFN Gallery, New York.*

4.24. **ALFRED LESLIE.** *Alfred Leslie.* 1974. Lithograph, 3'4" x 2'6" (1.02 m x 76 cm). *Published by Landfall Press, Inc., Chicago.*

accuracy of the facial features; the hair seems to be electrified by the intense raking light that illuminates the head. The reversal of values produces a spatial ambiguity between neck and chin where the light has washed out the shapes that normally differentiate the two.

PROBLEM 4.4

Value Reduction

Focus a spotlight on a still life using white objects with nonreflective surfaces. Study the subject carefully, and on a value scale from 1 to 10 (see *figure 4.2*), find its midpoint value. Squint your eyes to reduce color effects so that you see only patterns of light and dark. This drawing is to be a value reduction. You are to reduce all values in the still life to either black or white. Note both the actual values of objects and the light patterns on them, and classify these values as either black or white: Values from 1 to 5 will be white, from 6 to 10, black.

Draw the subject lightly in pencil; then use black acrylic or ink to make everything that is darker than the midpoint value a flat, unmodulated black. Erase the pencil lines, leaving the rest of the drawing white. Values will cross over objects and negative space; value will not necessarily be confined to an object. The finished drawing will be spatially flat, very dramatic, and somewhat abstract.

Ugo Rondinone has used value reduction and value reversal in his enormous drawing *(figure 4.25)*. The Swiss artist makes small sketchbook drawings directly from nature. Back in his studio he makes enlargements from the sketches. The final products resemble nineteenth-century picturesque illustrative drawings. Technique and scale convert them to unmistakably contemporary works.

4.25. **UGO RONDINONE.** *No. 135 VIERT-ERJUNINEUNZEHNHUNDERTNEUNUND-NEUNZIG (No. 135 Fourthofjuneninteennineteynine).* 1999. Ink on paper, 6'7" x 9'10" (200.6 cm x 299.7 cm). *Collection of Maja Hoffman.*

Four Divisions of Value

Coat your paper evenly with charcoal of four or five on the value scale *(see figure 4.2)*. If necessary go over the paper several times to create an evenly toned surface.

Using the same still life as in Problem 4.4, reduce the subject to four values—the gray of your paper, a darker gray, white, and black. The actual light patterns on the subject will govern your decisions. Establish the blacks and dark grays with compressed charcoal and create whites with a kneaded eraser. Values should cross over both objects and negative space.

PROBLEM 4.6

Categories of Light

In this drawing, use six values to depict the categories of light referred to in *figure 4.22*. Use geometric forms as in *figure 4.21* for the subject. Spheres, cones, pyramids, and cubes can be made of bristol board. Use a spotlight to produce a highlight, light, shadow, core of shadow, reflected light, and cast shadow.

Once you have observed your subject in detail, make four separate value scales of six values each, using these techniques: scribbling, stippling, crosshatching, and grouping parallel lines. *Density*, or closeness of marks, and amount of pressure exerted on the tool are the means of value change. Select one of the techniques and draw the still life with six values. Make the transitions gradual and smooth; match the actual values in the still life. Analyze Morandi's drawing (see *figure 4.14*) to see how the weight of the line and the closeness of marks create value change.

PROBLEM 4.7

Tonal Drawings

Use a backlit seated figure in a room as your subject to make an all-tonal drawing. Create a tonal transition from the bottom to the top of the picture plane—light to dark or dark to light. In your drawing, indicate the change of light across the figure and make values cross over both figure and negative space. Occasionally the edge of the figure should seem to disappear into the adjacent negative shapes or shadows.

In Sidney Goodman's charcoal drawing *(figure 4.26)*, value shifts in intensity from the bottom to the top of the picture plane. In the lower half of the drawing, the legs and lower torso dissolve into the background walls of the room. The lower arms are lost in the gray haze, and the upper arms are in relief against the black torso. The dark skull stands in relief against the white ceiling; the details of his face are lost in the dark value indicating the chest. The figure is in the act of dissolving in spite of the weight of the upper torso bearing down on the legs.

Value Used to Describe Space

Value is an indispensable element in describing space. As we have seen, spatial depiction has many manifestations; there is no single way to indicate space. One way to depict space is to use a progression of values from dark to light or light to dark. In

4.26. **SIDNEY GOODMAN.** *Man Waiting.*
1961. Charcoal on paper, 2'1⅝" x
1'7⅛" (65 cm x 49 cm). *The Museum of
Modern Art, New York. Gift of Mr. and Mrs.
Walter Bareiss (143.1962). Digital image
© The Museum of Modern Art/Licensed by
SCALA/Art Resource, New York.*

4.27. **SHARRON ANTHOLT.** *Tracing a
Stranger Self.* 1988. Charcoal on
paper, 3'3" x 4'8" (99.1 cm x 1.422 m).
Courtesy of the artist.

Sharron Antholt's charcoal drawing *(figure 4.27)*, we see a depiction of a hallway of
a Buddhist monastery. The atmospheric work is one of solemnity. The spiritual
dimension Antholt invokes is a result of a masterful control of value. A deep space
and carefully modulated values set the stage for a contemplative response.

Using Value to Describe Space

Focus on a spatial progression in a drawing that has several distinct levels of space. For your subject, arrange objects on a desk to indicate a foreground, middle ground, and background. Imagine your subject to be monumental objects in a landscape. In this drawing, exaggerate the scale of the various objects in order to create a deep space. Assume a low eye level rather than looking straight down onto the objects; this will help deepen the spatial field.

Manipulate the lighting to cast strong shadows; long, raking shadows can lend an air of mystery. Imagine the scene as taking place at night, so that the space behind the objects and beyond the desk will be dark and atmospheric. Aim for a gradual transition of values. Before you begin to draw, spend several minutes looking at the objects, and in your mind's eye transform them to looming objects in a landscape. This concentration will provide an imaginative beginning for the drawing.

EXPRESSIVE USES OF VALUE

An exciting aspect of value is its use as an expressive tool. We have discussed the principles of value, the observation of natural appearances, and the way this observation can help you use value. Value is a strong determinant in the depiction of emotions. An example is Howard Warshaw's *Red Man (figure 4.28)*. Fluid lines and layered washes work to achieve the special angst in his composition.

In his intimately scaled watercolor *(figure 4.29)*, Michael Flanagan evokes a lyrical feeling by using washes of close value to divide ocean and sky. Over the washes he imposes a delicate line drawing of three images—man, fish, and boat. The result is a sense of quiet containment.

Value can create mood through the use of *value reversal*, a technique that creates unusual spatial effects. In Dmitri Wright's stencil print *(figure 4.30)*, the emphasis shifts from the positive to the negative in a series of double takes. The work has the look of a photographic negative. Reverse values and spatial dislocation contribute to a feeling of loss or emptiness. As a base for the stencils, Wright has used a blueprint seen through the transparent figures. The mechanical drawing lying behind the figures and implements creates a second level of space that enhances the work. Space has been reversed; commonplace objects have become ghostlike. Wright presents us with an eerie vanishing act. By airbrushing stencils and actual objects, he has created a "memory" of the original objects. A halo encircles the shapes, contributing to the idea of absence and loss.

Before moving onto the next problem, review the illustrations in this chapter and analyze how value has been used as an expressive element in each drawing. There are as many expressive uses of value as there are felt expressions. It is up to the artist to determine mood and content and to figure out how best to use value to convey intent.

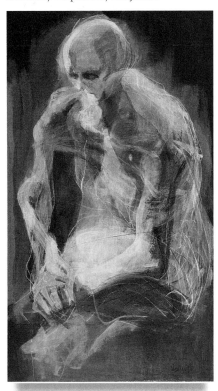

4.28. **HOWARD WARSHAW.** *Red Man.* 1967. Acrylic on paper, 5'5" x 3' (1.65 m x 91 cm). *Courtesy Francis Warshaw, Carpinteria, California.*

PROBLEM 4.9

Value Reversal

Using stencils or actual objects traced on found paper, make a drawing in which the value patterns are reversed. This is a good problem for mixed media; combine spray paint with such media as conté crayon, chalk, pastel, or white ink. Try for the effect of a photographic negative, as in the Wright stencil print.

4.29. **MICHAEL FLANAGAN.** *Ocean Silence.*
1980. Watercolor and pencil on paper,
10⅞" x 8½" (28 cm x 22 cm).
*Arkansas Arts Center Foundation Collection;
the Museum Purchase Plan of the NEA and
the Barrett Hamilton Acquisition Fund,
1981.81.24.*

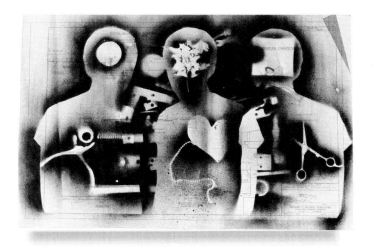

4.30. **DMITRI WRIGHT.** *Untitled.* 1970.
Stencil print, 1'11" x 3'⅛" (61 cm x
92 cm). *Brooklyn Museum, gift of the artist.
Acc. 74.183.*

PROBLEM 4.10

Value Used Subjectively

In this project, you will make a drawing that will subordinate visual appearances to emotive content. Project a strong feeling onto your subject using a value pattern that will underscore your attitude. Use simple, repeated, related abstract shapes as your subject. Make the forms occupy an illusionistic space. To achieve various levels of illusionistic space, employ a shift in scale, overlap, and value; use smudging, rubbing, and erasure to model the forms.

In an abstract drawing *(figure 4.31)*, Lee Bontecou transforms a simple ovoid that she enlarges and reverses from light to dark as it moves across the picture plane. Image, repetition, and shift in scale give her work its powerful character. Larger shapes loom behind the smaller ovoid forms in the foreground. Small, repeating elongated ovals resemble openings. Cavities, voids, sockets, and valvelike forms suggest the workings of an animated machine.

This problem could be expanded into a related series of drawings. Working in the same style and medium, use a similar vocabulary of shapes and values. Composition, shape, placement, size, and scale should vary from one drawing to the next.

SUMMARY

Spatial Characteristics of Value

Of all the art elements, value has the greatest potential for spatial development. When value defines light, structure, weight, or space, it is being used three-dimensionally.

If more than one light source is used, each source may cancel volumetric qualities revealed by another, resulting in an ambiguous space. A combination of flat value and modeled value also produces arbitrary space.

Flat patterns of light and dark confined within a given shape make the space seem shallow. Uniform lines within a shape keep the shape flat. In the same way, a uniformly textured surface pattern has a tendency to flatten.

However, volumes with gradual transitions from light to dark are seen as three-dimensional. When value defines the edges of planes and these planes behave according to the rules of perspective, the resulting space is illusionistic. Movement from foreground to background in a stepped progression of value planes produces a three-dimensional space. Irregular lines used to build lights and darks make a drawing more dimensional than do uniform patterns of line.

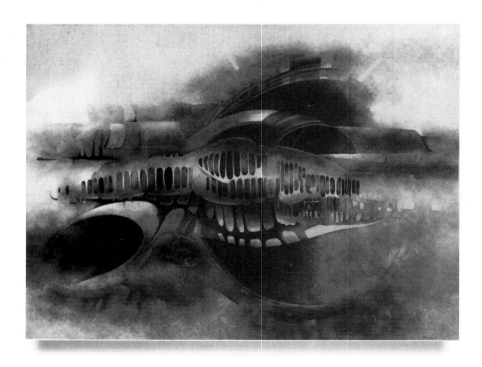

4.31. **LEE BONTECOU.** *Amerika.* 1966. Pencil and charcoal, 1'7¾" x 2'3⅛" (50 cm x 69 cm). *Albert J. Pilavin Collection, Museum of Art, Rhode Island School of Design.*

SKETCHBOOK PROJECTS

Now is a good time to begin using the sketchbook for thumbnail sketches. *Thumbnail sketches* are preparatory drawings in which you jot down ideas and options for final drawings. This practice is an economical one: It saves you time, materials, and effort. Additionally, it serves as a memory bank for ideas that come at odd times when you are out of the studio. Often these inspirational jolts are the most valid ones, so having a record of them can be a great help.

PROJECT 1

Thumbnail Sketches

Set yourself the task of drawing several thumbnail sketches every day. Establish the habit of keeping a sketchbook with you as you make your daily rounds. For ideas read Guide B, "Keeping a Sketchbook."

A look at some sketchbooks by Claes Oldenburg will be instructive in seeing how visual ideas develop through thumbnail sketches. Oldenburg is absorbed with the reduction of the image and with the conversion of ordinary objects into monuments (see *figures PG B.6* and *PG B.7*). In these quick sketches Oldenburg's wit and technical control are come through clearly.

PROJECT 2

Thumbnail Sketches Using Value Reduction

Working on-site using a cityscape as subject, make a series of thumbnail sketches. Change the size of the format from sketch to sketch. Concentrate on reducing the composition to simple value shapes. Use no more than three or four values. Squint your eyes to assess the actual landscape subject. This helps you see the larger shapes and most prominent value patterns. Vary the sketches by using stippling, crosshatching, and grouped lines to create value.

COMPUTER PROJECT

PROJECT 1

Converting Color to Value

An *appropriated image* is one that is taken from another source and recontextualized; that is, used in a different context or setting. Appropriation is a distinctive feature of postmodern art. Images to be used for this type of project can easily be found in photograph albums, magazines, old books, newspapers, postcards, and posters. Another source for images is the Internet—online encyclopedias often have illustrations, or clip-art software can be purchased or even found free on the Internet. Images from printed material can be scanned into the computer. Then they can be accessed, manipulated, and printed. These resource materials can serve as a physical base for your drawings or collages. Old letters or paper from old ledgers, for example, make interesting surfaces, or you can scan and print them on new paper.

Using Adobe Illustrator, find a color image that has a full range of values. Import the selected image into the desired program.

1. Print an unmanipulated color version to keep as a reference.

2. Go to the color control for the particular program in use. In Adobe Illustrator, color control is in the filter pull-down menu. Convert the color image to grayscale. This will reduce the image to a range of blacks, whites, and grays. Print this version. Notice how some detail has disappeared because certain colors and tonalities are the same value. Keep in mind that values need not be confined to an object; they can begin and end independently of an object. The computer has replaced the decision making in transforming color to a black and white value scale.

3. Experiment with the color and value controls in your program; create several variations on the value theme. Lighten and darken the image, changing the range of values. Reverse values; in Adobe Illustrator this is done under filter>color>adjust color>invert color. Midvalues can be changed to darker values, and the image can easily be reduced to two values—black and white, or any other two values on the value scale you choose. Print your experiments and add to your computer drawing file.

Even though the computer has done all the hard work in this project, you can benefit from careful comparison of the original color source and the converted image. You learn how to see color as value.

CHAPTER 5

A smudge is a trace of what was or is to come.
But a line is here. —MAY STEVENS

Line

n mathematics, a *line* is defined as a path between two points. However, in art, line is much more than a path between two points; it is the most direct means of establishing style. Line drawings are the purest form of drawing. They can convey elegance or raw energy, outrage or wit; they can be rude or polite. Jennifer Pastor's line drawing *(figure 5.1)*, for example, captures the raw energy and excitement—the trajectory of the bull and rider as they wheel through the arena—of a rodeo.

INTRODUCTION TO LINE

Line is valued both for its simple reductive power and for its potentiality for embellishment. In a lifelong career dedicated to line drawing, the Venezuelan artist Gego says, "I discovered that sometimes the in-between lines is as important as the line itself" (Gego, *Between Transparency and the Invisible*, Exhibition notes, 2005, International Center for the Arts of America, The Museum of Fine Arts, Houston). In *figure 5.2*, woven lines create layered blades of

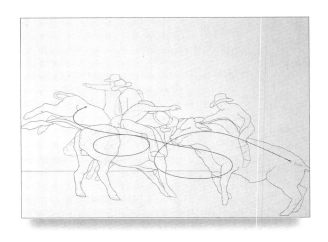

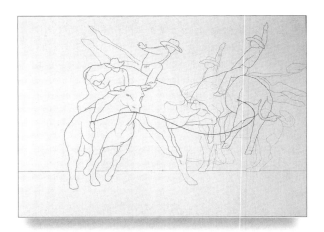

5.1. **JENNIFER PASTOR.** *Flow Chart for the "Perfect Ride" Animation.* 1999–2000. Pencil on paper, three of seven sheets, each 13½" x 17" (34.3 cm x 43.2 cm). *The Museum of Modern Art, New York.*

grass—a force field that activates the surface of the paper. The lines enclose white planes of varying shapes and sizes to stitch foreground to background.

Line can be put to analytical use as a means of converting abstract thinking into visual form. Using chance procedures and a noncompositional approach, Ellsworth Kelly made a series of drawings in which he eliminated visual control by not looking at the paper as he drew. The lines seen here *(figure 5.3)* indicate a view of rooftops and chimneys. The reduced vertical and horizontal lines state the edges of buildings; diagonal lines refer to slanted roofs, whereas curved lines indicate smoke.

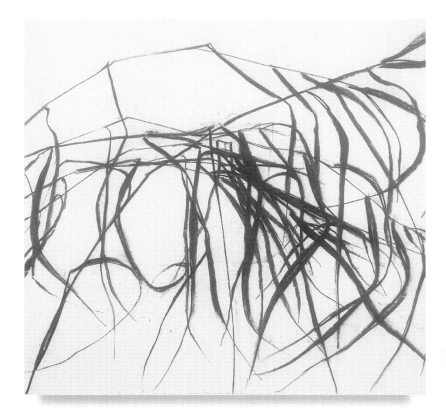

5.2. **SUSAN HARTNETT. *Sept. 19, 03 #2,*** ***Blue Joint grass (calamagrostis*** ***canadensis).*** 2003. Charcoal on paper. 22¼" x 29⅞". *Credit Photo: Alexandre Gallery, New York.*

5.3. **ELLSWORTH KELLY. *Smoke from*** ***Chimneys, Automatic Drawing from*** ***Rue Blainville.*** 1950. Pencil on paper, 19¾" x 25⅝" (50.2 cm x 64.9 cm). *Harvard University Art Museums, Cambridge, Mass.*

Kelly has used line as an economical indicator of space; it is a key element in establishing the relationship between the surface of the paper and the emerging or dissolving images on it. No better means can be found for translating the world of three dimensions into one of two dimensions.

Philip Guston's drawing uses line to communicate ideas and feelings through his cartoonlike self-portraits *(figure 5.4)*. His images are drawn with an exact, honest

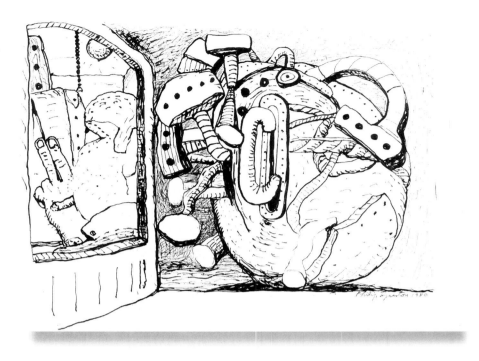

5.4. **PHILIP GUSTON.** *Untitled.* 1980. Ink on paper, 1'6¾" x 2'3⅜" (46.4 cm x 67 cm). *McKee Gallery; collection of Mr. and Mrs. Harry W. Anderson.*

crudeness. Guston states, "It is the bareness of drawing that I like. The act of drawing that locates, suggests, discovers" (Dabrowski, *The Drawings of Philip Guston*, p. 9). Guston's blunt, line reflects his interest in the comic strip and is in tune with his subject matter, a groping for personal meaning.

You have had considerable experience already in using line—gestural line; structural line; organizational line; analytical measuring line; directional line; outline; scribbled, tangled, and wrapping lines; continuous overlapping lines; automatic lines; crosshatched lines; and lines grouped to make value. This chapter deals with line quality, with the ways line can be used both objectively and subjectively as a carrier of meaning.

DETERMINANTS OF LINE QUALITY

To become sensitive to line is to recognize the inherent qualities of various linear drawing tools. Although materials sometimes can be made to work in ways contrary to their nature, recognizing the advantages and limitations of a medium is important. Some linear tools move effortlessly to create line: pencil, felt-tip marker, ballpoint pen, and pen and ink. Others produce a grainy, abrasive line such as charcoal, chalk, and conté crayon. China markers and lithographic pencils contain grease and can be smudged or dissolved. (See Guide A, "Materials" for further discussion of drawing media.)

Using ordinary media does not diminish the impact of a drawing, as can be seen in the ballpoint pen drawing by the Korean artist Il Lee *(figure 5.5)*. The dense mass created by compiling line upon line contrasts with the wispy lines that have escaped the confines of the weighted form.

The surface on which a line is drawn is another strong determinant of the quality of that line. The character of a line scratched into a surface is different from a drawn line, and a drawn line on paper is different from one on clay, as can be seen in *figure 5.6*. Michael Gross's exaggerated figures and incised line enliven the surface of the container.

5.5. **IL LEE.** *Untitled #601.* 2001.
Ballpoint pen on paper, 57" x 38".
*Courtesy of Art Projects International (API),
New York.*

5.6. **MICHAEL GROSS. *Be Smart, Buy Art.***
1986. Stoneware with slip and molded
decoration, 2'6" x 1'1½" diameter (76
cm x 34 cm). *The Arkansas Arts Center
Foundation Collection. The Decorative Arts
Museum Fund, 1986.*

Line quality is affected by the surface that receives the mark as well as by the
tool that makes it, as seen in Eve Aschheim's mixed-media drawing *(figure 5.7)*.
Aschheim superimposes lines made with various media on transparent paper. Some
lines bleed through diluted gesso; others lie on the surface of the paper. What

5.7. **EVE ASCHHEIM.** *Lurker.* 1999. Pencil, gesso, black gesso, wax crayon, ink on Duralene mylar, 12" x 9". *The Judith Rothschild Foundation Contemporary Drawings Collection, 2005. (TR 12112.2538).*

would seem to be a deep illusionistic space, a long hall, is undermined by linear complexities and contradictions in the composition. The white semicircular lines prevent an optical illusion of space and keep the attention on the surface of the drawing.

Other major determinants of line quality and drawing style are the times and societies in which the artist lives. This is most apparent with artists who deal with social commentary, such as George Grosz, a caustic critic of the conditions in Germany after World War I *(figure 5.8)*. His powerful indictments make use of exaggerated lines to convey biting commentary. His caustic accusations are conveyed by his crabbed line. Grosz said of those years that he felt the ground shaking under him and the shaking was visible in his work. Grosz's quaking line is the identifying characteristic of his drawings. An artist's linear style can be as personal as handwriting; familiarity with that style makes it easier to identify the artist. Grosz and Picasso are two artists with distinctive linear styles.

The technology of a given period exerts influence on contemporaneous drawing style and line quality as well. Just as scientific discoveries early in the century affected art styles, in today's world, the computer explosion certainly has had an equal effect on art. We are bombarded with computer-generated graphic images; it is no surprise that artists have exploited this new technology. Victor Newsome's gridded drawing of a head *(figure 5.9)* is an example of such influence. Unmistakably a contemporary drawing, its lines resemble those generated by a computer; the grid lines themselves are another reference to a mechanically generated surface. The line quality derives from technological influence.

5.8. **GEORGE GROSZ.** *Exploiters of the People from the series for The Robbers by Friedrich von Schiller.* 1922. Photolithograph. 2'2⅜" x 1'6⅜" (67 cm x 47 cm) (sheet); 1'7⅛" x 1'2¾" (49 cm x 37 cm) (image). *Print Collection, Miriam and Ira O. Wallach Division of Art, Prints, and Photographs, New York Public Library, Astor, Lennox, and Tilden Foundations. 83.9. © Estate of George Grosz/Licensed by VAGA, New York.*

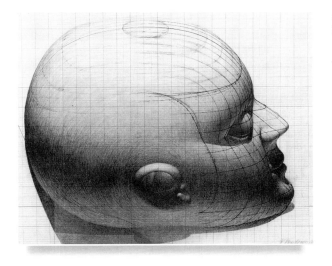

5.9. **VICTOR NEWSOME.** *Untitled.* 1982. Pencil and ink on paper, 1'1½" x 1'5¼" (34.3 cm x 43.8 cm). *The Arkansas Arts Center Foundation Purchase, 1983. 83.9.*

EXTENDED CONTEMPORARY USES OF LINE

A contemporary art phenomenon determining line quality is the relationship that drawing shares with the other disciplines of art—painting, printmaking, sculpture, and photography. Drawing, especially the linear element, extends to other disciplines and other media. The marks that define drawing are now incorporated into work by sculptors and photographers.

An example of the parallel relationship between two art disciplines can be found in a combination photo-drawing by Ian McKeever *(figure 5.10)*. In a work whose subject is the processes of erosion of the natural world, gestural line unites photography and drawing. McKeever likens drawing and photography to the landscape itself in that they both "expose and obscure, reveal and conceal . . . they are like the agents of land erosion breaking down and rebuilding surfaces" (Tony Godfrey, *Drawing Today*, p. 33). McKeever's active lines convey the idea of a world in flux.

Vik Muniz extends the use of line in even more experimental ways. He "draws" iconic subjects using thread or wire. Here, in *figure 5.11*, he has re-created the etched lines of an eighteenth-century Giovanni Piranesi print. Muniz photographs the thread drawings, enlarging them to huge prints, and then discards the original work. Muniz's work is about displacement from one cultural viewpoint to another and from one medium to another.

5.10. **IAN MCKEEVER.** *Staffa—Untitled.*
1985. Pencil and photograph on paper,
2'6" x 1'10" (76.2 cm x 55.9 cm).
Collection of the artist.

5.11. **VIK MUNIZ**. *Prison XIII, the Well, After Piranesi.* 2002. Cibachrome, 72" x 100" (182.9 cm x 25.4 cm).
From Vitamin D: New Perspectives in Drawing *by Emma Dexter (London: Phaidon Press, 2005).*

TYPES OF LINE

In our study of line quality, we will categorize some line types and learn to use them as well as recognize them in other artists' work. Remember, an artist seldom confines the use of line to one particular type of drawing. This statement can best be illustrated by William T. Wiley's tongue-in-cheek drawing *Mr. Unatural Eyes the Ape Run Ledge (figure 5.12)*. Wiley puns on the role of line with a sign in the drawing: "Suite out a line, sweet out a line" (Sweet Adeline). Wiley's works are filled with both visual and verbal puns. His dual roles as artist-magician and artist-dunce are underscored by his whimsical line quality.

Contour Line

In Chapter 2, we discussed the two basic approaches to drawing: the quick, immediate, gestural approach that sees forms in their wholeness, and the slower, more intense contour approach. Contour involves an inspection of the parts as they make up the whole. Contour, unlike outline, is spatially descriptive. It is *plastic*; that is, it emphasizes the three-dimensionality of a form. (See *figure 5.1*.)

Juan Gris's *Portrait of Max Jacob (figure 5.13)* is an example of contour; every line is fluently drawn. Slow and accurate observation is the key. The composition is subtly unified by a sidewise figure-eight shape; the clasped hands find their echoes in the bow tie and in the eyes. The form builds from the hands to the head. Gris has used contour lines of varying width to describe changes of texture, value, and color. Heavier, darker lines create accents (usually where the line changes direction, the mark is darker); lighter lines describe the less dominant interior forms.

5.12. **WILLIAM T. WILEY.** *Mr. Unatural Eyes the Ape Run Ledge.* 1975. Colored pencil and wax on paper, 3' x 2'4¾" (91 cm x 73 cm). *Collection Robert and Nancy Mollers, Houston. Walker Art Center, Minneapolis, Minn.*

5.13. **JUAN GRIS.** *Portrait of Max Jacob.* 1919. Pencil, 1'2⅜" x 10½" (36.5 cm x 26.7 cm). *The Museum of Modern Art, New York; gift of James Thrall Soby. Photograph © 1997 The Museum of Modern Art, New York.*

Not all contour drawings are drawn from life, however. An interesting pairing with the portrait of Max Jacob is another Gris drawing, the abstracted, mental construct *Personnage Assis (figure 5.14)*. In the first drawing, Gris used intermittent dark lines; in the second one, the darker lines are not merely accents; they play the

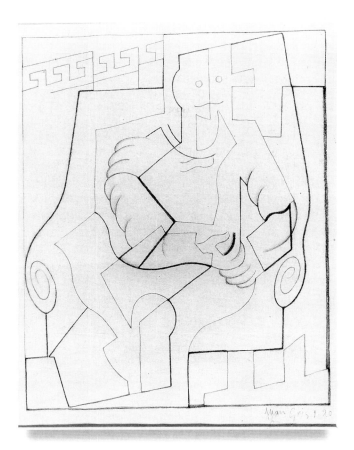

5.14. **JUAN GRIS.** *Personnage Assis.*
1920. Pencil on paper, 1'1½" x 10⅝"
(34.3 cm x 27 cm). *Arkansas Arts Center*
Foundation Collection, The Tabriz Fund, 1987.
87.47.2.

dominant role in the composition, and spatially they set up a series of interchanging foreground, middle ground, and background planes. It reminds us once again of that ever-present issue in the drawing: figure/ground relationships.

Before moving onto specific line-drawing problems, review the steps involved in contour-line drawing below.

REVIEW: STEPS IN CONTOUR-LINE DRAWING

1. Use a sharp-pointed implement (such as a 2B pencil, or pen and ink) to produce a single incisive line.
2. Keep your eyes on the subject.
3. Imagine that the point of your drawing tool is in actual contact with the subject.
4. Do not let your eyes move more quickly than you can draw.
5. Keep your implement in contact with the paper until you come to the end of a form.
6. Keep your eye and hand coordinated.
7. Begin at the outside edge of your subject, and when you see the line turn inward, follow it to its end.
8. Draw only where there is an actual, structural plane shift or where there is a change in value, texture, or color.
9. Do not enter the interior form and draw nonexistent planes or make meaningless lines.
10. Do not worry about distorted or inaccurate proportions; they will improve after a number of sessions dedicated to contour.
11. Do not retrace already stated lines, and do not erase for correction.
12. Keep in mind line variation in weight, width, and contrast.

The next five problems present variations of contour-line drawing. They are slow contour, exaggerated contour, quick contour, cross contour, and contour with tone. Remember, the same general instructions given in Chapter 2 for blind contour are applicable for all types of contour.

PROBLEM 5.1

Slow Contour Line

Make a slow contour drawing of a machine part, keeping in mind the steps listed earlier. Draw slowly, searching for details. Do not look at your paper. Glance briefly at the drawing for realignment when you have come to the end of a form. Do not trace over already stated lines.

Make several slow contour drawings, increasing the time you spend on each drawing. You should eventually be able to spend as much as an hour on a single drawing. Experiment with different implements.

PROBLEM 5.2

Exaggerated Contour Line

Normally in contour drawings, the artist avoids intentional distortion; however, exaggerated contour line takes advantage of these distortions, intentionally promoting them. It is the preferred technique of caricaturists, who make sharp commentary on prominent personalities.

David Levine, the caricaturist for *The New York Review of Books*, is an accomplished draftsman whose drawings depict the major cultural and political figures of our time. In *figure 5.15*, Levine depicts Clement Greenberg, the most influential art

5.15. **DAVID LEVINE.** *Clement Greenberg.*
Ink on thin board. *Lescher and Lescher, Ltd.*
© *1975 by David Levine. Originally appeared in* The New York Review of Books.

critic of his time, in the costume of a pope. In Levine's caricatures, the scale of the head dominates the picture plane; the remainder of the body is drawn in a highly reduced scale. Certain salient features of the subject's physiognomy are also exaggerated. Levine captures the essence of physical shape as well as cultural roles.

For this drawing, use a model as your subject. Your model should either stand or sit on a high stool. Use exaggerated contour line, and reverse Levine's procedure by enlarging the lower half of the model's body and reducing the scale in the upper half of the figure.

Before you start to draw, lightly dampen your paper. Use pen and ink and begin by drawing the model's feet. Using a contour line, draw until you have reached the middle of the page (you should be at knee level on the figure). Now you must radically adjust the scale of the figure to fit it in the remaining space. The resulting drawing will appear as if made from an ant's eye view. There should be a monumental feeling to the figure, as in Milton Avery's *Untitled (Male Figure)* *(figure 5.16)*.

You will notice that a different kind of line quality results from the dampened paper. You will have a darker line along the forms where you exerted more pressure or where you have lingered, waiting to draw. This line of varying width is one you should intentionally employ from time to time.

5.16. **MILTON AVERY.** *Untitled (Male Figure)* from *Eleven Provincetown Sketches.* n.d. Pencil on paper, 11" x 8½" (28 cm x 22 cm). *Collection of the Modern Art Museum of Fort Worth; gift of Sally Michel Avery. © 2007 Milton Avery Trust/Artists Rights Society (ARS), New York.*

Quick Contour Line

Quick contour drawing is a shorthand version of slow contour. A single line is still the goal; however, the movement of the line is faster and less determined. In quick contour drawing, you are trying to catch the essence of the subject.

In Gaston Lachaise's quick contour drawing *(figure 5.17)*, the speed with which the figure was drawn is apparent. No more than a few seconds were required to make the sketch that is complete in essential information. Lines of varying weight and value serve as spatial indicators that would be absent in a contour line of maintained width. The line emphasizes the figure's repeating circular forms from head to hip; the body's masses are lyrically stated.

Make several quick contour drawings on the same page, experimenting with point of view, scale, size, and media. Alternate the time from 15 seconds to three minutes. Animals are good subjects for quick contours. Simplify their shapes to capture the essence of their poses.

5.17. **GASTON LACHAISE.** *Back of a Nude Woman.* 1929. Drawing, pencil preparation, quill pen and India ink on brush wash, 1'5⅞" x 1' (45.5 cm x 30.9 cm). *Brooklyn Museum of Art, Gift of Carl Zigrosser.*

PROBLEM 5.4

Cross-Contour Line

Cross-contour lines describe an object's horizontal contours, or cross contours, rather than its vertical edges. They emphasize an object's turn into space. You are undoubtedly familiar with contour maps, which describe the earth's land surface with their undulating lines that rise and recede. Diana Jacobs's drawing presents a visual definition of cross contour *(figure 5.18)*. The warped center of the drawn weaving is made up of cross- and vertical-contour lines, creating a spatial illusion.

In Henry Moore's drawing, *Forest Elephants (figure 5.19)*, the lines economically map the contours of the elephants, "stitching" the animals to their supporting surface. Cross-contour lines give the elephants dimension so that they seem to be emerging from a dark space.

Make a cross-contour drawing using a reclining model as subject. Imagine the line as a thread that wraps the body horizontally, encasing its mass. Refer to the Newsome drawing (see *figure 5.9*) to see how reductive cross and vertical contours can be teamed to build a three-dimensional illusion.

PROBLEM 5.5

Contour with Tone

After you have had some practice with contour drawing, you can add value or tone. Be selective in your placement of value. Don Bachardy's poignant drawing of his dying friend Christopher Isherwood *(figure 5.20)* is a good example of contour with tone. It is a compilation of quick contour, slow and exaggerated contour, cross contour, and an economical use of value. Pale washes create a focal point.

Select several old contour drawings and add a focal point by using value. The added tone should be compatible with the medium of the original.

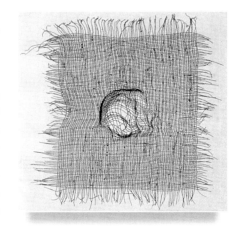

5.18. **DIANA JACOBS.** *Event.* 2001. Etching, 2'6" x 2'6" (76 cm x 76 cm). *Goya-Girl Press, Baltimore, Md.*

5.19. **HENRY MOORE.** *Forest Elephants.* 1977. Charcoal, chalk on white heavy-weight wove, 1'1/12" x 1'37/12" (30.7 cm x 39.6 cm). *Acquired by The Henry Moore Foundation.*

5.20. **DON BACHARDY.** *Christopher Isherwood.* October 20, 1985. Black acrylic wash on ragboard, 3'4" x 2'8" (1.01 m x 81 cm). *Collection of the artist. Photo by Dale Laster.*

5.21. **STEVE GIANAKOS.** *Gorillas #10.* 1983. Ink and colored pencil on paper, 3'4" x 5' (1.02 m x 1.52 m). *Barbara Toll Fine Arts, New York.*

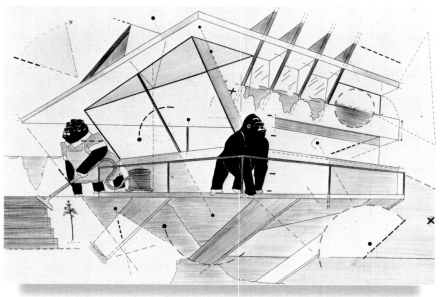

Mechanical Line

Mechanical line is an objective, nonpersonal line that maintains the same width along its full length. An example of this type of line would be an architect's ground plan in which various lines indicate different materials or levels of space. Steve Gianakos, who studied industrial design, uses a number of drafting techniques in his work *(figure 5.21)*. The carefully plotted arcs and angles are a source of humor in the work; no doubt they are intended to make some tongue-in-cheek remark on architectural drawings. Note the mechanical application of line; each individual line is unvarying, deliberate, and controlled.

PROBLEM 5.6

Using Mechanical Line

Draw multiple views of an object—top, bottom, and sides—using mechanical line. You may keep the views separate, or you may overlap and superimpose them. Keeping in mind that mechanical line remains the same throughout its length, select a drawing tool that will produce this kind of mark, such as a pencil, felt-tip marker, ballpoint pen, or lettering pen. It would be amusing to convert an unexpected object, such as a toy or an article of clothing, to a mechanical drawing.

Structural Line

Structural lines reveal how planes connect to build volume and create a three-dimensional effect. Although a drawing can be made using only structural lines, these lines are usually found in combination with organizational or contour line. Structural lines can be grouped to create value; they can also be put to abstract use, as in Marcel Duchamp's pencil-and-wash drawing *(figure 5.22)*. Here an idea of simultaneity and sequential motion is conveyed by structural and diagrammatic lines. Change, Duchamp's recurring theme, is given graphic form through the use of structural lines.

PROBLEM 5.7

Using Structural Line

For this problem use *scratchboard*, a clay-coated paper whose surface is made to be scratched into. Use sharp implements to make white lines. The finished drawing will resemble a print, since the line is actually incised into the surface. Cut a 2-inch strip from the scratchboard to experiment with various implements before beginning

5.22. **MARCEL DUCHAMP.** *La Mariée Mise a Nu Par Ses Celibataires.* 1912. Pencil and wash, 9⅜" x 1'⅝" (23.8 cm x 32.1 cm). *Musée National d'Art Moderne, Paris. © 2007 Artists Rights Society (ARS), New York/ADAGP, Paris/Succession Marcel Duchamp. Photograph by Philippe Migeat, Centre G. Pompidou.*

the drawing. Lightly transfer the basic shape of your composition onto the scratch-board before you start making heavier incised structural lines.

Make a drawing of a figure using structural lines to indicate changes of planes, to create values, and to build volume. Use parallel lines, cross-hatching, or grouped contour lines; they can be angular or curved.

In the print by the Canadian artist Cecil Tremayne Buller *(figure 5.23)*, we see how suited structural line is to woodcut. The reduction to black and white and the interchange of values result in a structural effect. The abstract patterning remains flat within a plane but the overall effect is one of interlocking volumes, both within the figures and in the print as a whole.

Lyrical Line

Lyrical drawings are intimate and reflect a sensitivity of expression. Lyric verse is akin to songs, the earliest ones accompanied by the lyre, from which the word *lyric* is derived. *Lyrical lines* are ornate, intertwined lines that flow gracefully, like arabesques.

Contour line and decorative line are frequently combined to create a lyrical mood. Lyrical drawings produce a mood of lightness and gaiety. Repeating curvilinear lines establish rhythmic patterns fitting a relaxed theme. Generally, the more deliberately controlled a line, the more objective it is. The more spontaneously a line is stated, the more subjective it is. Lyrical line falls under the subjective category and is characterized by sensitivity of expression.

Lyrical line and the drawings of Henri Matisse are synonymous. In Matisse's distinctive pen-and-ink drawing *(figure 5.24)*, the line flows effortlessly across the page. The white ground of the paper is activated by the forms that float across the surface. Matisse's line embodies his wish to make art that is as "comfortable as an armchair." We see a model, her back reflected in a mirror in the background, a door

5.23. **CECIL TREMAYNE BULLER.** *Je suis à mon bien-aimé et mon bien-aimé est à moi, lui qui se nourrit parmi les lis.* 1929–1931. Wood engraving, 10¹¹⁄₁₂" x 7⁴⁄₉" (27.8 cm x 18.9 cm). *Courtesy, The Montreal Museum of Fine Arts. Photo: The Montreal Museum of Fine Arts.*

5.24. **HENRI MATISSE.** *Nude in the Studio.* 1935. Pen and ink, 1'5¾" x 1'10⅜" (46 cm x 57 cm). *Location unknown. © 2007 Succession H. Matisse, Paris/Artists Rights Society (ARS), New York.*

to another space, another room, a window to an outside space, and in the lower right-hand corner a shorthand description of the scene just described, an even more abstract handling of space than in the dominant composition—and a notation of the artist's hand holding a pen, a reference to still another space.

PROBLEM 5.8

Using Lyrical Line

Choose a room interior as subject. Use lyrical lines to create decorative patterns. A free-flowing implement such as brush and ink or pen and ink is recommended. Draw while listening to music. The goal is spontaneity. Take a relaxed attitude.

Constricted, Aggressive Line

Constricted line makes use of angular, crabbed, assertive marks, aggressively stated. The lines should be rough and scratchy, carriers of a bitter expression; they can convey the feeling of extreme emotion, as in George Grosz's work (see *figure 5.8*).

PROBLEM 5.9

Using Constricted, Aggressive Line

The abraded surface and rugged line quality in Jean Dubuffet's drawing *(figure 5.25)* is a result of the images scratched into the surface, a technique called

5.25. **JEAN DUBUFFET.** *Subway.* 1949. Incised ink on gesso on cardboard, 1'⅝" x 9⅞" (32.1 cm x 23.5 cm). *Collection, The Museum of Modern Art, New York. The Joan and Lester Avnet Collection. © 2007 Artists Rights Society (ARS), New York/ADAGP, Paris. Photograph © 1997 The Museum of Modern Art, New York.*

grattage. The French artist was intent on a return to expressionistic, fetishistic, primitive art that he tagged *Art Brut*. Dubuffet aimed for immediacy and obsessiveness in his work. Aggressive, constricted marks, abraded surfaces, and grotesque imagery provided Dubuffet primitive means for primitive intent.

Coat a piece of bristol board with a layer of gesso over which you then apply a coat of black ink. Use found implements such as old pens, nails, or razor blades as scrapers to depict an event or situation toward which you feel great antipathy. Aim for a drawing style and a line quality that will underscore a bitter message.

Handwriting: Cursive and Calligraphic Line

In the Orient, artists are trained in calligraphic drawing by first practicing the individual strokes that make up the complex characters of their writing. Subtleties of surface, value, and line quality are promoted. The marks can range from rigorously severe to vigorously expressive, as in the calligraphic drawing by Isamu Noguchi *(figure 5.26).*

Ink and brush is the traditional medium of calligraphy where instrument, media, surface, and technique all play crucial roles. Variations of line encompass the full range from bold to delicate, from thick to thin. Noguchi's lines are sweepingly graceful. A Chinese saying sums up the drawing: "A line is a force."

5.26. **ISAMU NOGUCHI. *Untitled (from the Peking Drawing Series).*** 1930. Pen and ink on paper, 4' x 3' (1.22 m x 91.4 cm). *Perimeter Gallery, Chicago. Photo by Michael Tropea. © 2007 The Isamu Noguchi Foundation and Garden Museum, New York/Artists Rights Society (ARS), New York.*

Using Handwriting or Calligraphic Line

On a sketch pad, practice writing with ink and a bamboo-handled Japanese brush. Hold the drawing tool near the end, away from the brush, and at a 90-degree angle to the paper. Your paper should be on a horizontal surface. Change the scale of your marks, making the transitions gradual and graceful. Apply different amounts of pressure to create flowing motions. Turn the brush between your fingers as you write. Experiment with the way you hold the brush and with the amount of ink loaded onto it.

After you have some control of the technique, make a composition of written words. Choose a text that is appealing to you—a poem, a passage from a novel, or your own original writing. In your drawing, layer the words and obscure their legibility, allowing them to be read only occasionally.

To differentiate the layers, use black, white, and sepia ink on light gray or buff paper.

Implied Line

An *implied line* is one that stops and picks up again. It can be a broken contour; the viewer conceptually fills in the breaks. Refer to the Sarmento drawing (see *figure 3.7*) to freshen your memory of implied shape.

In *figure 5.27*, David Hockney makes use of a fragmented, or implied, line. Hand, dress, and chair dissolve into a series of accent marks; their individual shapes are not clearly defined. Hockney's implied line is a weighted, broken contour line.

5.27. **DAVID HOCKNEY.** *Celia Inquiring.* 1979. Lithograph, 3'4" x 2'5" (1.016 m x 73.7 cm). *Ed: 78. © David Hockney.*

Implied line results from an interchange between positive and negative shapes. It brings the negative space into the implied positive shapes, creating spatial ambiguity. This lost-and-found characteristic requires a viewer's participation since missing lines and shapes are filled in mentally.

PROBLEM 5.11

Using Implied Line

With a still life as subject, use a felt-tip marker to alternate drawing between the left and right side of the objects in the still life; leave the opposite side empty. This technique results in implied shapes. Lighten the pressure on your drawing tool as the line begins to break. The lines should change from light to dark along their length. Use a minimal amount of line to suggest or imply shape.

Blurred Line

Blurred lines are smudged, erased, or destroyed in some way, either by rubbing or by erasure. They are frequently grouped to form a sliding edge; they are not as precisely stated as implied lines. Blurred and smudged lines create an indefinite edge, thereby resulting in an ambiguous space.

Hockney, in the study of a friend *(figure 5.28)*, uses blurred and erased lines to build the figure. Lines are grouped in a single direction within each shape, binding

5.28. **DAVID HOCKNEY.** *Henry in Candlelight.* 1975. Crayon on paper, 17" x 14". *Private collection, France.* © *David Hockney.*

the figure to its space. There is an unfinished quality to the drawing, owing to the disruption of the contours. The strokes seem to emerge from the surrounding space. Hockney's technique of blurred line is especially appropriate when we note the title, *Henry in Candlelight*. The flickering quality of the light is translated into the drawing by means of the blurred line.

Blurred, erased gestural marks are signatures of Willem de Kooning's work *(figure 5.29)*. De Kooning creates a spatial ambiguity through a textural surface of built-up and erased line in both his drawings and paintings. His style gives us a strong clue as to why the Abstract Expressionists were called *Action Painters*. De Kooning was a master draftsman, yet he found it necessary to rein in his natural facility to hone his pictorial skills.

This discussion of blurred line would not be complete without mentioning what is arguably the most discussed drawing of the twentieth century, Robert Rauschenberg's 1953 *Erased de Kooning Drawing*. Rauschenberg was interested in disintegration, in obliterating the artist's hand and artistic presence from his own work, so he devised a project that would be a perfect vehicle for implementing his theories. Rauschenberg requested that de Kooning give him one of his drawings, one that de Kooning would not like to part with; the other stipulation was that it should be a drawing that would be difficult to erase. De Kooning gave the request long and serious consideration before complying. Rauschenberg spent two months trying to eliminate all traces of de Kooning's marks by carefully erasing

5.29. **WILLEM DE KOONING.** *Woman.*
1952. Pastel and pencil, 1'9" x 1'2" (52 cm x 36 cm). *Private collection, Boston. © 2007 The Willem de Kooning Foundation/ Artists Rights Society (ARS), New York. Photograph by Barney Burstein, Boston.*

the entire drawing. The erased surface persisted in retaining memories of the original drawing.

PROBLEM 5.12

Using Blurred Line

With a 4B pencil and a white plastic eraser, make a drawing in which you use blurred, smudged, and erased line. Using the eraser as a drawing tool, make sweeping motions that go counter to the pencil marks. Erase and blur the already established lines. Alternately redraw and erase until the drawing is finished.

In a second drawing, make a toned ground for a blurred-line drawing. Develop clusters of line with charcoal; conté crayon, stick; and eraser. In this technique, the positive and negative shapes merge; positive shapes dissolve into the ground of the toned paper. Compose your drawing so that a light, positive shape adjoins a light, negative shape; and a dark, positive shape adjoins a dark, negative shape. This will result in an ambiguity of edge.

Whimsical Line

A playful, whimsical line quality is appropriate for a lighthearted approach. This subjective line is both intuitive and directly stated. A whimsical line changes its width arbitrarily. Whimsy is more a feeling than a technique. Exaggeration and unexpected juxtapositions play a major part in creating a whimsical mood.

In a drawing rooted in the humorous vein *(figure 5.30)*, the Portuguese-born artist Paula Rego uses quick contours, insets, shifting scale, sketchy characters,

5.30. **PAULA REGO.** *Aïda.* 1983. Acrylic on paper, 7'10½" x 6'7¹¹/₁₂" (2.4 m x 2.03 m). *Collection of the artist.*

exaggerated proportions, and odd costumes—all of these elements convey a whimsical account of the nineteenth-century opera *Aïda*. Rego plots the narrative in both vertical and horizontal registers (note the inserts); she interrupts the theatrical flow with her subversive imagery and compilation of riotous activity. Like other artists (Walt Disney among them), Rego uses animals to underscore human foibles. A synchronic presentation replaces the linear unfolding of the opera scene by scene; in Rego's drawing the whole story is squeezed into a single, action-packed page.

PROBLEM 5.13

Using Whimsical Line

Make a drawing based on a childhood story and give it a humorous twist. Aim for caricature-like distortions, using a naïve, whimsical line. Use colored pencils or felt-tip markers.

Elizabeth Layton, a woman in her nineties, illustrates such a story in her retelling of *Cinderella (figure 5.31)*. Her shaky line may come from a hand that is trembling, but its direction is sure.

SUMMARY

Spatial Characteristics of Line

Although each problem in this chapter has generally been confined to the use of one kind of line, most artists do not limit the types of lines they use. Anna Sigmond Gudmundsdottir combines drawing and graffiti to create elaborate environments in which images from popular culture collide with text and

5.31. **ELIZABETH LAYTON.** *Cinderella.*
1986. Lithograph, 1'10" x 2'6" (56 cm x 76 cm). *Lawrence Arts Center, Kansas. Gift of the artist.*

5.32. ANNA SIGMOND GUDMUNDSDOTTIR.
From "The offer no one can refuse, only because the majority was invented."
2003. Mixed media on wall. *Installation at O.K. Centrum fuer Gegewartskunst, Linz, Austria.*

mythic figures *(figure 5.32)*. Web sites and archives available online are the source for her images, which she reworks in a variety of line qualities and recycled styles.

What follows is a brief summary of what you have learned about the spatial characteristics of line. Subjective lines are generally more dimensional than objective lines. This is because a subjective line changes width, changes from light to dark, and is more suggestive of space than a flat line of maintained width. Outlining makes shapes appear flat; contour line is more dimensional than outline.

A contour line of varying width and pressure is more dimensional than one of uniform weight. A discontinuous, or broken, line is more spatial than an unvarying one.

When line is stated primarily horizontally and vertically, that is, when it remains parallel to the picture plane, a shallow space results. If, however, lines penetrate the picture plane diagonally, a three-dimensional space is produced. Generally, a buildup of lines is more volumetric than a single line.

When lines are grouped in a single direction to create value, the resulting space is flatter than if the lines are not stated uniformly. Lines that create a repeating pattern of texture make a flatter space than those stated less predictably.

Remember that you must look at all the lines in a drawing together to determine its spatial effect.

As we stated at the start of this chapter, line is the most direct means of establishing style. It is as personal as handwriting and should be practiced, analyzed, and refined throughout your drawing career.

SKETCHBOOK PROJECT

Every problem in this chapter is appropriate for the sketchbook; daily contour drawings are strongly recommended. They are ideal for the sketchbook since they can be done with any subject matter and in the shortest time periods. Keep your sketchbook handy and fill it with the various types of contour drawings.

The more lines you draw, the more sensitive you will become to line quality. Being involved in simple mark making will improve your sensitivity to line. Line used abstractly as well as concretely to describe an object in the real world requires practice on a regular basis. You will begin to find possibilities for new line applications the more you draw.

PROJECT 1

The Cadavre Exquis (The Exquisite Corpse)

The *cadavre exquis* was a drawing technique devised by the Surrealists in which a group of artists work on the same drawing, each unaware of what the others have drawn. In the same drawing there will be different styles, different ideas, and mixed images. The result can be surprisingly coherent, funny, and strange at the same time.

The person who begins is to cover the beginning segment of the drawing by taping a piece of blank paper over the initial image. A line or two can be left visible so that the second person can attach the second part to the first part. Continue the process of drawing and concealing until the third person has finished. Unmask the drawing to reveal the composite drawing.

You might want to make a few rules beforehand, although this is not necessary. You could, for example, restrict what kind of imagery is to be used: parts of the body, animals, plants, or machines. Limiting the medium will make for a more visually coherent drawing. Because this exercise is designed to make you more comfortable in working with line, you should make several exquisite corpse drawings that employ line only.

COMPUTER PROJECT

PROJECT 1

Computer Drawing and Line Quality

Like the other computer exercises, much depends on the particular programs available to you. Most graphic programs allow the user to control line by width, and sometimes the user can control line quality *(figure 5.33)*. Programs are increasingly responsive to artists who require line quality to resemble physical drawing and painting media. The 12 examples shown here are from Adobe Illustrator Brush Library. The names are: Fountain Pen, Dry Brush—Thick, Dry Ink, Calligraphic Round, Calligraphic Flat, Charcoal, Fire Ash, Scroll Pen, Chalk, Train Tracks, and Dashed. Experiment with the programs available to you and create your own inventory of line quality.

5.33. Computer drawing creating line.
Courtesy of Tom Sale.

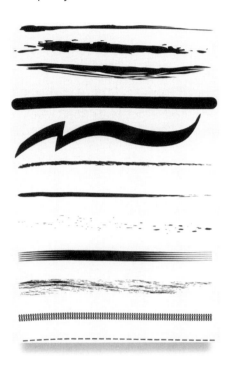

CHAPTER 6

Oil, watercolor, pencil, fabric, paper, photographs, metal, glass, electric light fixtures, dried grass, steel wool, necktie, on wood structure with four wheels, plus pillow and stuffed rooster.

—CATALOG ENTRY DESCRIBING MEDIA USED IN ROBERT RAUSCHENBERG'S

COMBINE ODALISK, 1955–1958

Texture

THE ROLE OF TEXTURE IN CONTEMPORARY ART

Before beginning our discussion on the role of texture in contemporary art, we need to define the term. *Texture* in its most literal meaning refers strictly to the sense of touch. For the artist, however, the *visual* appearance of a work, its surface quality, is most important. Although the actual texture of surface and medium may have a subtle tactile quality, the visual quality is what contributes to the textural character of the work.

The catalog entry cited above shows the multitude of textures available to the contemporary artist. The predominant role of texture in drawing before the twentieth century was illusionistic, imitating textures in the natural world. Today, however, texture does not just imitate the real world. Artists use real-world textures in their art. Consider the following artists and how they have incorporated these new techniques into their works of art.

The old world of texture and the new come together in Susan Turcot's drawing *(figure 6.1)*. On one side of her two-part drawing, Turcot uses texture to transcribe a landscape; on the other side, with her eyes closed, she makes

6.1. **SUSAN TURCOT. From the series**
Divided Subjects #8. 2003. Graphite
on paper. 30 cm x 40 cm (unframed),
TUR0094. *Courtesy Amdt & Partner,*
Burlin/Zurich.

nonreferential gestural marks. The two types of texture, on imitative and one the
actual texture of the pencil, set up a dichotomy between form and chaos. The
scribbles play a conceptual role in suggesting disintegration and fragmentation.
The clash of textures carries the meaning of the work.

Richard Long's work furnishes insight into the extremes of modern-day texture
(figure 6.2). Extending the landscape tradition established in the last century, Long
evokes a romantic response in his work made of actual mud, rock, and dirt. In the
work shown here, Long uses the silt of the Mississippi River as a medium for his
large drawing; the rivulets of actual mud flowed over Japanese rice paper bring to
mind the ebb and flow of the river itself.

Contemporary art runs the gamut from illusionistic veracity to cartoon styl-
ization. Two examples furnish insight into these extremes. Roy Lichtenstein's
Tablet (figure 6.3) is symbolically represented; the reflected glass is indicated by
vertical lines that contrast with the curvilinear lines that represent the fizzing
tablet. The background space is filled with the artist's trademark benday dots;
the static glass is inserted in a texturally patterned background. The spatial and
textural clues are conventions; we know how to read them from interpreting
comic strips.

In contrast, Serse's life study of a water droplet *(figure 6.4)* is more realistic and
texturally complex. His technique with graphite and eraser results in a three-
dimensional illusion. As opposed to Lichtenstein's static image, Serse's drawing captures a real moment in time.

6.2. **RICHARD LONG.** *Untitled.* 1992. Mississippi mud on rice paper, 6'6" x 3'7" (1.98 m x 1.09 m). *Modern Art Museum of Fort Worth; gift of the Director's Council.*

Pattern and Decoration

A significant impulse that began in the latter part of the twentieth century and that continues today is an emphasis on decorative textural patterning. Miriam Schapiro took the lead in a movement that is called Pattern and Decoration, which developed new strategies for women's work and introduced new images, content, techniques, and materials. In *figure 6.5*, Schapiro uses acrylic paint, paper cutouts, and fabric glued on paper to create a room-sized book. Each page, 9 feet by 12 feet (!), is made up of different sets of patterns. The pages resemble a group of quilts laid end to end.

Another artist who uses pattern and decoration in her work is the German artist Rosemarie Trockel. Trockel presents knit panels, clothing, sculpture, drawings, photographs, and video art that are distinctly political and feminized. It is a surprise to learn that the image in one of her ironic works shown here *(figure 6.6)* is drawn, not knitted. Trockel's trick-the-eye texture closes the gap between high and low art.

Object as New Genre

The *object* emerged as a distinct genre in the late twentieth century. This novel development introduced a new kind of art formulation. Although art objects are three-dimensional, they are not strictly sculpture. Artists' one-of-a-kind books fall into this crossover category between drawing, printmaking, photography, and sculpture. In this new genre of objects—including cubes, boxes, trays, and containers as well as books—real texture on real objects has displaced the illusionistic function of texture. Dottie

6.3. **ROY LICHTENSTEIN** American, 1923–1997. *Alka Seltzer.* 1966. Graphite with scraping, and lithographic pochoir on cream woven paper, 751 mm x 567 mm. (image); 763 mm x 567 mm. (sheet), *Margaret Fisher Endowment, 1993.176. Reproduction, The Art Institute of Chicago. Photo: Robert E. Mates and Paul Katz.*

6.4. **SERSE.** *Studio dal vero,* 1997. Graphite on paper. 150 cm x 100 cm.

6.5. **MIRIAM SCHAPIRO.** *Rondo* **(excerpt).**
1989. Artist's book, acrylic paint,
paper cutouts, and fabric on paper,
9' x 12' (2.74 m x 3.66 m) per page.
Published by Bedford Arts Publishers. Courtesy of the artist.

6.6. **ROSEMARIE TROCKEL.** *O.T 1996.*
1996. Acrylic on paper, 2'3⁄4" x 2'83⁄8"
(62.9 cm x 82.2 cm). *Photo courtesy of Barbara Gladstone Gallery, New York.*
© 2007 Artists Rights Society (ARS), New York/VG Bild-Kunst, Bonn.

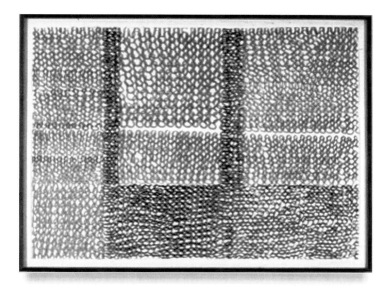

Love's book, *All There Is (figure 6.7),* is made of materials associated with neither books nor art but out of more base materials that avoid connotations of art. Pages are formed of layered pieces of glass, acetate, and mirror, which are held together by soldered lead and encased in a glass container embedded in another glass case filled with dirt. The viewer is given a tactile reward by actually handling the work.

CATEGORIES OF TEXTURE

Textural quality in a drawing depends on the surface on which it is drawn, the inherent character of the medium, and the artist's control of that medium. In addition to reinforcing the content of a work, texture gives information about materials and media. In this role, it surpasses the other elements. Some basic categories of texture, beginning with the traditional ones of actual, simulated, and invented, will lead us to a clearer understanding of texture.

6.7. **DOTTIE ALLEN.** *All There Is.* October, 1986. Glass, lead, dirt, photocopies on acetate. Overall (glass box): 5⅜ x 8¼ x 9¾ in. (13.7 x 21 x 24.8 cm). Overall (Each Slide): 4¹⁄₁₆ x 5½ in. (10.3 x 14 cm). *The Museum of Fine Arts, Houston. Gift of Len E. Kowitz.*

Actual Texture

Actual texture refers to the surface of the work (smooth or rough paper, for example), the texture of the medium (such as waxlike crayons, which leave a buildup on the surface), and any materials, such as fabric or paper, added to the surface of the work.

In Jiri Georg Dokoupil's drawing *(figure 6.8)*, texture is created by controlling the carbon deposits from a candle collected on the paper. This technique is called

6.8. **JIRI GEORG DOKOUPIL.** *Bosnian Refugees Arriving in Germany.* 1992. Candle soot on canvas, 4'2" x 3'4¼" (1.27 m x 1.02 m). *Tony Shafrazi Gallery.* © 2007 Artists Rights Society (ARS), New York/VG Bild-Kunst, Bonn.

fumage. A stencil or piece of paper is used to block out the white areas. By shifting the stencil and by controlling the thickness of the carbon deposits, a range of values can be created. The soot creates a soft and velvety texture; the imprecise edges of forms suggest they are emerging from darkness. Dokoupil's work deals with emigration; his style brings to mind old black-and-white newsreels.

Willie Cole's medium and image are one and the same: He scorches the surface of the paper with a hot clothes iron to create repeated forms *(figure 6.9)*. The burnt iron shapes, each differing according to their commercial brand, suggest masks, boats, shields, or missiles. For Cole, they also suggest the African ritual of scarification. To underscore their domestic function, Cole places the drawing in an actual window frame. The word *domestic* has a double meaning in Cole's work. The first meaning refers to scarification, but it also refers to a servant. Cole labels the individual iron imprints to give them a "tribal identity."

We can see that texture not only conveys information about the artist's medium but also gives information about subjective and expressive intent. Finally, any real material added to the surface of the work is, of course, actual texture.

6.9. **WILLIE COLE.** *Domestic I.D., IV.* 1992. Iron scorches and pencil on paper mounted in recycled painted wood window, 35" x 32" x 1⅜" (88.9 cm x 81.3 cm x 3.5 cm). *The Museum of Modern Art, New York.*

Simulated Texture

Simulated texture is the imitation of a real texture. Simulation can range from a suggested imitation to a highly believable *trompe l'œil* (trick-the-eye) duplication. Leo Joseph Dee employs a contemporary handling of the *trompe l'œil* technique where verisimilitude is the goal *(figure 6.10)*. A torn segment of an envelope is realistically rendered; an isolated detail of the crumpled paper emerges from the blank picture plane. By the title, *Paper Landscape*, we are given directions to interpret the drawing as a metaphorical stand-in for a landscape. Careful control of the tool, silverpoint on prepared board, and a concentrated observation result in a trick-the-eye texture.

Julie Saecker Schneider's imitation of real textures results in a three-dimensional image. In her graphite drawing *(figure 6.11)*, hair and snakes are so meticulously rendered that a shocking effect is produced, appropriate for the subject, Medusa.

The contrasts between rough and smooth, coarse and glossy, or soft and hard can be communicated without actually using glossy or rough media. In Jeanette Pasin Sloan's drawing of glasses and bowls *(figure 6.12)*, each object is richly patterned by reflections that echo the striped cloth on which they have been placed. The reflected verticals undergo a series of transformations owing to the curvature of each particular piece. On the convel shape of the black goblet, the reflected space of the room has been drawn in miniature. The drawing succeeds both as an illusionistic duplication of a still life and as an abstract composition of contrasting and repeating forms.

Invented, Conventional, or Symbolic Texture

Invented, conventional, symbolic, or *decorative, textures* do not imitate textures in real life; rather the artist invents the textural patterns. Invented textures can be used as

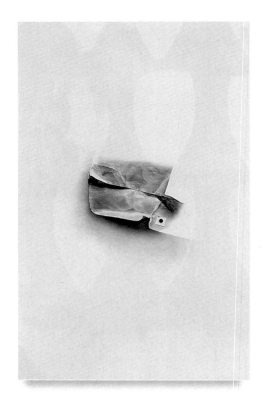

6.10. **LEO JOSEPH DEE. *Paper Land-scape.*** 1972. Silverpoint on gesso-coated museum board, 2'11⅛" x 2'2" (88 cm x 66 cm). *Yale University Art Gallery, New Haven, Conn. Purchased with the aid of funds from the National Endowment for the Arts and the Susan Morse Hilles Matching Fund. © Joseph Szaszfai.*

6.11. **JULIE SAECKER SCHNEIDER.**
Medusa II. 1995. Graphite on paper,
23" x 29". *Private collection. Marsha*
Mateyka Gallery, Washington, D.C.

6.12. **JEANETTE PASIN SLOAN. *Chicago***
and Vicinity. 1985. Colored pencil on
paper, 2'10" x 1'10½" (86.4 cm x
57.2 cm). © *Jeanette Pasin Sloan.*

6.13. **DAVID HOCKNEY.** *The Rake's Progress.* June 1975. Cut-and-pasted papers and ink on paper, 19¾" x 25⅝". *Gift of R. L. B. Tobin. (281.1978). Digital Image © The Museum of Modern Art/Licensed by SCALA/Art Resource, NY. © David Hockney.*

nonrepresentational patterns, as in David Hockney's sketch for the stage designs for *"An Assembly" from The Rake's Progress (figure 6.13)*. Or they also may be abstracted to symbolize real textures; for instance, Hockney uses symbolic notations for hair, fabric, and crocodile skin.

James Rosenquist's work is a concise compendium of texture—actual, simulated, and invented *(figure 6.14)*. Texture is again the subject of the work. The image on the left is an example of invented texture; the image in the center simulates crushed paper; and the third image makes use of actual texture in the marks and

6.14. **JAMES ROSENQUIST.** *Iris Lake.* 1974. Lithograph, 3'½" x 6'2" (93 cm x 1.88 m). *Marian Goodman Gallery. © James Rosenquist/Licensed by VAGA, New York.*

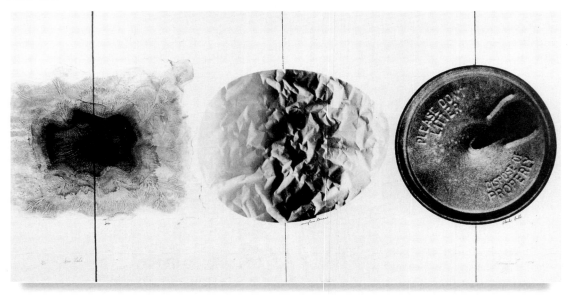

rubbings. The pictorial space is ambiguous because the illusionistically three-dimensional elements are placed in a flat, white field. The shapes can be read as lying on top of the plane or as holes in its surface.

Texture is a critical element whether used referentially or independently of the subject depicted. Just as we could make a scale of artistic choices with realism at one end and nonobjective art at the other, there are gradations in the use of texture, too. Texture, although it can be used to record the observed phenomenon of external reality, always relays information concerning media and surface.

PROBLEM 6.1

Using Actual Texture

In this problem, focus on the texture of the drawing medium itself, its inherent qualities. Cut several pieces of 18-inch-square mat board. Using pencil, chalk, pastel, charcoal, or a combination in conjunction with a flat, water-based house paint, begin with a gestural network of lines using various media. Then overlay some sections with paint. Use scumbling, drips, abrasion, drawing, redrawing, and repainting until you have achieved an interesting surface. Think of a wall with scaling paint, or some weathered surface. You are not copying or imitating a found surface; you are involved in a process in which the surface is a record of your activity. Do not develop a focal point; however, the texture should vary from section to section. The transitions between one area and another should be subtle. (See David Jeffrey, color *plate 7.6.*)

At a later time, you might want to use this technique for building a surface on which to draw.

PROBLEM 6.2

Using Simulated Texture

After closely examining David Musgrave's accurately rendered leaf *(figure 6.15)*, choose as your subject a flat, textured surface, such as a weathered piece of wood, an old piece of wallpaper, or a large leaf. Photocopy these textures on letter-size paper and make a finished drawing on the same size paper, imitating as closely as possible the original object. Mount the photocopy and drawing side by side as a diptych.

PROBLEM 6.3

Using Invented Texture

For this drawing, invent a mythological creature. Fill the entire picture plane with invented textural patterns. Use black-and-white acrylic on fabric. The absorbent quality of the cloth will provide a softer and much different texture from paper. Appropriate fabrics are muslin, duck, sailcloth, or canvas.

Outsider art is a particularly rich source for textural inventions. The Tasmanian tiger made by William L. Hawkins presents an uninhibited use of invented texture *(figure 6.16)*. Repetition builds the body of the beast, which has seductive collaged eyes. A white line separates the tiger from a scumbled background shape; the whites are distributed throughout the drawing in varying shapes and sizes. Hawkins

6.15. **DAVID MUSGRAVE.** *Dirty Leaf.*
2004. Graphite on paper, 16⅞" x
13¼" (42.9 cm x 33.8 cm).

6.16. **WILLIAM L. HAWKINS.** *Tasmanian
Tiger #3.* Enamel and mixed-media construction on masonite, 48" x 48" x 4"
(122 cm x 122 cm x 10 cm). *Ricco-
Maresca Gallery, New York.*

has created an active, energetic surface texture by a lively application of paint and repetition. See Michael Abyi's drawing on fabric, *figure 1.5*, for another interpretation of this approach.

PROBLEM 6.4

Using Conventional or Symbolic Texture

Represent various textures in an imaginary landscape using conventional or symbolic texture. A comic-strip style would be appropriate for this problem.

In David Hockney's *Cubistic Bar (figure 6.17)*, symbolic texture enlivens the scene. In insets a palm tree and ocean scene are cursorily indicated; clouds are cubed to echo the title of the drawing, and randomly textured planes created by colored crayons advertise a seaside bar.

CONTEMPORARY TEXTURES

Additive Materials to Create Texture

We have seen how flexible additive materials can be in retaining a sense of their previous identity while functioning compositionally within the work (see Rauschenberg's combine, *figure II.14*).

6.17. **DAVID HOCKNEY.** *Cubistic Bar* from *Les Mamelles de Tiresias.* 1980. Crayon, 18⅞" x 23⅞". © *David Hockney.*

Let us now divide additive materials into two classifications: *collage* and *assemblage*. *Collage* is the addition of any flat material, such as paper or fabric, to the surface of a work. (See Lance Letscher, *plate 7.12*.) *Assemblage* is the use of dimensional material attached to a piece of artwork by any means—glue, nails, wire, or rope.

An example of assemblage is the work of the German artist Joseph Beuys who, in a performance piece, incorporates a hare, rods, felt, and fat to a drawing on chalkboard *(figure 6.18)*. He uses mythic imagery to express a state of transition through ephemeral materials.

Before moving on in our discussion, several definitions of terms will be useful when talking about texture. *Papier collé* is a term for pasting paper to the picture plane; *photomontage*, as its name implies, uses only photographs; *collage*, like *montage*, is any flat material put together to create a composition. Works using papier collé, collage, montage, and photomontage usually remain flat, although they can be built up in low relief.

These techniques are actively used in contemporary art, as in Barbara Kruger's work with its exposé of establishment values *(figure 6.19)*. By making the words deny the image, she urges the viewer to reassess accepted ideas.

Jacques de la Villéglé's work *(figure 6.20)* is an offshoot of collage. He calls his work *décollage* (unpasting); he pulls down and reveals hidden, layered posters from Parisian walls, executing his art without scissors or paste. Villéglé stresses the impersonal character of his work; he described himself as an "anonymous lacerator."

Another technique used in contemporary art is *bricolage*. *Bricolage* is the art of making do with whatever is at hand. In drawing, bricolage manifests itself in found

6.18. **JOSEPH BEUYS.** *Eurasia,* from *Siberian Symphony.* 1966. Mixed media performance with action tool: board with chalk drawing, wedges of felt, fat, hair, and rods. *Private collection. Photo: © 2007 Artists Rights Society (ARS), New York/VG Bild-Kunst, Bonn.*

6.19. **BARBARA KRUGER.** *Untitled (When I Hear the Word Culture I Take Out My Checkbook).* 1985. Photograph, 11'6" x 5' (3.51 m x 1.52 m). *Mary Boone Gallery, New York.*

surfaces. Judy Pfaff uses pages from a Japanese book as the background for her drawing *(figure 6.21)*. Overlaying the found paper with ink, oil stick, and collage, Pfaff presents a variation on scientific illustration. The double-page format suits Pfaff's subject of bivalves.

In collage, montage, photomontage, assemblage, and installations, bizarre and unlikely combinations press the viewer to interpret, to find meaning in the disparate pieces. The breakdown of conventional categories such as Rauschenberg's Combines (see *figure II.14*) and predetermined rules for art has helped close the gap between art and life, a steadfast goal of the artists of our era.

PROBLEM 6.5

Using Papier Collé

For this problem, reassemble old drawings to create a new work. For example, you might tear up old figure drawings and rearrange the pieces to make a landscape.

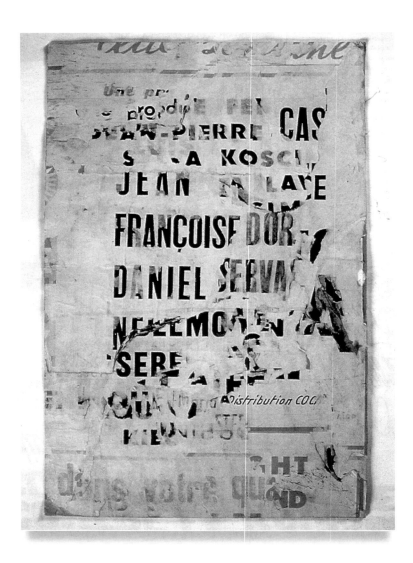

6.20. **JACQUES DE LA VILLÉGLÉ.** *Metro Saint-Germain.* 1964. Torn posters, 1'7" x 1'1½" (48.3 cm x 34.3 cm). *Zabriskie Gallery, New York. © 2007 Artists Rights Society (ARS), New York/ADAGP, Paris.*

Pay attention to the shapes of the torn paper and to the marks drawn on them. Use glue or masking tape. Redraw over the old drawings to integrate the papier collé.

Francis Alÿs's torn and reconstituted drawings *(figure 6.22)* suggest possibilities for other configurations. He attaches the torn sheets with masking tape and redraws between layers of tracing paper. The accidental quality of the work is reinforced by the irregular format, the result of the layered papers.

PROBLEM 6.6

Using Collage

Make copies of real objects on a photocopy machine. Try for a wide range of textural variety. Cut out the shapes of the copied objects and incorporate them into the drawing, using media compatible with the collage.

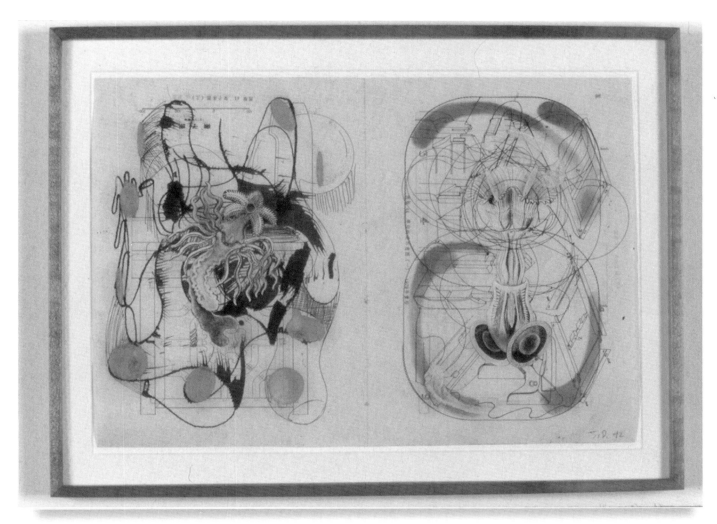

6.21. **JUDY PFAFF.** *The Bivalves A.* 1992. Ink, oil stick, collage on found paper, 10¼" x 14¼".

PROBLEM 6.7

Using Photomontage

Taking a clue from the work of Amelié von Wulffen *(figure 6.23)*, glue a photograph on found paper. Extend the attached image by drawing out from its edges. Alter the scene of the original photograph with added imagined elements such as Von Wulffen has done.

Transferred Texture

Related to both actual texture and simulated texture is the transfer of a texture from one surface to another, a technique called *frottage*. This transfer is made by taking a rubbing from an actual textured surface or by transferring a texture from a printed surface onto the drawing. Transferred textures cannot clearly be categorized as actual texture or simulated texture because they possess elements of both; they belong to a crossover category.

The technique of stone and bronze rubbing is an ancient one, popular in earlier times for making transferred images of tombstones and low-relief sculptures found

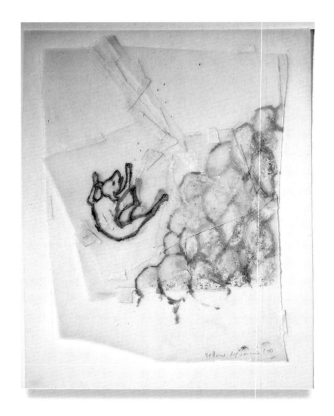

6.22. **FRANCIS ALŸS.** *Study for Falling Dog.* 2001. Pencil on tracing paper, 6⅜" x 7" (16 cm x 18 cm). *Lisson Gallery.*

6.23. **AMELIÉ VON WULFFEN.** *Untitled (Madchen im Garten) (Maid in the Garden).* 2004. Photograph, book page, acrylic, ink on paper, 39" x 41⅜" (99 cm x 105 cm).

6.24. **ANN PARKER & AVON NEAL.** *Timothy Lindall. Salem, Massachusetts . . . 1698/9.* 1963. Stone rubbing, 1'6½" x 1'11¾" (47 cm x 60.3 cm). *Amon Carter Museum, Fort Worth, Texas.*

in churches and churchyards *(figure 6.24)*. Rather than rubbing, Kiki Smith has inked a crocheted doily and transferred its texture to paper *(figure 6.25)*. She sees the mandala shape as a metaphor for a rose window as well as for anatomical parts such as eyes and cells. Smith chose the image for its reference to the feminine craft tradition.

Transfer from a printed page is a widely used contemporary technique. The image to be transferred is coated with a solvent, then laid face down onto the drawing surface and rubbed with an implement such as a wooden spoon, brush handle, or pencil. The directional marks made by the transfer implement provide additional textural interest in a drawing. Robert Rauschenberg developed the technique of transfer from a printed surface in the 1950s as a means of reintroducing representational imagery different from other realist techniques. In an illustration for Dante's *Inferno: Canto XXI, Circle Eight, Bolgia 5, The Grafter (figure 6.26)*, Rauschenberg made his earliest experiments with transfers, combining them with gouache, collage, graphite, red pencil, and wash. The marks made by the implement in transferring the images provide textural unity for the composition. The overall sameness of line direction has the effect of flattening out the images. At the same time, the streaked lines build on one another to make an agitated surface, creating a nervous movement throughout the work.

PROBLEM 6.8

Using Rubbing

Using an oil stick, make rubbings of several textured surfaces, combining them into one composition. Oriental papers are good for rubbed drawings. They are strong and can withstand friction without tearing, and they are texturally interesting. Consult Guide A, "Materials" for a list of papers. For additional information, refer to Kiki Smith's doily transfer (see *figure 6.25*).

6.25. **KIKI SMITH.** *Grace.* 1994.
Collaged lithograph on Nepal paper.
37½" x 19½" (95.3 cm x 49.5 cm).
Photography by: Ellen Page Wilson, Courtesy
PaceWildenstein, New York. © Kiki Smith,
Courtesy PaceWildenstein, New York.

PROBLEM 6.9

Transfer from a Printed Surface

Before you begin this problem, read the list below in its entirety. Also, be sure that you work in a well-ventilated space.

■ Using pictures from current magazines or newspapers, create a drawing made of transferred images.

■ Alcohol can be used for transferring photocopies, turpentine or Nazdar for newspaper and magazine images. Lightly brush the solvent on the back side of the image to be transferred, and let it set a minute so that the ink will soften before beginning to rub. Lay the image face down on the picture plane and transfer by rubbing with a wooden spoon, brush handle, or pencil.

■ Distribute the transferred images throughout the picture plane. You can keep all the lines going uniformly from right to left, across, or up and down; pay attention to the patterns the lines themselves make regardless of the image. You can turn your paper and work from all sides for a different textural effect.

■ You may find that the transferred images need no additional drawing, or you may integrate the composition by using gouache, graphite and turpentine, watercolor,

6.26. **ROBERT RAUSCHENBERG.** *Illustration for Dante's* **Inferno: Canto XXI, Circle Eight, Bolgia 5, The Grafter.** 1959–1960. Red and graphite pencil, gouache, cut-and-pasted paper, wash, and transfer, 1'2⅜" x 11½" (37 cm x 29.3 cm). *Collection, The Museum of Modern Art, New York. Given anonymously. © Robert Rauschenberg/Licensed by VAGA, New York. Photograph © 1997 by The Museum of Modern Art.*

or ink wash. Graphite sticks and pencils make more subtle additions to the transferred images. Be selective in your additive marks. The very nature of transfer is its rather blurred and indistinct quality. The negative marks, the white marks that show between the intermittent rubbed lines, allow the paper to come forward and to create an ambiguous space.

■ Work on several drawings at a time, creating a thematic relationship between them by using related images in each piece. Base your theme on a favorite story or song.

■ A good-quality heavy rag paper is ideal for this problem. You can even transfer images onto silk, cotton, or other fabrics. Consult the paper list in Guide A, "Materials."

CONCLUSION

Contemporary artists do not always confine their use of texture to one category. We conclude our discussion of texture with a description of two works in which texture serves multiple functions. In Judy Pfaff's drawing (see color *plate 7.1*), the multiple motifs are biological cells, plants, herbs, medical illustrations, mandalas, mantras, old manuscripts, and architectural details. In her work, the structure is complicated by textural variety. Underlying her work is the idea that all things are connected; this is conveyed through her web of textures.

Cy Twombly's work could be mistaken for a page from a notebook except for its large size (see color *plate 7.2*). The title of the series, *Mushrooms, No. V*, comes from *Natural History, Part I.* This title gives a clue that the work stems from a botanical source. The empty background, the gridded papers, the blank label, and the color scale provide subtle textural variety. The simulated texture of the mushrooms, the photomontage, and the loose scribbles build an enigmatic turn on traditional botanical illustration.

As noted at the beginning of this chapter, texture refers to the visual appearance of a work, its surface quality being the most important. New technologies and concepts have opened the door to textural innovations. We explored a range of textural categories and additive materials in this chapter. Texture is an element that pays rich rewards in both making and viewing art.

SUMMARY

Spatial Characteristics of Texture

Generally, uniform use of textural pattern and invented texture results in a relatively shallow space. A repeated motif or texture that remains consistent throughout a drawing tends to flatten it.

The use of simulated and invented texture in the same drawing results in arbitrary space, as does a combination of simulated texture and flat shapes.

Simulated texture is more dimensional than invented texture. If sharpness of textural detail is maintained throughout the drawing, space will be flatter. Diminishing sharpness of textural detail results in a more three-dimensional space. Objects in the foreground that have clearer textural definitions than those in the background usually indicate an illusionistic space.

In summary, simulated texture is generally more three-dimensional than invented texture. Repeated patterns or textural motifs result in a flatter space. Spatial ambiguity can result from a use of simulated and invented texture in the same work.

SKETCHBOOK PROJECTS

PROJECT **1**

Identifying Textural Techniques Used in Depicting Water

This assignment goes beyond the actual sketchbook. Go to the library and look for texts that show how artists depict images of water. The notebooks of Leonardo da Vinci, for example, with their scientific and visual investigations, deal with of the properties of water. Hockney has used the theme of water extensively in his prints, paintings, and drawings.

In your sketchbook, take written and visual notes of how the various artists have approached the problem of depicting this symbolically loaded element. Classify the textures according to the various categories discussed in this chapter. Note the scale of textural variety from photorealistic to illusionistic to symbolic to abstract. Describe the kinds of marks, styles, and media used to achieve various textural effects.

Transcribing Textural Techniques

Make a list of different kinds of water images—for example, swimming pools, waterfalls, natural pools, lakes, oceans, droplets, water running from spigots, bathtubs, showers, sprinklers, birdbaths, boiling water, ice water in a glass, steam, fog, rain, splashing water, standing water, turbulent water, and so on—the list should be as comprehensive as possible. Write descriptions of the characteristics and properties of each item on your list.

Choose a minimum of seven kinds of water to transcribe into drawn textures in your sketchbook. The size of each textural notation should be at least four inches square (10.16 by 10.16 cm), or it can fill a full page. Experiment with different kinds of media and with different kinds of marks. Scale is an interesting aspect of this project. In some of your transcriptions, try for an accurate description; in others, synthesize the information in a nonconventional approach. Make five drawings for each category.

Variations on this problem can be done with an endless number of textural challenges: urban textures and manufactured surfaces; natural, organic textures, such as animals, plants, or minerals; and secondhand textures drawn from found printed surfaces, such as photographs or illustrations. You might want to devote a special notebook to textures for reference in later work.

Both transcribing visual textures and inventing ways to symbolize texture will sharpen your perceptual and conceptual skills.

COMPUTER PROJECT

Creating Texture on the Computer

Paper selection is the only control the computer graphic artist can exert in regard to the actual physical texture of a computer drawing. However, the computer has limitless possibilities for simulated and invented textures. Use the computer to generate texture samples for a collage.

There are many ways to create textures on the computer: Actual textures can be photographed with a digital camera and downloaded to your computer; objects can be scanned directly into the computer; textural images can be found on the Internet and printed; and finally, textures can be created with graphics programs, such as Adobe Illustrator and Photoshop.

Here are some ideas for creating texture samples on the computer. They may be printed in black and white or color. Use the controls in your scanner program to manipulate color and value. Scan into your computer some flat actual material, such as old papers, wrinkled foil, textured fabric, and weathered wood.

Using a digital camera, photograph grass, pebbles, rusty metal, and animal fur. Fill the entire frame with a single texture. Create your own textures in Adobe Illustrator. Use various line qualities available to create a textured network of lines. Make at least five samples, ranging from light to dark and from organized to chaotic. This can be done quickly with cut-and-paste tools.

Install a wall of textures using samples from the class. Take note of new ways to create texture.

Using sample textures, cut and tear shapes to create a collage. Pay attention to contrasting values and to contrasting textures, such as smooth and rough. Use a spray adhesive or glue stick to attach the shapes to the picture plane. You may add some actual texture (such as string) to the finished piece.

CHAPTER 7

Color is a vital necessity. It is raw material indispensable to life, like water and fire. —FERNAND LÉGER

Color

FUNCTIONS OF COLOR

Our language is filled with references, analogies, metaphors, descriptions, and allusions to color. Wassily Kandinsky described his city scenes as "yellow enough to cry" (Eleanor Munro, "Where Postmodern Art and Schizophrenia Intersect," *New York Times*, March 31, 2002, Art/Architecture 34). Whether shrill or cacophonous, sweet or somber, saturated or pale, color speaks in an evocative voice. More than any other element, color has a direct and immediate effect on us, on the emotional, intellectual, psychological, even the physiological level. It evokes associations and memories; it can provoke the full gamut of physical responses, such as anger, excitement, sadness, peacefulness, and joy.

In our everyday conversations, adjectives relating to color are legion: gaudy, bright, intense, fresh, deep, gay, brilliant, lustrous, florid, flashy, glaring, soft, subdued, tender, dull, lifeless, leaden, muddy, pale, sallow, faded, lackluster—we could go on for pages. Color lies at the core of our sensual, visual, and conceptual experiences.

Contemporary artists prize color not only for its aesthetic function but for its symbolic significance as well. Consider the works of Judy Pfaff and Cy Twombly. Pfaff's richly colored surfaces take time to decipher. The overall use of green unifies the disparate images, styles, and surfaces in her work. In *Untitled* (*plate 7.1*), the actual organic material incorporated into the drawing springs from the layered ground. Twombly's theme is also natural history, but his mushroom drawing has a more informational, scientific feel (*plate 7.2*). Subtly colored mechanical drawing papers, the label, and the botanical drawings form a contrast to Twombly's stuttering handwriting. A color chart provides the muted color scale used in the drawing. The expressive, symbolic, and associative powers of color evoke a visceral response.

Attitudes toward color are culturally and historically revealing. Born in Pakistan and now living in New York City, Shahzia Sikander was trained in the traditions of Indian and Persian, Mughal and Rajput, miniature painting. Using the format and formal devices of miniatures, Sikander uses vegetable color, dry pigment, and watercolor tea on hand-prepared wasli paper to make drawings (some only inches high) that echo the vibrant colors and expressive subjects of their predecessors (*plate 7.3*). Miniature painting is a convention-bound art form that demands the use of hand-prepared pigments and burnished paper to give the colors their distinctive luminescent quality. Sikander places the much-used image of traditional miniatures—women awaiting the arrival of a lover—in a chaotic contemporary condition. Color, technique, format, and formal devices point us to a world that is more distant than miles would indicate.

In contemporary art, technology has provided new impetus for dealing with color, as seen in the drawing by Tom Burckhardt, *Geisha Hair* (*plate 7.4*). Burckhardt makes digital scans of images and then prints them onto pages of old books, adding his own drawn images in colored ink. Two dissimilar categories of images appeal to the artist: industrial equipment and Eastern decorative objects. In the drawing shown here, it takes a while to realize that the zany biomorphic shapes are actually part of the headdress of a Japanese geisha. Burkhardt deals in contradictions, between found images and drawn additions, between hand-drawn forms and digitized scans, between East and West, between the industrial and the decorative. Color enriches and ties together the disparate techniques, images, and ideas.

The overriding lesson that contemporary artists have learned is that color is relative; it interacts with and is affected by its surroundings. Since colors are always seen in a context, in a relationship with other colors, artists must make use of this knowledge of color relationships.

Color Media

The importance of materials in the use of color cannot be overestimated, since an artwork is as much a product of what it is made of as how or why it is made. Involvement, practice, and experimentation with color media will give you new respect for the integral nature of each medium.

Color media include but are not limited to pastels, watercolors, gouaches, acrylic and oil, ink-and-brush, and oil crayons. Each medium has its own defining characteristics. Pastels are dry and chalky; watercolors are transparent; gouaches are opaque; acrylic and oil can be used as thin and fluid washes or they can be applied in a thicker, flatter, more opaque state; ink-and-brush drawings can be fluid, stippled, rubbed, or dabbed; oil crayons leave a waxy buildup.

Color evokes visceral, instinctual, or intuitive responses. We respond not only to the color but also to the medium itself. In art, the very signs of spontaneity signify the speed of execution, the singularity of a particular, unique moment. In Melissa Meyer's work, the transparent hues of watercolor convey light, gesture, and touch (*plate 7.5*). The drawing represents a mirror of time, a conjunction of action and material.

In their continuing efforts to expand the role of drawing and to overturn accepted practices, many artists have considered the properties of paper as an end in itself. Rather than using the paper merely as a ground or field for the action of drawing, artists have treated the manipulated paper as the finished work of art. In many contemporary drawings, lines or marks on the surface are a scaffold that holds a suspended, disembodied background wash in check, or the ground can be a textured surface that forms an underpinning for linear elements. Washes can provide neutral backgrounds—blues, sepias, umbers, and grays are traditional wash colors.

In his subtle work (*plate 7.6*), David Jeffrey has stacked several sheets of paper of various sizes on top of each other and cut them into distorted, squarish shapes. Rather than pressing the papers flat, he has allowed them to warp and bulge. From being folded and refolded both vertically and horizontally, the surface of the paper eventually rips, exposing the underlying layers. The paper at this point is very fragile. Jeffrey manipulates the paper mass through the use of wax, charcoal, and rust, which is applied in irregular tints. The surface resembles stain or mold. Color, in spite of its muted, fleeting appearance, is an essential element in the final drawing.

The blast of color in Sam Durant's diptych (*plate 7.7*) is an unexpected intrusion in what would otherwise be a rigidly controlled monochromatic graphite drawing. The stacked mirror images of the cages offer two possibilities for their use (hence the title, *The Possibilities Are Endless*). One use of such cages is to hold unruly wards; another is to imprison subjects, such as the detainees in Abu Ghraib prison. The violent spray color shots are symbols of protest and heightened emotion.

Before beginning the problems in this chapter, examine *plates 7.1* through *7.16*; note the medium used in each work, how it is applied, and what effects are achieved. Your experiments with color application should be based on the knowledge and experience you have gained from working with various media.

Here are some suggestions to follow when working with color.

GUIDELINES FOR WORKING WITH COLOR

1. Avoid filling a shape with a single color unless you desire a spatially flat effect.
2. Experiment with layering colors and combining multiple colors to build mixed hues and a rich surface.
3. Think not only in terms of color but value as well.
4. Familiarize yourself with a variety of color media and their characteristics. Experiment with watercolor, oil pastels, colored pencils, felt-tip markers, gouache, acrylic, and colored inks.
5. Color is an eye-catching and dominant element; do not forget, however, what you have already learned about the role of shape, value, line, and texture.
6. Color can be used to develop a focal point in an otherwise achromatic drawing; it can be used to direct the eye of the viewer through the composition; and it can be an effective tool for creating spatial tensions in a drawing.
7. Consider your personal response to color and how you can broaden your color tastes.

Using Color Media

For this problem, you are to make four drawings using different color media in each. Look at the drawing by Andy Warhol (*plate 7.8*).

Cut a piece of good rag paper (Arches, for example) into four pieces. Use gouache or acrylic for the first sheet, watercolor or colored inks for the second, pastels for the third, and colored pencils for the fourth. Arbitrarily create some colored shapes such as Warhol has done. The shapes should be made quickly. In one drawing, use pastel shapes. In the second, use intense saturated colors. In the acrylic drawing, mix colors to produce "no-name" colors. And in the watercolor, layer color over color to state transparent washes. After you have made the colored surfaces, impose pencil or ink drawings of commercial products such as those you might find in a bathroom cabinet or on a writing desk. Arrange the objects flat, as if on a tabletop. Do not confine the objects to the colored shapes, and leave some color shapes as they are. Drawn objects may cross over two or more background colors.

COLOR TERMINOLOGY

Some basic definitions of terms are necessary before moving on in our discussion of color.

Color has three attributes: *hue*, *value*, and *intensity*.

■ *Hue* is the name given to a color, such as violet or green.

■ *Value* is the lightness or darkness of a color. Pink is a light red; maroon is a dark red. A color can be heightened, darkened, or modified by mixing or overlaying two or more hues to create value.

■ *Intensity* refers to the saturation, strength, brilliance, or purity of a color.

The *Munsell color wheel* (*plate 7.9*) is a circular arrangement of 12 hues, although one can imagine an expanded gradation of color. These 12 colors are categorized as primary, secondary, and tertiary.

■ *Primaries* (red, blue, and yellow) cannot be obtained by mixing other hues, but one can produce all the other hues by mixing the primaries.

■ *Secondaries* (green, orange, and violet) are made by mixing their adjacent primaries; for example, yellow mixed with blue makes green.

■ *Tertiaries* are a mixture of primary and secondary hues; yellow-green is the mixture of the primary yellow and the secondary green.

Local color and *optical color* are terms used to describe color. *Local color* is the known or generally recognized hue of an object regardless of the amount or quality of light on it—for example, the red of an apple, the green of a leaf. The local color of an object will be modified by the quality of light falling on it. Bright sunlight, moonlight, or fluorescent illumination can change a color. For example, the local color of an intense red object changes under moonlight to a deep red-violet, which is its *optical*, or *perceived*, color. The distinction between local and optical color is that the former is known (conceptual) and the latter is seen (perceptual).

Walton Ford uses both actual and optical color to depict the birds' plumage in his watercolor, gouache, pencil, and ink drawings (*plate 7.10*). The birds are evenly lit with a minimal suggestion of shadow to emphasize their dimensionality. The background is tinted with an orange glow reflecting the setting sun's diffused light. Ford's drawings relate to field notes taken on site by naturalists in the nineteenth century. But their huge size, up to 18 feet wide, place them firmly in a contemporary context.

PROBLEM 7.2

Using Local and Optical Color

In this problem, duplicate as closely as you can the perceived or optical color of an object. In verbal descriptions of the color of an object, it is usually enough to name a single hue, as in "a red apple." But an artist must describe the apple more accurately, using more than one hue.

The subject of this drawing will be, in fact, a red apple. Tape off a segment on the surface of the apple—a rectangle 2 inches by 3 inches (5 cm by 8 cm). Use pastels to make a drawing of this selected area, enlarging the section to 18 inches by 24 inches (46 cm by 61 cm). Use a buff-colored paper such as manila. The drawing will be a continuous-field composition, focusing on color and textural variations.

Carefully examine the portion of the apple to be drawn, analyzing exactly which colors are there. You may see an underlying coat of green, yellow, maroon, or brown. Tone your paper accordingly and build the surface of your drawing using layers, streaks, dabs, and dots of pastels. The longer you draw and look, the more complex the colored surface will appear. Sustain this drawing over several drawing sessions. If you extend the drawing time to several days, you will find the apple itself has undergone organic changes and will have changed colors as a result. Adjust your drawing accordingly.

COLOR SCHEMES

Color schemes require a special vocabulary. Although there are other kinds of color schemes, we will discuss only *monochromatic, analogous, complementary, primary*, and *secondary* color schemes.

■ A *monochromatic color scheme* makes use of only one color with its various values and intensities. Heide Fasnacht is an artist whose monochromatic drawings are based on photographs of explosions, detonations, and natural phenomena such as geysers and volcanoes (*plate 7.11*). She is interested in subjects that seem impossible to stabilize and that are at the border of visibility. Her drawings capture a split second in time. Although the finished work depicts a flash of the eye, the work may take several months to complete. Using a colored pencil, Fasnacht makes her monochromatic images of smoke and clouds built up of crosshatched and parallel lines.

■ An *analogous color scheme* is composed of related hues—colors adjacent to one another on the color wheel. For example, among blue, blue-green, green, and yellow-green, the shared color is blue. In Lance Letscher's collage (*plate 7.12*), an analogous color scheme predominates. Note the larger boat shape in the upper third of the picture plane; it is built, as are the other boats, of strips of analogous color. (The strips themselves resemble a color scale.) The background surface is built of aged, yellowed papers that support the colors used in the overlaid images. Letscher occasionally adds strips of green as accents, as a complement to the overall reddish-brown tones. A repetition of colors and shape plays a dominant role in organizing the picture plane. Analogous colors, analogous shapes, and analogous sizes furnish the structure for the drawing.

- *Complementary color schemes* are based on one or more sets of complements. Complementary colors are contrasting colors that lie opposite each other on the color wheel. Blue and orange, red and green, and yellow-green and red-violet are complements. Complementary colors in large areas tend to intensify each other. Small dots or strokes of complementary hues placed adjacently neutralize or cancel each other. The viewer blends these small areas of color optically and sees them as a grayed or neutralized tone. (Note these effects in Letscher's drawing with the accented areas that make use of green and red complements.) Daniel Zeller's muted complementary color scheme conveys the notions of refined systems that are at the same time microscopic and macroscopic views of a three-dimensional world (*plate 7.13*). Details and color are built up of lines made with a Rapidograph pen. The image seems to grow organically out of the obsessively stated lines. Inch by inch, the cellular forms seem to eat up the adjacent color cells.

- A *primary color scheme* uses the primary triad of yellow, red, and blue. Not only does a color scheme organize a work by directing the eye of the viewer (like attracts like), but a color scheme is also a carrier of meaning, as in *Your Own Blush and Flood* (*plate 7.14*), a work by the California artist William T. Wiley. Triangular forms occur repetitively in Wiley's work. He includes three-pronged forked limbs and a triangular tabletop. On one of the three central blocks, there are three symbols, one of them a triangle. There are also three cut logs behind the bucket. We can assume that the triadic color scheme has symbolic meaning. He directs us through his allegorical maze by both shape and color; the reds call our attention from one object to the next, whereas the complicated blue value patterns unify the jumbled composition. The crystalline colors are in keeping with the fragmented, broken quality of the images. The brittle, jagged edges echo the fragmentation inside the picture plane. Much of Wiley's work relies on paradox, on something being two things at once. Wiley learned from Zen Buddhism that opposites are reconciled when seen as a part of a continuous chain. Wiley's work is full of contradiction, complexity, humor, and metaphor.

We have by no means exhausted the number of color schemes available to the artist. The chosen color scheme contributes to the overall mood and meaning in a work. Although a color scheme in a given work is related to aesthetics and psychology, it must suit the demands of the artist's personal vision.

PROBLEM 7.3

Using a Monochromatic Color Scheme

From a magazine or newspaper, choose a black-and-white photograph with at least five distinct values. Enlarge the photograph to a drawing with no dimension smaller than 12 inches. You may use a copier to make the enlargement. Convert the photograph to a monochromatic drawing, duplicating the original values; for example, you might choose an all-blue or an all-red monochromatic color scheme. Take note of the value variations within a given shape and try to match them in your chosen color. A close inspection of Fasnacht's monochromatic drawing (see *plate 7.11*) will be informative.

Coat your drawing surface (paper or board) with gesso, and use acrylic paint. You will need to apply the paint in varying consistencies to achieve a range of values. Begin with a light wash to lay out the composition. Then, by adding and subtracting, brushing and rubbing, try to imitate the original value patterns. You can wipe off the paint to create lighter values and use a buildup of paint for the darker ones. Mark Tansey uses a variety of implements to achieve various textures; you, too, should experiment with found implements.

Color photocopy machines can convert black-and-white images to a monochromatic color. After you have completed your drawing, photocopy the original black-and-white photograph using one of the primary colors and then compare the two versions.

PROBLEM 7.4

Using a Complementary Color Scheme

Create an imaginary organism as if seen through a microscope. Using repeated images of the organism, make a drawing based on a complementary color scheme. Use pen and colored ink or fine felt-tip pen. You can use a white pen to resist the color laid on it and thus leave the white of the paper as an added element to the complementary colors. (Note that in *Parasitic Symbiosis* [see *plate 7.13*], Zeller's choice for paper is Strathmore 500 series plate surface bristol board.)

The organism should undergo slight changes in contour and scale as it moves across the picture plane. The motif should be of one color and the background its complement. Use invented texture to fill the entire picture plane.

WARM AND COOL COLORS

Colors can be classified as warm or cool. *Warm colors*, such as red, orange, and yellow, tend to be exciting, emphatic, and affirmative. In addition to these psychological effects, optically they seem to advance and expand. In Elizabeth Peyton's portrait (*plate 7.15*), the figure seems to be dissolving into a sea of red. From the stance of a fan, Peyton depicts friends and celebrities with an eye to fashion.

Cool colors—blue, green, and violet—are psychologically calming, soothing, or depressive and unemphatic; optically, they appear to recede and contract. These characteristics are relative, however, since intensity and value also affect the spatial action of warm and cool colors. Intensely colored shapes appear larger than duller ones of the same size. Light-valued shapes seem to advance and expand; dark-valued shapes seem to recede and contract. Analyze Melissa Meyer's drawing (see *plate 7.3*) for these effects.

PROBLEM 7.5

Using Warm and Cool Colors

In this problem, use two sources of light: one warm and one cool. Seat a model in front of a north window from which natural, cool light enters. On the side of the model opposite the window, place a lamp that casts a warm light. Alternate the light sources; draw using the natural light for three minutes, then close the window shade and draw using the warm artificial light for three minutes. Continue this process until the drawing is completed.

Use colored pencils or pastels and no fewer than three warm colors and three cool colors. There will be areas in the figure where the warm and cool shapes overlap; here you will have a buildup of all six colors. Work quickly, using short strokes, overlapping colors where appropriate. Focus on drawing the light as it falls across the form. Draw the light in the negative space and on the figure. Do not isolate the figure; draw both negative and positive forms. Try to imagine the light as a colored film that falls between you and the model. Do not use black for shadows. Build value changes by overlays of color.

Note how the short strokes unify the drawing and limit the space. By concentrating on the quality of light, you will find that you can achieve atmospheric effects.

PROBLEM 7.6

Using a Warm or Cool Color to Create a Color-Field Composition

Divide in half a 22" by 30" sheet of Strathmore cold press paper. On one half of the paper, draw a self-portrait using either local or arbitrary color. On the other half, use a continuous field of color. Aim for the same mood on both sides.

Use media of your choice, giving consideration to the color you need, including not only the hue but also its proper value and intensity. You may layer the color in washes, build the color in overlapping strokes, or use a saturated single color. Consider the textural quality of the finished surface. (Note the variations and subtle changes in tone in Peyton's portrait, *plate 7.15*.) Use color for its psychological and symbolic impact.

SUMMARY

Spatial Characteristics of Color

In the twenty-first century, we find artwork that gives the illusion of three-dimensional space, works that are relatively two-dimensional, and works that are spatially ambiguous. Color is a major determinant of spatial illusion.

When unmodulated flat patterns of color are used, or when colors are confined to a shape, the shapes remain relatively parallel on the surface of the picture plane. On the other hand, when colors are modeled from light to dark, a more volumetric space results; and when bright colors are used in the foreground and less intense values are used in the background, color contributes to a three-dimensional illusion of space.

As a general rule, warm colors come forward and cool colors recede. This rule, however, is relative because the intensity and value of a hue may affect the spatial action of warm and cool colors.

An ambiguous space results when using flat color shapes and modeled color volumes in the same composition. When bright colors occur in the background of an otherwise three-dimensional work, the background will seem to come forward, flattening the picture plane to some extent. Space becomes ambiguous when colors cross over shapes; a flattening takes place.

SKETCHBOOK PROJECT

PROJECT 1

Using Color for Quick Landscape Sketches

For this exercise, make a series of landscape sketches, *pochades*, using various color media. Choose a convenient site, one you can visit easily and frequently over the period of a week or so. Visit the setting at various times of the day (or night), and, if possible, under different weather conditions. Make a series of quick, abbreviated sketches using color to convey both the quality of light and the feel of the place. In the initial drawings, let the optical color determine your palette. As you familiarize yourself with the actual setting and its compositional relationships, expand your color choices.

Vary the color schemes, using dry media for one session, wet media for another, and combinations of wet and dry at other times. In spite of being quickly drawn, colors can be layered. You might make several drawings simultaneously, especially if you are working with wet media; then go back over them as they dry.

Staying with the same subject, in order, frees you for color experimentation within self-set limits. At the end of the time designated for this project, choose one of the more successful sketches or combine elements from a number of sketches in a larger, finished drawing that you complete in the studio. By this time, your familiarity with the scene and your memory of it will enhance the preparatory sketches.

COMPUTER PROJECT

PROJECT 1

Using the Computer to Create Matisse Cutouts

The Internet can be a quick and accessible way to research ideas for your projects. This color exercise is based on Matisse's cutouts *(figure 7.1)*. Before beginning this project, use the Internet to research Matisse's work and to find examples of his paper cutouts. (The computer skills needed for this project are similar to those used in the computer problem on shape in Chapter 3.)

7.1. Matisse at work on a paper cutout. © *Bettmann/Corbis.*

1. Using a program such as Adobe Illustrator, create a variety of shapes using Matisse as inspiration. (His cutouts included figurative as well as biomorphic, abstract shapes.) Simplified figures, flowers, and stars, as well as the negative shapes created between them, can be used along with shapes of your own design.
2. Choose a color scheme to work with based on those discussed in this chapter. You may add black and white if needed.
3. Fill the shapes with solid colors and arrange them on a colored picture plane. Experiment with several compositions and print them out. Be selective: you may find that certain shapes work better than others, or you may prefer certain color arrangements over others. Save your file so you will be able to make changes based on suggestions that arise during a class critique.
4. If the printout quality is not good, make a construction paper version or a painted paper version for your finished drawing. In reconstructing the computer version, you will probably want to change the scale of the finished drawing.

Plate 7.16 is an example of what can be done with this project using Matisse-like shapes and colors.

PLATE 7.1. **JUDY PFAFF.** *Untitled.* 1998.
Oil stick, encaustic, organic matter,
photograph, found paper, approxi-
mately 48" x 80" (121.9 cm x
203.2 cm), framed.

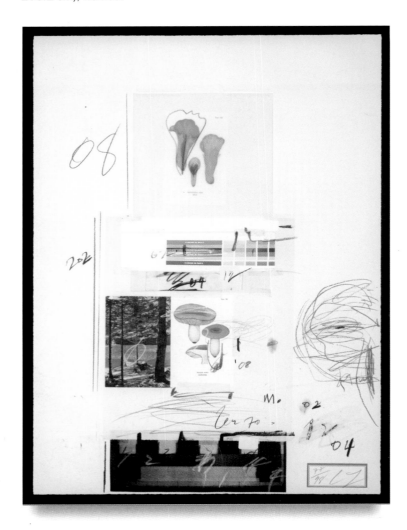

PLATE 7.2. **CY TWOMBLY** (1928–).
© Copyright. No. V, 1974. From **Natural
History, Part I, Mushrooms.** Lithograph
and mixed media on paper, 758 mm x
558 mm. Purchased 1981. *Photo Credit:
Tate Gallery, London/Art Resource, NY. Tate
Gallery, London Great Britain.*

PLATE 7.3. **SHAHZIA SIKANDER.** *Riding the Ridden.* 2000. Vegetable color, dry pigment, watercolor tea on hand-prepared wasli paper, 8" x 5½" (20 cm x 14 cm). *Courtesy of the artist and Sikkema Jenkins & Co., New York.*

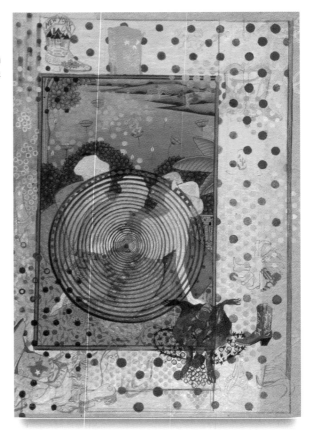

PLATE 7.4. **TOM BURCKHARDT.** *Geisha Hair.* 2001. Ink, colored pencil, and digitized image on paper, 1' x 1'6½" (30 cm x 47 cm). *Private collection. Courtesy Tibor de Nagy Gallery, New York.*

PLATE 7.5. **MELISSA MEYER.** *Akron 2* **from *The Akron Series.*** 2003. Water-color on paper, 10" x 7" (25.4 cm x 17.8 cm). *Courtesy Joyce and Charles Shenk, Columbus, Ohio.*

PLATE 7.6. **DAVID JEFFREY.** *Untitled.* 1995. Wax, charcoal, and rust on two sheets of translucent vellum paper, 2'5" x 2'7½" (73.7 cm x 80 cm). *Fogg Art Museum, Cambridge, Mass. Gift of Sarah-Ann and Werner H. Kramarsky, 2001.241. © President and Fellows of Harvard College.*

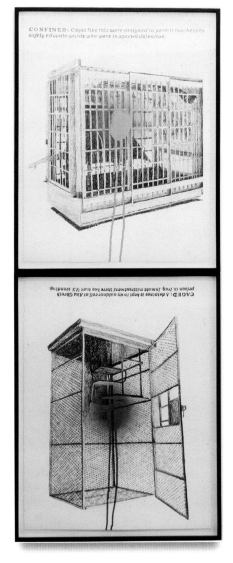

PLATE 7.7. **SAM DURANT.** *The Possibilities Are Endless.* 2004. Graphite and spray enamel on paper, diptych, each 30" x 22" (76.2 cm x 55.9 cm).

PLATE 7.8. **ANDY WARHOL** (1928–1987).
Untitled (Beauty Products), 1960.
Gouache and pencil on paper, 736 mm
x 580 mm. Purchased 1988. *Photo
Credit: Tate Gallery, London/Art Resource,
NY. Tate Gallery, London, Great Britain.*

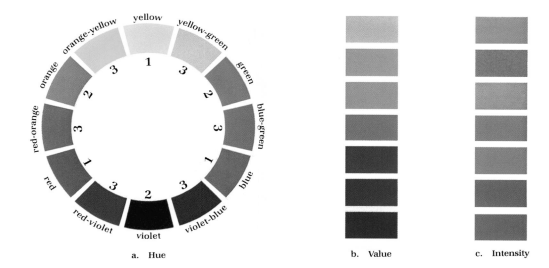

a. Hue

b. Value

c. Intensity

PLATE 7.9. The major elements of color: hue (as expressed in the Munsell color wheel), value, and intensity.

PLATE 7.10. **WALTON FORD.** *The Starling.* 2002. Watercolor, gouache, ink and pencil on paper, 60½" x 119½" (153.7 cm x 303.5 cm). *Courtesy of the artist and Paul Kasmin Gallery, New York. Photo Credit: Adam Reich.*

PLATE 7.11. **HEIDE FASNACHT.** *Hotel Demolition.* 2000. Colored pencil and paper, 5' x 3'4" (1.52 m x 1.02 m). *Courtesy of the artist and Kent Gallery, New York.*

PLATE 7.12. **LANCE LETSCHER.** *Boats.* 2002. Collage on Masonite, 1'9⅛" x 2'7¼" (53.6 cm x 79.3 cm). *Private collection, courtesy of Howard Scott Gallery, New York.*

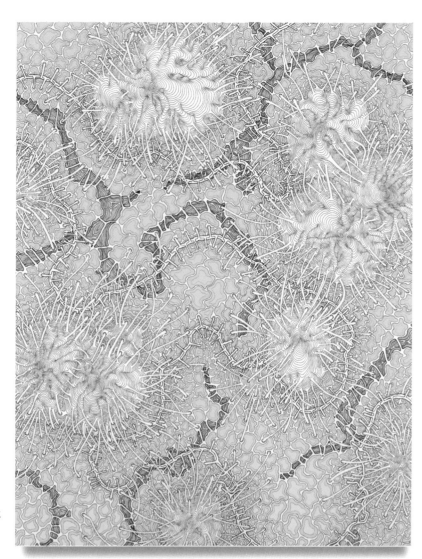

PLATE 7.13. **DANIEL ZELLER.** *Parasitic Symbiosis.* 2003. Ink on paper, 13½" x 11" (34.3 cm x 27.9 cm). *Image courtesy of the artist.*

PLATE 7.14. **WILLIAM T. WILEY.** *Your Own Blush and Flood.* 1982. Watercolor on paper, 1'10" x 2'6" (55 cm x 75 cm). *Collection Byron and Eileen Cohen, Shawnee Mission, Kansas. © Photo by Schopplein Studio SFCA/Morgan Gallery, Kansas City, Missouri.*

PLATE 7.15. **ELIZABETH PEYTON.** *Scott Walker.* 1996. Watercolor on paper, 10" x 7" (25.4 cm x 17.8 cm). *Courtesy Gavin Brown's enterprise.*

PLATE 7.16. **TOM SALE.** Computer color cutouts. *Courtesy of the artist.*

Perspective: Just another lie invented by dead European white males. —CHARLES BARSOTTI

Antiperspective: The Triumph of the Picture Plane

CONTEMPORARY CHALLENGES TO TRADITIONAL PERSPECTIVE

The artist Wayne Thiebaud says he is amazed—and amused—that a city's massive apartment complexes are designed to have "100 views rather than several . . . it's really rather silly—or sublime—depending on your point of view" (Beal, *Wayne Thiebaud Painting*, p. 5). Thiebaud's quote demonstrates the challenges artists face when translating three-dimensional visual data from the real world onto the constraints of a two-dimensional surface. Artists must make a number of choices about how to express the experiences and ideas of the phenomenal world. Some of these choices are made intuitively and others consciously. Some are personally determined; others are culturally influenced. In this chapter, we will look at the different ways artists express their experiences and ideas of the phenomenal world. We will examine the rejection of the centuries-old tradition of fixed-focus vision (i.e., perspective), and finally, we will coin a new term: antiperspective and the new ways artists wring from the world their spatial images.

Bill Haveron is one such artist who demonstrates that optical appearance and traditional perspective are

8.1. **CHARLES BARSOTTI.** *Perspective. The New Yorker* Magazine, June 22, 1992. © 2002 The New Yorker *Collection from cartoonbank.com. All Rights Reserved.*

insufficient for the artist who wants to express more about an object than a strict visual description taken from a single viewpoint *(figure 8.2)*. Haveron renders dense vignettes through multilayered images and multiple standpoints. In a realist style, he creates a kaleidoscopic mix of imagery and perspective. East Texas landscape collides with exotic wildlife; inset tableaux come from disparate times and places. This particular graphite drawing is derived from a dream in which a friend offers advice, "Don't let the tigers smell you bleeding. Don't let the buzzards see you fall down." Contracting and expanding space, Haveron denies the convention of perspective.

In contemporary art, there have been three major challenges to the traditional convention of perspective. However, before defining those challenges, let's take a step back and explain what we mean by perspective.

The word *perspective* comes from the Latin *prospectus*, which means "to see through or into." In traditional art, perspectival relationships that exist in the real world are transcribed onto the confines of the two-dimensional picture plane. In looking at a work of art that employs traditional perspective, we as viewers can project ourselves through our imaginations into that illusion of real space.

As we mentioned above, contemporary art challenges this traditional convention in three ways. The first challenge is the predominance of photo-derived imagery in which spatial representation is determined by the camera. The second is the conceptual approach in which images are drawn not from real life but from the imagination; and third, the influence of comics and other subcultures on mainstream art. Raymond Pettibon is an artist whose primary medium is drawing influenced by a comic book style *(figure 8.3)*. Pettibon uses exaggerated perspective and a combination of image and text; his extreme point of view adds a sense of menace to the images. Current events along with sub- and pop cultures provide the grist for Pettibon's themes. In this illustration, the train is hurtling through space; all points converge to the lower right corner of the drawing. Radical means support a melodramatic tale.

8.2. BILL HAVERON. *Two Tourniquets for a Prosthesis* (Dedicated to Jim Magee). 2005. Graphite on paper, 60" x 84" (152 cm x 213 cm). *Gerald Peters Gallery, Dallas.*

8.3. **RAYMOND PETTIBON.** *No Title (The shrilling whistle...).* 2003. Pen and ink on paper, 22¼" x 16½" (56.5 cm x 41.9 cm). *Courtesy the artist and Regen Projects, Los Angeles and David Zwirner Gallery, New York.*

ANTIPERSPECTIVE—THE FLATBED PICTURE PLANE AND SUPERFLAT

As we stated earlier, we are coining a term for a new category of perspective; that term is *antiperspective*, which will allow us to cover more recent developments in handling space. Throughout this book, we have presented challenges to linear perspective by artists who intentionally subvert its traditional conventions. One such artist who challenged linear perspective was Rauschenberg.

Leo Steinberg characterized Rauschenberg's working surface as a "flatbed picture plane." Steinberg likened it to a flat, horizontal surface on which anything can be placed. Jasper Johns, with whom Rauschenberg worked, made equally revolutionary advances in his work in overturning traditional attitudes and approaches to illusionistic space. In the 1950s, Johns also chose commonplace objects—"things that were seen and not looked at": flags, targets, alphabets, numbers (see *figure 2.18*). Where Rauschenberg's work was exuberant and all-inclusive, Johns's images turned in on themselves. The very choice of subject matter resulted in work that allowed "no air or empty space." Steinberg said that in Johns's work he saw "the end of illusion"; the work, he concluded, was profoundly important (Steinberg, *Other Criteria*, p. 13).

According to Johns's logic, since the surface of a drawing or painting was flat, he would paint only flat images on it. And, like Rauschenberg, if he needed something three-dimensional, he would add the actual object to the flat surface. In 1956, Johns incorporated the first objects to an otherwise flat picture plane. Not only did Johns dispense with perspective, he seemingly dispensed with structure. So the picture plane triumphed in its battle with perspectival illusionism.

In describing the popular work of a new generation of Japanese artists (whose major influence has been comic books and animated movies), Takashi Murakami offers a new twist on Leo Steinberg's flatbed picture plane with the concept of "superflat," Murakami's term for a computer-generated desktop graphic in which a number of distinct layers merge into one (Raphael Rubinstein, "In the Realm of the Superflat," *Art in America*, June 2001, pp. 111–115). Flatness can, after all, have many dimensions.

DEFINITIONS AND GUIDELINES

In this chapter we will discuss eye level and baseline; aerial, linear, multiple, axonometric, and stacked perspective; and foreshortening. Through the eyes of contemporary artists, we will look at various perspectival conventions of representing three-dimensional objects as they appear to recede into space on a two-dimensional surface.

Linear perspective, a theory developed in the Renaissance, is a quasi-mathematical system based on the observations that parallel lines seem to converge as they move into space and that all lines going in the same direction into space appear to converge or meet at a single point on the horizon. This discovery of perspective provided art with a forceful and exciting impetus at a time when many former ideas and ways of interpreting the world were being replaced with new observations and theories.

Artists use many clues to indicate space. These clues include diminution in size, occultation (where a closer object blocks the view of a more distant object), and overlap—a device that even young children use in their drawings. According to the conventions of perspective, objects appear larger or smaller in relation to their distance from the viewer. This recession into space can be relayed by the artist according to certain rules. Of course, perspective is based on what the eye sees; it is not simply a mathematical rule. Some knowledge of perspective can be helpful for the artist, but it also has limitations. Perspective can be used as an aid in seeing, but it should not be a formula to be substituted for visual acuity.

Keep in mind that linear perspective is only one of many systems of spatial representation and is not always the most appropriate choice for a particular idea. In different historical times and cultures, different perspectival systems have been dominant. In non-Western art, in children's art, in the art of the Middle Ages, and in the art of the twentieth century, the dominant system of representation has not been linear perspective.

EYE LEVEL AND BASELINE

A drawing of a scene from real life differs from the actual scene; it is a two-dimensional translation from a three-dimensional subject. It *re-presents* the scene as viewed from a particular position. This viewing position taken by the artist is an inherent part of the depiction, or representation. The viewing position not only determines how the scene is composed by the artist, but it also determines how the picture is perceived by the viewer. The first important matter that the artist must consider in the treatment of space is the use of eye level. The term *eye level* refers to an imaginary horizontal line that is parallel to the viewer's eyes. When we look straight ahead, this line coincides with the horizon. If we tilt our heads, if we move our angle of sight to a higher or lower position, this eye-level line will also change on the picture plane, thereby making the horizon line seem higher or lower.

Two extremes of eye level, the ant's-eye view and the bird's-eye view, are exploited in the exuberant works by Ann Parker from her "Northern Sports Series" *(figures 8.4* and *8.5)*. The first print is from an ant's-eye view, or better said, from a sturgeon's view. The fish are lures, ornately carved and decorated to attract real sturgeons. From beneath the ice we look to the surface where the frigid fisherman is patiently staked out, trident in hand. We perceive the fish and sportsman as occupying two different levels of space, and two different states of mind: the decoys seem more animated than the fisherman.

8.4. (left) **ANN PARKER.** *Sturgeon Stake Out.* 1991. Linocut, 4'2" x 2'6" (1.27 m x 76 cm). *Courtesy of the artist.*

8.5. (right) **ANN PARKER.** *The Prize* **from "Northern Sports Series."** 1991. Linocut, 4'2" x 2'6" (1.27 m x 76 cm). *Courtesy of the artist.*

Parker's second print, titled *The Prize*, makes use of an overhead viewpoint (or a bird's-eye view); forms diminish in size as the space recedes from top to bottom of the picture plane. The ice fisherman proudly displays his catch while the lures seem to share in his achievement; the prize itself seems somewhat skeptical. A conceptually deeper space is indicated by the dark hole in the ice occupied by the sturgeons who witness the boast; this inset does not make use of the bird's-eye perspective; it is indicated by a recession of space from front to back. A third kind of space is used in the sketchy background where Parker has distorted the space to wrap around the fisherman and his catch. This circular notation of Lake Winnebago and its surrounding woods holds the key to a visual pun. In photography, the lens that compresses a 360-degree view onto a rectilinear format is called a "fish-eye lens." The prizewinner is posing for a documentary photograph, but who is behind the camera?

Throughout history, artists have been occupied with the problem of how to re-create a distorted image as it might be found in the real world, as in a convex mirror, for example. In contemporary art, this distortion takes on new connotations. In *The Inertia of Night (Self Portrait as a Slat)* by the Australian artist Mike Parr *(figure 8.6)*, the oblique figure on the left reminds us of the distortion that occurs when a slide is projected at an angle, when the parallax is not true. We feel that if we could shift our viewing angle, the distortion would disappear. Parr makes reference to space and flatness in his use of the word *slat* in the work's title. The scale of the drawing (nine feet by six feet) relates more to a projected film image than to the

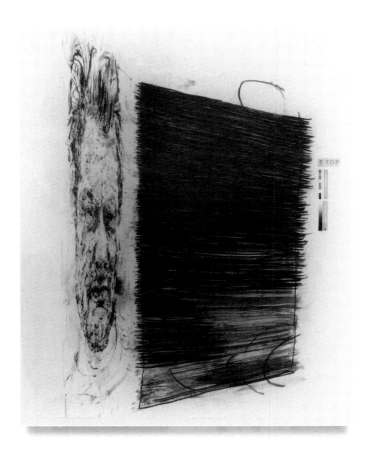

8.6. **MIKE PARR.** *The Inertia of Night (Self Portrait as a Slat).* 1983. Charcoal and Girault pastel on paper, 8'11⅞" x 6' (2.74 m x 1.83 m). *Collection of Roslyn and Tony Oxley, Sydney, Australia. Photograph from Sherman Galleries.*

human figure. It is the unsettling point of view that manipulates the viewer's sense of space, making this work intriguing.

We have seen several examples of subjective manipulations of vantage point. Eye level is much more than a spatially descriptive tool for these artists; it is a major means of conveying conceptual, psychological, and emotive ideas.

Another important consideration is *baseline*, the imaginary line on which an object sits. Baseline and eye level are closely related. If all the objects in a given picture share the same baseline—that is, if the baseline remains parallel to the picture plane—space will be limited (see *figure 8.24*). In *figure 8.7*, however, Tony Hepburn has aligned objects along a sharply receding baseline. A flat rectangular plane reinforces the fixed base line; otherwise the objects maintain a fixed relationship to the picture plane.

If objects sit on different baselines, and if these lines penetrate the picture on a diagonal, the resulting space will be deeper. In Judy Youngblood's *Foreign Correspondents*, horizon lines, eye levels, and baselines play a crucial role. The horizon is placed progressively lower in each print in the series. In *figure 8.8*, bundles of twigs are distributed in a random fashion. In *figure 8.9*, the bags have sprouted legs. These striding anthropomorphic figures occupy different baselines on a low horizon. The figures seem to be standing on the rim of the horizon. Cast shadows connect the animated sacks in a series of diagonal lines that penetrate the picture plane.

Eye level is only one determinant of pictorial space. The space an artist uses is relative; it is not possible to determine the spatial quality of a work by eye level alone. In fact, the same eye level can result in a shallow or deep space, depending on other determinants in the work such as scale, proportion, texture, value, and color.

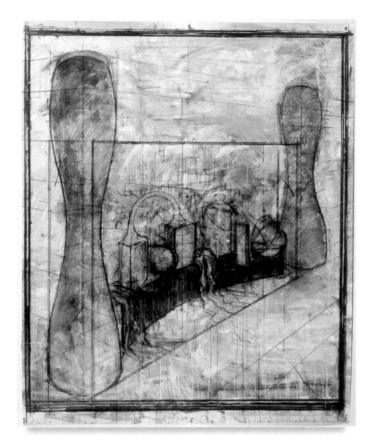

8.7. **TONY HEPBURN.** *Draw Shave II.*
1992. Charcoal, acrylic, conté crayon
on paper, 60" x 47¾" (152 cm x
121 cm). *Collection Dolores and Milton
Fishman. Photograph Dirk Bakker. Photograph
courtesy of the artist and paulkotulaprojects.*

PROBLEM 8.1

Using Eye Level and Baselines

Before beginning this problem, complete Sketchbook Project 1, found at the end of this chapter.

Make a triptych, a three-part drawing, using the invented forms taken from the preparatory work in your sketchbook. Use a different image for each panel of the triptych and a different horizon line for each panel. Combine a distant view of a group of objects with a close-up, magnified view of the same objects.

The three sections of the drawing should relate to one another thematically. Keep the negative space simple; focus on the relationship of the objects within that space. The triptych can be arranged side by side or stacked.

AERIAL PERSPECTIVE

There are two distinct types of perspective, aerial and linear. *Aerial perspective* is the means by which the artist creates a sense of space through depicting the effects of atmospheric conditions. Various atmospheric conditions affect our perception of shape, color, texture, value, and size at different distances. For example, compare your memory of a bright, sunny summer day and a cold, drizzly winter night.

8.8. (left) **JUDY YOUNGBLOOD.** *Foreign Correspondents #1.* 1979. Etching with aquatint and drypoint, 11¾" x 1'2¾" (30 cm x 37 cm). *Courtesy of the artist. Photo by Danielle Fagan, San Antonio, Texas.*

8.9. (right) **JUDY YOUNGBLOOD.** *Foreign Correspondents #4.* 1979. Etching with aquatint and drypoint, 11¾" x 1'2¾" (30 cm x 37 cm). *Courtesy of the artist. Photo by Danielle Fagan, San Antonio, Texas.*

8.10. **APRIL GORNIK.** *Swamp Light.* 2000. Charcoal on paper, 50" x 38" (127 cm x 97 cm). *Gift of Neda Young to the Friends of Art and Preservation in Embassies, "Gift to the Nation" Collection.*

In aerial perspective, objects in the foreground are larger and their details are sharp; objects in the background are diminished and less distinct. As the objects recede into space, their color and value become less intense and their textures less defined.

April Gornik has employed aerial perspective in her charcoal drawing, *Swamp Light (figure 8.10)*. A brooding, diffused light bathes the scene, while the swamp disappears in the fog above the horizon line. The horizon line is faintly suggested.

The natural landscape offers three vital forms: earth, air, and water. The light is barely perceptible; a mist clouds the landscape; the water particles in the air soften the distant landscape.

Aerial perspective demands that as the distance increases textural definition decreases. Gornik's spatially illusionistic drawing is a contemporary evocation of an age-old theme.

PROBLEM 8.2

Using Aerial Perspective

Using charcoal and erasure on toned paper, make a landscape drawing on site. Depict a specific time of day or night and season of the year. Look for atmospheric clues to establish a mood. The main subject might be the sky, in which case you could use a low horizon line. Or you might focus on a field of grass with a high horizon line. Pay particular attention to the size, value, and scale of your marks; make them smaller and closer together as they recede into space.

Other devices that create a sense of atmosphere are diagonals penetrating the picture plane, overlapping forms, diminution of size as the forms recede, gradual value changes, blurring in focus from front to back, and changes in texture from foreground to background.

In a second drawing, create an imaginary setting from a 1950s film noir. In that genre emptiness, bleakness, mystery, and obscurity apply. The scene could take place at night in an abandoned cityscape. Imagine a movie set in which a streetlight, a shaded backlit window, or car lights faintly illuminate the scene. Ominous shadows lend a sense of mystery. You might opt for an enveloping fog as in the Gornik drawing.

LINEAR PERSPECTIVE

Filippo Brunelleschi, the Italian Renaissance architect, is credited with the invention of *one-point* or *linear perspective*, the system of translating three dimensions into two. The critic Michael Kimmelman describes Brunelleschi's method as follows. The Florentine architect painted a view of, for example, the Baptistery of San Giovanni on a wooden panel. He then drilled a hole in the center of the panel; by standing directly in front of the baptistery and viewing it from the back of the panel, he could see the church. With a mirror held in front of the reverse side of the panel, he could see the painted version. The mirror blocked Brunelleschi's vision of the church and presented the painted image; removing the mirror allowed him to see the actual three-dimensional image. By this simple device, Brunelleschi proved that a microcosm of the world could be re-created on a flat surface (Michael Kimmelman, "Everything in Perspective," *New York Times Magazine*, April 18, 1999, p. 86).

The architect Rem Koolhaas and his collaborating team offer a lesson in one-point perspective in a modern version of the technique *(figure 8.11)*. Rigid lines of maintained width lead to the vanishing point in the center of the picture plane. A cut-away plan in reverse values (white on black) intrudes forcefully on the background landscape of black on white. The drawn cubicles in the foreground structure impose a second level of one-point perspective. Spatially the work is complex and this complexity is compounded by the addition of the black and white photographs.

M. C. Escher, the master of perspectival games, mixes the rational with the antirational in his spatially ambiguous work. In *figure 8.12*, he has maintained an extreme bird's-eye view in the upper half of his drawing, aptly named *High and*

8.11. **REM KOOLHAAS, ELIA ZENGHELIS, MADELON VRIESENDORP, AND ZOE ZENGHE-LIS.** *Exodus, or The Voluntary Prisoners of Architecture. The Baths Project. Plan.* 1972. Cut and pasted paper, photo-lithograph, and gelatin silver photographs, with ink on paper, 16⅛" x 11½". Patricia Phelps de Cisneros Purchase Fund, Takeo Ohbayashi Purchase Fund, and Susan de Menil Purchase Fund. *Museum of Modern Art, NYC. (369.1996) Photo credit: Digital Image © Museum of Modern Art/ Licensed by SCALA/Art Resource, NY.*

8.12. **M. C. ESCHER. Study for the litho-graph** *High and Low.* 1947. Pencil, 5'8¾" x 4'2½" (2.71 m x 1.99 m). *© 2006 The M.C. Escher Company–Holland.*

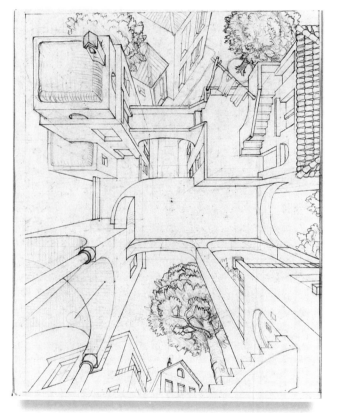

Low. In keeping with his unwavering involvement with spatial ambiguity, in the lower half of the drawing he has abruptly changed eye level to an equally extreme ant's-eye view. Within each segment the eye level is strictly maintained. Escher employs contour line along with a rigidly controlled one-point perspective to set up an exaggerated spatial contradiction.

Let's now look at two practices that can be helpful in drawing linear perspective: using a see-through pane and remaining stationary in order to make a consistent drawing, and using a viewer for framing and sighting.

Using a See-Through Pane

First, in order to establish a horizon line, place an acrylic plastic sheet, like a pane of Plexiglas, at a fixed distance directly in front of you. Ideally, the pane should be the size of your drawing paper. If you do not maintain a fixed distance from the pane, the measurements change. Attach the pane to the edge of your easel, or on a tripod. Be careful to keep it perfectly perpendicular to the ground and directly in front of your eyes. The glass is perpendicular to your sight line; that is, if you drew a line from the center of your eyes, it would intersect the plane of glass. If you look up, the horizon line is below the direction of your sight; if you look down, the horizon line is above your sight line. The pane of glass is always perpendicular to your line of vision; in other words, your line of vision will always intersect the clear plane at a 90-degree angle.

This pane of glass represents the picture plane; you are transferring the visual information seen through this imagined plane onto your drawing surface. The see-through plane is identical with the picture plane. The information you record on the glass is the same as the information you draw on your paper.

Your viewing position is of the utmost importance. Two relationships are crucial: your distance from the subject being drawn and your angle in relationship to the subject. Ask yourself: Are you directly in the middle front and parallel to the subject, or are you at an angle to it? Manipulate the distance between you and the subject by looking through the glass at various different viewing angles and from various different stances.

Always locate the horizon line, even if it falls outside the picture plane. Its position will describe the viewer's position—whether the viewer is looking up, down, or straight ahead. (On the pane of glass, using a water-soluble felt-tip marker, draw the horizon line. The water-soluble marks can be wiped clean with a damp rag.)

Perspective hinges on the fact that lines that in reality are parallel and moving away from us appear to meet at some point on the horizon. That meeting place is called the *vanishing point*, or the point of convergence. Parallel lines of objects above the horizon line will converge downward; those of objects below the horizon will converge upward. Lines perpendicular and parallel to the picture plane do not converge unless the viewer is looking up or down, tilting the picture plane. Draw those lines on the glass plane. In Escher's drawing, the vanishing point is in the exact center of the picture plane; all parallel lines both above and below converge at the mark. Compare the two views of the tree, stairs, and passageway connecting the buildings on either side of the composition and trace their converging lines.

Once the horizon line has been determined, find the vanishing point by pointing with your finger and tracing the direction of the receding lines until you reach the horizon line (or more graphically, draw the receding lines on the clear glass). The vanishing point is located at the juncture of the traced line and the horizon line. True one-point or linear perspective (see *figure 8.11*) will have a single vanishing point in the middle of the picture plane.

One-point perspective is useful chiefly in situations in which subjects are parallel or perpendicular to the picture plane, as in the Antholt drawing (see *figure 4.27*). Antholt's use of aerial and one-point perspective is the means to represent an esoteric idea. Her formal technique is a means to a metaphysical end with symbolism as its "point of departure"; her subject is "the conditions of spirituality within a house." A strict use of one-point perspective is a means to promote "an appreciation of sterner, more eternal conditions." Antholt's use of aerial perspective lends a tone of solemn purpose to the work. As one reviewer has written, "An atmosphere of sublimity pervades every picture like a fragrance" (J. W. Mahoney, "Sharron Antholt at Franz Bader," *Art in America*, March 1989, pp. 155, 156).

If you are standing in front of a building parallel to the picture plane and you move to the right or left so that the building is seen at an angle, you will have changed to a *two-point perspective*. There are now two sets of parallel lines, each with a different vanishing point (see *figures 8.17* and *8.18*). There may be multiple vanishing points in two-point perspective; any number of objects set at an angle to the picture plane can be drawn, and each object or set of parallel lines will establish its own vanishing point. All planes that are parallel share the same vanishing point. (Take your pane of glass outdoors in your neighborhood or on campus, and trace a number of one-point perspective scenes. You can lay the glass on your sketchbook or on a clean sheet of paper and you will easily see the various angles to be drawn; the conversion of angles, or the angles of the parallel lines as they move into the distance, have been indicated accurately on your "window into space.")

Objects in *three-point perspective* have no side perpendicular to the picture plane, so there will be three sets of receding parallel lines, which will converge to three vanishing points, two sets on a horizon line and one set on a vertical line (see *figures 8.19* and *8.20*).

Using a Viewer for Framing and Sighting

Using a sighting viewer is a convenient way to crop a composition. Cut a six- by nine-inch opening in a larger rectangle of mat board. (Make several of these viewers, cut to the proportion of your drawing paper, such as a square and a longer rectangle to be used in long, horizontal, or vertical formats.)

Attach two taut strings (with either glue or tape), one vertically from top to bottom, and the other horizontally from side to side to bisect the opening both horizontally and vertically. This crosshair divider is helpful in marking reference points for placement in the initial stages of a composition. It offers you a plumb line to check verticals and horizontals and their relationships to each other. It is helpful in taking proportional measurements; for example, a head might be the unit of measurement to determine the height or width of a particular pose.

Make measurement marks along the sides, indicating one-inch intervals to help you more correctly determine heights and widths. You can attach strings along these axes to create a grid that will be useful in establishing relative height and width.

Remember in sighting (and in using the glass pane) to use only one eye because binocular vision interferes with a single sight line. Keep the glass pane and the sighting device in your drawing kit for checking proper size and scale.

PROBLEM 8.3

Locating Vanishing Points

Cut six strips of stiff paper ¼ inch by 11 inches (.6 cm by 28 cm). Use them to determine where the vanishing points fall on the horizon. Locate vanishing points and horizons in each illustration in this chapter by laying the strips along the converging lines. Horizon lines and convergence points frequently fall outside the picture plane. Note whether the artist has taken liberties with a strict perspective in each drawing.

8.13. **RON DAVIS.** *Bent Vents & Octangular.* 1976. Acrylic on canvas, 9'6" x 15' (2.9 m x 4.57 m). *The Museum of Contemporary Art, Los Angeles. Gift of Robert A. Ravan, photo by Squidds & Nunns.*

Ron Davis has left traces of all the lines of measurement used in making his drawing *(figure 8.13)*. He has left in the drawing extended verticals, horizontals, and angled parallel lines moving into space; these multiple lines trace vanishing points of every angle of the faceted forms of his subject. They make up a lively spatial grid into which the objects are logically fitted. Davis uses an overhead light source to differentiate the planes of the forms and to further enhance the spatial quality of the drawing. The overhead view results in a three-point perspective with three vanishing points falling outside the picture plane.

One-Point Perspective

A tongue-in-cheek reference to the time-honored one-point perspective is the sketch by David Macaulay, *Locating the Vanishing Point (figure 8.14)*, taken from his book *Great Moments in Architecture*. It certainly was a great moment in art when Italian artists discovered this new means of describing the visual world, but in the world of contemporary art it is frequently seen as a cliché.

One-point perspective, as we have seen, is a convention in which parallel lines (lines parallel in actuality) located diagonally to the picture plane converge at a single point on the horizon *(figure 8.15)*. The humor in Macaulay's drawing stems from the fact that the railroad tracks converge before they reach the horizon. This contradiction sets up a complicated response in trying to explain the paradox.

In addition to a point of convergence, other devices—overlapping, reduction in the size of objects as they recede, and blurring of detail in the distance—contribute to the sense of spatial recession. In many drawings, especially cartoons, these devices are exaggerated, as in *figures 8.3* and *8.16*.

Figure 8.16 shows us an example of one-point perspective with an escalator forming the lines of convergence in a panel from the comic book *The Sarcophagus* by Enki Bilal. There is nothing comic in Bilal's pessimistic strips; they deal with the individual in conflict with monolithic powers. In spite of a one-point perspective, Bilal confounds a logical spatial interpretation with extreme shifts of scale.

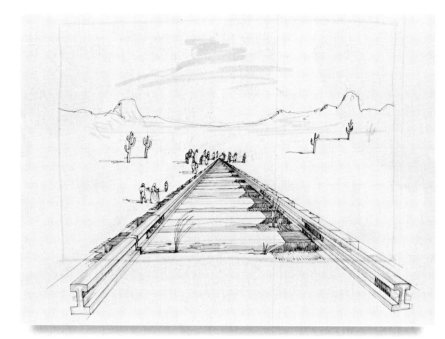

8.14. **DAVID MACAULAY. Final preliminary sketch for Plate XV, *Locating the Vanishing Point* (Macaulay's intentionally misplaced horizon line), from Great Moments in Architecture.** 1978. Ink and felt-tip marker. *Copyright © 1978 by David Macaulay. Reprinted with permission of Houghton Mifflin Company. All rights reserved.*

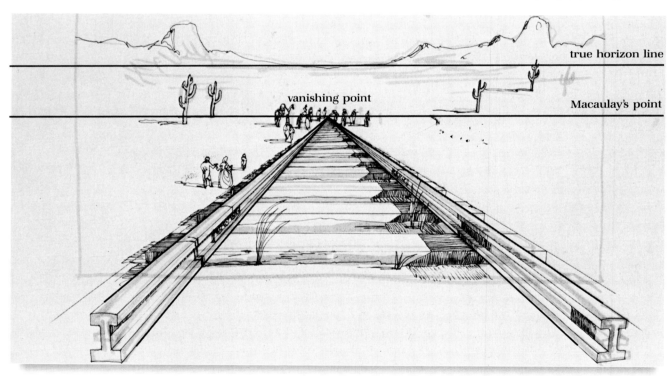

8.15. Diagram—One-point perspective superimposed on David Macaulay's final preliminary sketch for Plate XV, *Locating the Vanishing Point* (Macaulay's intentionally misplaced horizon line).

PROBLEM 8.4

Using One-Point Perspective

It is important to position yourself so that your angle of vision encompasses both the height and width of your subject. Use the transparent pane and sighting device to help you track vanishing points and horizon line.

■ Station yourself directly in front and center of a building or a long hall; your angle of vision will be the center of the drawing. If you place the picture plane too

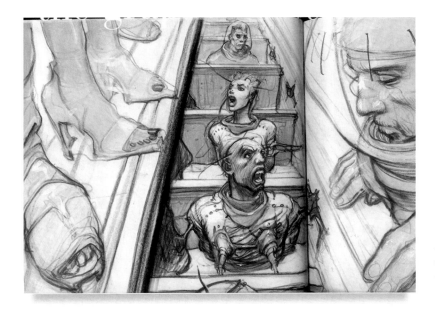

8.16. **ENKI BILAL. A page from *The Sarcophagus.*** 2000. Drawing, 6'8⅝" x 8'8⅓" (2.05 m x 2.65 m). © *Bilal and Christin—Dargaud, Paris.*

close to your line of vision, the objects in the foreground will be so large that they will crowd out the objects in the distance.

■ First, locate the horizon line, even if it is off the paper. Establish the height of the verticals in proper proportion to each other using the sighting device.

■ Trace the parallel lines to their vanishing point on the horizon line.

■ Use contour line.

■ Maintain a fixed point of view. Close one eye to rid yourself of the problem of binocular vision in tracing vanishing points.

You might enliven this somewhat mechanical drawing with collage elements, as in the work by Paolini (see *figure 8.11*).

Two-Point Perspective

A view that uses *two-point perspective* has two vanishing points on the horizon, rather than the single point of convergence in one-point perspective. Two-point perspective describes objects that are oblique to the picture plane, that is, are turned at an angle to the picture plane. This is clear when we look at Edward Ruscha's *Double Standard* (made in collaboration with Mason Williams; *figure 8.17*). The verticals all remain parallel to the vertical edges of the picture plane, but the two sides of the service station lead to two vanishing points, one to the right and the second to the left *(figure 8.18)*. The vanishing point on the right is at the exact lower right corner; the one on the left falls outside the picture plane. The horizon line coincides exactly with the bottom edge of the picture plane. For two-point perspective, any number of objects may be oblique to the picture plane, and each object will establish its own set of vanishing points on the horizon line. (In Ruscha's depiction, the X presents a "double standard.") The baseline is at the exact bottom edge of the print. The scale of the building and the extreme upward view emphasize the ant's-eye view and diminish the scale of the implied viewer.

8.17. **EDWARD RUSCHA (Collaboration with MASON WILLIAMS).** *Double Standard.* 1969. Color silkscreen printed on mold-made paper, 2'1¾" x 3'4⅛" (65 cm x 1.02 m). *Edition of 40.* © *Edward Ruscha/Licensed by VAGA, New York.*

vanishing point 1   horizon line   vanishing point 2

8.18. Diagram—Two-point perspective superimposed on Edward Ruscha's *Double Standard.*

PROBLEM 8.5

Using Two-Point Perspective

For this project, make an arrangement of various sized boxes. Experiment with placement. If you arrange the boxes on a table, the horizon line and vanishing points will be different than if you place them on the floor. Give real consideration to eye level and baselines (see *figure 3.32*).

■ Position yourself so that you are able to see both front and sides of the boxes.

■ Using two-point perspective, register the horizon line by checking your angle of vision.

■ Estimate the height of the vertical nearest you, and draw it. This step is crucial; it establishes the scale of the drawing, and all proportions stem from this measurement.

■ Next trace the vanishing points. Remember that you may have several sets of vanishing points (all facing on one horizon line) if you are drawing a number of objects that are set at an angle to the picture plane.

■ After you have finished the drawing, look through the see-through pane from the same perspective you made the drawing. Hold the pane at a fixed distance from your eyes; close one eye and trace the scene, concentrating on the objects in perspective. Establish the horizon line and lightly extend the diagonals to their vanishing points on the horizon. Place the glass on which you have traced the horizon line and diagonals on top of your drawing and compare the two. This device will help serve as a corrective to clarify the angles and points of convergence. Using a transparent picture plane will help you solve some problems in seeing. Do not, however, use this as a crutch to prevent you from developing your own visual acuity.

Three-Point Perspective

In *three-point perspective*, in addition to lines receding to two points on the horizon, parallel lines that are perpendicular to the ground appear to converge to a third, a vertical, vanishing point. In Hugh Ferriss's study for a skyscraper *(figure 8.19)*, we can easily trace the vertical vanishing point. Each tower has its set of stacked parallel, horizontal lines receding downward to two points on the horizon line, whereas the vertical lines of each tower converge at a single point above the central tower *(figure 8.20)*. The angle or speed with which the lines converge produces a sense of vertigo, not unlike the effect the tourist experiences in New York City looking upward at the vertical architectural thrusts. Ferriss counters this pyramidal effect with rays of beacon lights, which converge downward. The cleanly modeled forms change in value, from light at the base to a flat, dense black at the top, further emphasizing the building's verticality.

8.19. (left) **HUGH FERRISS. *Study for the Maximum Mass Permitted by the 1916 New York Zoning Law, Stage 4.*** c. 1925. Carbon pencil, brush and black ink, stumped and varnished on illustration board, 2'2³⁄₁₆" x 1'8" (66.5 cm x 50.8 cm). *Cooper-Hewitt National Design Museum, Smithsonian Institution, New York; gift of Mrs. Hugh Ferriss.*

8.20. (right) Diagram—Three-point perspective superimposed on Hugh Ferriss's *Study for the Maximum Mass Permitted by the 1916 New York Zoning Law, Stage 4.*

Using Three-Point Perspective

Assume an ant's-eye view and arrange several objects on a ladder. Position yourself at an angle to the ladder so that your view is looking upward. Again, trace with your finger the vanishing points that will fall on the horizon line, and then trace a third vanishing point, the vertical one. Keep in mind all three vanishing points even though they may fall outside the picture plane. The forms will be larger at the bottom of the ladder (and at the bottom of the picture plane). When you reach midpoint on your paper, check the scale and draw in the remainder of the ladder and objects. Employ aerial perspective to further enhance the feeling of space.

AXONOMETRIC PERSPECTIVE

In an *axonometric view*, an object's horizontal and vertical axes are drawn to scale, but its curved lines and diagonal are distorted. Imaginary cities have always been a magnet for artists; from Hieronymus Bosch to Rem Koolhass the metaphor has been a powerful one. Koolhaas and Vriesendorp make use of axonometric perspective in the drawing, *The City of the Captive Globe (figure 8.21)*. The bird's eye view and axonometric perspective of the city form a diagonal grid with ghostly

8.21. REM KOOLHAAS AND MADELON VRIESENDORP. *The City of the Captive Globe Project.* Axonometric view. 1972. Gouache and graphite on paper, 12½" x 17⅜". Gift of The Howard Gilman Foundation. *Museum of Modern Art, New York. (1206.2000) Photo credit: Digital Image. © Museum of Modern Art/Licensed by SCALA/Art Resource, NY.*

buildings projecting skyward. This unusual perspective announces an imaginary idealized city.

MULTIPLE PERSPECTIVES

Since the beginning of the twentieth century, artists have felt that strict, one-point perspective is lifeless, that any fixed, single viewpoint is too limiting, too narrow, and too isolated to adequately render our ever-changing, interconnected world. Thus, they improvised various perspective systems—all within a single work of art.

The disorienting effect achieved by changing eye levels and perspectives within the same work can be seen in the drawing by Mel Bochner *(figure 8.22)*. Bochner deals with the manipulation of perspective as a theme throughout his work. In *Split Infinity*, eight sheets of paper are composed around an empty square. What we expect to be a mirroring of the images, Bochner turns into multiple perspectives. Erasure and a canceling out of forms gives a sense of motion. The cascade of falling boxes is confounded by the projecting background grids.

PROBLEM 8.7

Using Multiple Perspectives

Make a drawing in which you use changing, or multiple, eye levels within the same drawing. The resulting space will be ambiguous. Draw an urban freeway, changing eye level and perspective from one section of the drawing to another. The roadways might vanish on an extreme diagonal into space; billboards could be out of scale and have multiple vanishing points. Keep in mind the disorienting effects of a multiple perspective with its highly ambiguous space. Use extremes of perspectival space to mirror the disorientation of city life. Look at the stacked perspective in the

8.22. **MEL BOCHNER.** *Split Infinity.* 1992–1993. Charcoal and pastel on paper, 35" x 70" (88.9 cm x 177.8 cm). *Private collection.*

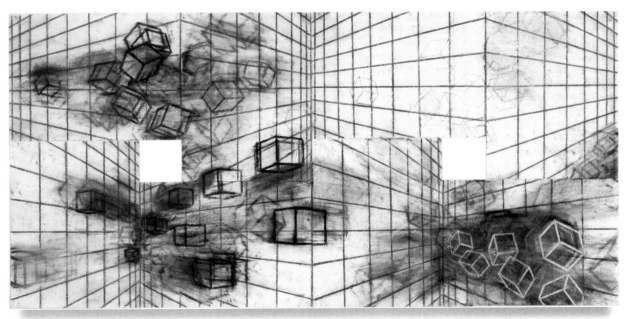

8.23. **WAYNE THIEBAUD. *Down 18th Street (Corner Apartments).*** 1980. Oil and charcoal on canvas, 4' x 2'11⅞" (1.218 m x 91.2 cm). Hirshhorn Museum and Sculpture Garden, Smithsonian Institution, Washington, D.C. Museum purchase with funds donated by Edward R. Downe Jr., 1980. Lee Stalsworth, photographer. Acc. 80.66. © *Wayne Thiebaud/Licensed by VAGA, New York.*

cityscape of Wayne Thiebaud *(figure 8.23)* for ideas of how to handle images from urban landscape, although Thiebaud does not use multiple perspectives.

Stacked Perspective

Anyone who has read comic books is familiar with stacked perspective—stacked panels or frames on the same page create a space that is predominantly two-dimensional. A parallel grouping of squares or rectangles, stacked one on top of the other, encourages a reading from top to bottom across the page in a sequential order. These parallel frames reinforce the two-dimensionality of the picture plane. In comic strips, there can be abrupt changes in horizon line from frame to frame and pronounced shifts in eye level, from high to low. Perspective is frequently exaggerated; extreme angles are used often to suggest a deep space.

In *figure 8.23*, we see a modified stacked perspective view in a drawing of San Francisco's topography by Thiebaud. An uphill view is combined with an extreme compression of space from bottom to top. Thiebaud's work, as one critic notes, reads more like a waterfall than a four-lane street. His cityscapes deny the convention of perspective. He says, "What interests me is how an artist can interrupt that convention, orchestrate or augment it" (Beal, p. 4). The "urban landscapes," as he calls them, allow Thiebaud to integrate horizontal and vertical planes, like a series of stacked flat planes lined up behind one another. Thiebaud builds his images unconstrained by exact representation, taking "a piece here and a piece there and [organizing] it like a stage. Working with specific information I can . . . manage the landscape" (Beal, p. 3).

Thiebaud is interested in what he calls a "concept of extremism" (Beal, p. 4), whether in dealing with color, light, or perspective. This stretched-out, or rather stretched-up, vertical space seems to be further extended by the long freeway that dissects the picture plane. The snakelike movement of the adjoining roads weaves upward through the composition.

PROBLEM 8.8

Using Stacked Perspective

Stack several objects on shelves. Using multiple parallel baselines draw two or three objects on each baseline. Make use of repeated shapes, repeating values, invented texture, and outlining to create a relatively shallow space. Place some of the objects parallel to the picture plane, and set others at an angle. Change scale and proportion from shelf to shelf.

Macaulay's *Fragments from the World of Architecture (figure 8.24)* could have been made in response to this problem. For subject matter he has chosen common building materials—acoustical tiles, Formica, fake brick, Styrofoam, and AstroTurf. You, too, might go on an "archaeological dig" in search of subject matter for this drawing.

FORESHORTENING

Perspective is concerned with representing the change in size of objects as they recede in space. *Foreshortening* is the representation of an object that has been extended forward in space by contracting its forms through overlapping. Beginning with the form nearest the viewer, shapes are compiled from large to small, one overlapping the next, in a succession of steps. Georges Rohner's twentieth-century

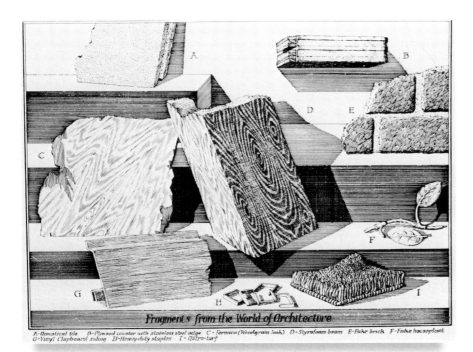

8.24. **DAVID MACAULAY.** *Fragments from the World of Architecture, from Great Moments in Architecture.* 1978.
Copyright ©1978 by David Macaulay. Reprinted with permission of Houghton Mifflin Company. All rights reserved.

version *(figure 8.25)* of Andrea Mantegna's fifteenth-century Christ presents an example of extreme foreshortening. The forms are compiled one behind the other from foot to head. The leg on the left is more severely foreshortened than the one on the right, which is presented in a side view. The leg on the left is compressed, each anatomical segment maintaining its own discrete shape; there is no flowing of one form into the other as we see in the other leg.

Foreshortening does not apply to the figure exclusively; any form that you see head-on can be foreshortened. In foreshortening, spatial relationships are compressed, rather than extended. Foreshortening heightens or exaggerates the illusion of spatial projection.

PROBLEM 8.9

Using Foreshortening

Observing a model, combine four or five views of arms or legs in a single drawing employing foreshortening; that is, begin with the form nearest you, enclose that form, then proceed to the adjacent form, enclosing it. Be careful to draw what you see, not what you know or imagine the form to be. For example, in drawing the leg, analyze the parts that compose the form: foot, ankle, calf, knee, thigh, hip connection. This is unlike a profile drawing where you are presented with a side view and each form flows into the next. In foreshortening, distance is achieved by the succession of enclosed, overlapping forms. Make careful sightings when making horizontal and vertical measurements. Note the relationships in height and width between each level of overlap. For example, in a reclining pose such as Rohner has used, compare the height and width of the foot with the calf immediately behind it, the length and width of the calf with the thigh, and so on. Use the sighting device to help determine measurements.

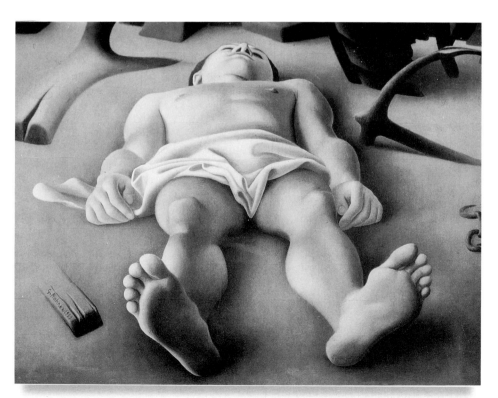

8.25. **GEORGES ROHNER.** *Drowned Man.* 1939. Oil on canvas, 1'11¾" x 2'7⅝" (60 cm x 80 cm). *Courtesy Galerie Framond, Paris.*

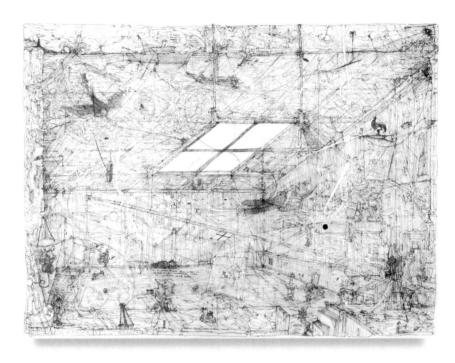

8.26. **WILLIAM T. WILEY.** *Slightly Hysterical Perspective.* 1979. Acrylic and charcoal on canvas, 7'5" x 8'6" (2.26 m x 2.59 m). *Sharon and Thurston Twigg-Smith, Honolulu. Photo by eeva-inkeri. Courtesy of George Adams Gallery, New York.*

Conclusion

The type of space an artist uses is relative; it is seldom possible to classify a work as strictly two- or three-dimensional. As a student you may be required to create a flat or an illusionistic or ambiguous space in a given problem, but as an artist your treatment of space is a matter of personal choice. Mastery of the spatial relationships of the elements and knowledge of perspective will give you freedom in that choice. Your treatment of space should be compatible with the ideas, subject, and feeling in your work. The more you draw from life, the more you see. Soon rules drop away and you internalize order.

William T. Wiley's drawing, *Slightly Hysterical Perspective*, will have the final word in this chapter *(figure 8.26)*. That proverbial window-into-space has been turned topsy-turvy; rather than looking out, it looks down—down into a jumbled studio filled with a conglomeration of images and spaces. Wiley's drawing seems a perfect metaphor for the many perspective choices available to the contemporary artist.

Sketchbook Project

The sketchbook projects at the end of each of the preceding chapters can be done at any time during your study of each element. The following two projects, however, should be done after you have read the introductory material to chapter 8, and in preparation for problem 8.1.

PROJECT 1

Invented Spatially Illusionistic Forms

Although your approach in keeping a sketchbook is serious, playful invention should not be minimized. Look at the improvisations by Arshile Gorky *(figure 8.27)*, an artist known for his biomorphic variations.

8.27. **ARSHILE GORKY.** *Virginia Landscape (Untitled, Study for Pastoral Series).* 1943. Graphite and pastel and crayon on paper, 20" x 27" (51 cm x 69 cm). *Private collection.* © 2007 Artists Rights Society (ARS), New York.

In your sketchbook draw several pages of invented organic forms. Imagine them from various angles as they turn in space. Concentrate on making them dimensional. Indicate front and sides either by planar connections or by volumetric modeling. Imagine a light source casting shadows to enhance the three-dimensionality of the forms.

PROJECT 2

Employing Different Horizon Lines

Make quick sketches in which you arrange three or four invented shapes in an imagined space. Employ different horizon lines. In the first drawing, arrange the forms on a low horizon line. Remember that if all the forms share the same baseline, that is, if they are lined up along a single line parallel to the picture plane, space will be limited. A diagonal or angular distribution of the forms penetrating the picture plane will result in a more spatial illusion.

In the second group of sketchbook drawings, raise the horizon line, locating it somewhere in the upper third of the picture plane. Be aware that you are manipulating the viewer's stance. Determine whether the forms are being viewed from above or below. Indicate a light source to achieve the spatial effect you desire.

Overlapping forms and shifts in size and scale of the objects distributed throughout the composition will produce a three-dimensional space.

This group of preparatory sketches provides material to be used in problem 8.1, so you can save the finishing touches for that problem.

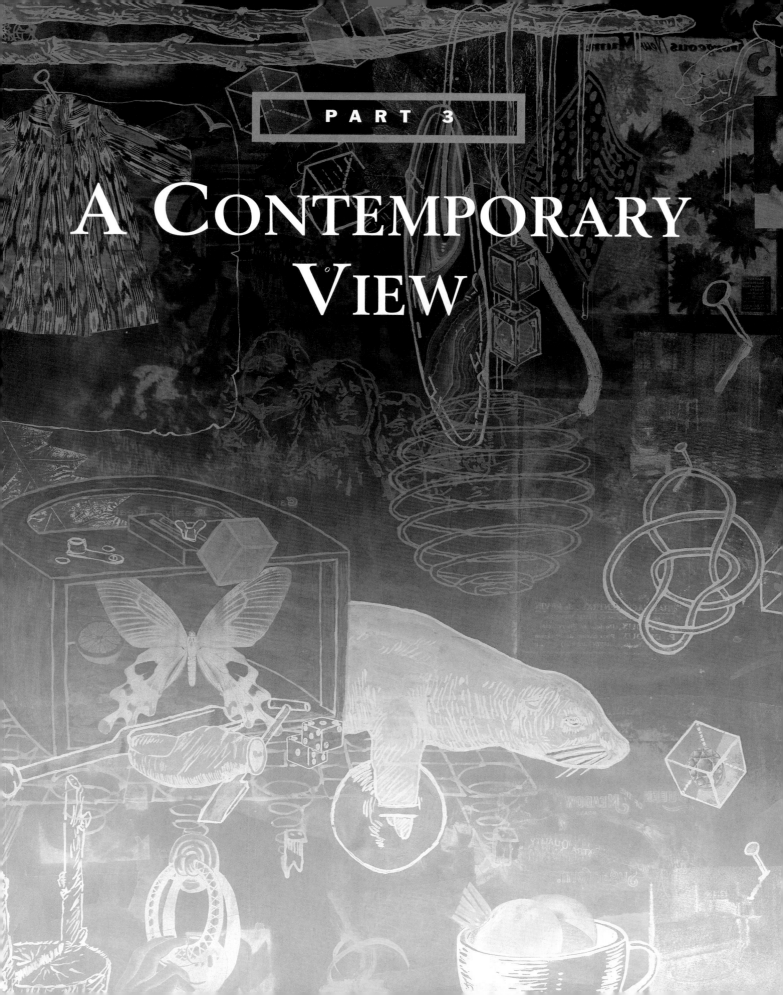

PART 3

A CONTEMPORARY VIEW

CHAPTER 9

Time doesn't flow, it ticks. Space is not a surface but a grid.
— STEPHEN WOLFRAM, PHYSICIST

Organizing the Picture Plane

CHALLENGES TO TRADITIONAL COMPOSITIONAL APPROACHES

John Baldessari, a major influence on conceptually based photography, directs us to *A Different Kind of Order (figure 9.1)* in his retelling of a story about the well-known jazz pianist Thelonious Monk. Baldessari framed five photographs of various disasters found in press files, matted them crooked in their frames, and hung them askew. In the sixth frame is the narrative:

> There's a story about Thelonious Monk going around his apartment tilting all the pictures hanging on the wall. It was his idea of teaching his wife a different kind of order. When she saw the pictures askew on the wall she would straighten them. And when Monk saw them straightened on the wall, he would tilt them. Until one day his wife left them hanging on the wall tilted.

There is more to this anecdote than meets the eye, so to speak. Baldessari points to our adherence to an accepted rule in art without giving consideration to why we are committed to it. The artist shows us both visually and verbally that there is more than one kind of order in the world. In every work of art, we find at least two different

9.1. JOHN BALDESSARI. *A Different Kind of Order (The Thelonious Monk Story).* 1972–1973. Five gelatin silver photographs and one typewritten sheet, individually framed; each image: 6⁹⁄₁₆" x 9¹³⁄₁₆" (16.7 cm x 24.9 cm); each frame: 11⅝" x 14¹¹⁄₁₆" (29.5 cm x 37.3 cm). *The Museum of Fine Arts, Houston, Texas; purchased with additional funding provided by the National Endowment for the Arts.*

9.2. ROBERT MORRIS. *Blind Time XIX.* 1973. Powdered graphite and pencil on paper, 2'11" x 3'10" (89 cm x 1.17 m). *Virginia Wright Fund. The Washington Art Consortium: Henry Art Gallery, University of Washington, Seattle; Museum of Art, Washington State University, Pullman; Northwest Museum of Arts and Culture, Spokane; Seattle Art Museum; Tacoma Art Museum; Western Gallery, Western Washington University, Bellingham; Whatcom Museum of History and Art, Bellingham. Photo by Paul Macapia, © 1977. © 2007 Robert Morris/Artists Rights Society (ARS), New York.*

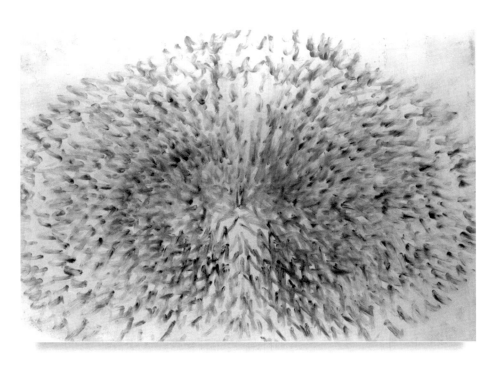

kinds of meanings, the semantic one and the visual-aesthetic one. (*Semantics* is a branch of linguistics that deals with the study of meaning and the relationships between signs and symbols and what they represent.) Visually, the mounted photographs ask a question that can be answered only in a qualified way: Is it the photographs or the frames that are crooked?

Art derives its vitality from new ideas; it challenges previously accepted conventions, styles, techniques, and definitions. So the rules of composition are not fixed; they need to be used or discarded as the visual idea requires.

Multiple formats, such as the divided picture plane and the grid, are characteristic of contemporary art. Sequence and serial development lie at the heart of Minimalism. Impermanence, change, and transition in the culture are mirrored in the art of our times.

Let us look at an extreme example of a challenge to traditional composition. Robert Morris, in making his *Blind Time* drawings *(figure 9.2)*, blocked his vision, making a disconnect between hand-eye coordination. This coordination has always been the core of art making. Not only could Morris not see the marks he was making, he could not see the shape of the sheet he was drawing on. No implement intervened between his hands and the paper. He made 98 "task-oriented" drawings, each within a preset time period. He records the activity in a legend in the corner of each drawing. His aim was "to relinquish control and distance, authorship and ego" (Connie Butler, *Afterimage*, p. 97).

CONTEMPORARY TREATMENT OF THE PICTURE PLANE

Contemporary artists have stretched, distorted, layered, punctured, and warped the rectangular picture plane. At the same time, they have developed and expanded imagist themes; figurative imagery hangs alongside abstract forms.

The picture plane makes formal demands on the artist. Certain concerns must be dealt with in working on a flat, two-dimensional surface. *Form* is the interrelationship of all the elements. In art, form and meaning are inseparable; form is the carrier of the meaning. It is the design or structure of the work, the mode in which the work exists. It is an order created by the artist. A two-dimensional work announces itself in two ways. First, it asserts its presence as a two-dimensional object; and second, it conveys a spatial tension between its internal forms.

Dominance of the Edge

The most obvious challenge to the rigidity of the perimeters of the traditional picture plane has been the breakup of its regular shape. Nancy Rubins's large pencil-on-paper drawing resembles a Baroque sculpture more than it does a drawing, with its heroic scale and billowing three-dimensional forms *(figure 9.3)*. Rubins covers heavy sheets of paper with graphite marks densely overlaid to create a leaden luster. The irregularly torn sheets of paper, which resemble sheets of metal, are crumpled, folded, bent, and twisted into giant three-dimensional shapes and attached to the

9.3. NANCY RUBINS. *DRAWINGS.*
2000–2001. Pencil on paper, 14' x 24' x 3' (4.27 m x 7.32 m x 91.4 cm).
Courtesy Paul Kasmin Gallery and the artist.

9.4. **RICHARD ARTSCHWAGER.** *Northwest Passage.* 1994. Acrylic, Formica, Celotex, and wood, 6' x 4'11" (1.83 m x 1.5 m). *The Eli and Edythe L. Broad Collection. © 2007 Richard Artschwager/Artists Rights Society (ARS), New York.*

wall by pushpins. She has introduced actual mass and weight to her work, characteristics not usually associated with drawing.

Richard Artschwager's work *(figure 9.4)* demonstrates the dominance of the outside edge of the picture plane. He intentionally uses offbeat materials, such as Celotex and Formica, to diminish an aesthetic response to the work. The drawing could be taken from a real estate ad. The frame is an integral part of the work; it calls attention to the object-hood of the piece. Artschwager's painted faux-wood window frame dissects the scene and locks the viewer's attention on the frame rather than on the depicted scene. This window serves a triple function: It frames another image, it reiterates the size and shape of the picture plane, and it is a contemporary window into a contemporary space.

PROBLEM 9.1

Shaped Picture Planes

In the library, look at catalogs and books that focus on contemporary artists who use nontraditional shaped formats in their work. Frank Stella, Elizabeth Murray, and

Neil Jenny are examples of the many current artists working with shaped picture planes. Neil Jenney's work (see *figure 3.22*) is associated with dominant irregularly shaped frames that alter the look of the traditional format.

In your visual research, pay close attention to the motif or image and how it relates to the shape of the support. You will discover a broad range of subject matter being used on these structures, from nonobjective to recognizable. Determine how subject, content, and support are welded in each work.

PROBLEM 9.2

Confirming the Flatness of the Picture Plane

Make a drawing on gessoed board, cardboard, or Masonite. Choose a common, everyday object as subject; enclose it in a drawn frame or patterned border. Combine solid value shapes, outlining, and invented texture to emphasize the flatness of the picture plane. Jim Nutt is a good artist to study before beginning your drawing (see *figure II.10*).

Continuous-Field Compositions

One solution in dealing with the edge of the picture plane is to negate its limitations by making a *continuous-field composition*; that is, if we imagined the picture plane to be extended in any direction, the image would also extend to produce a continuous field. There is no single focal point.

Andrea Way's drawings are indicative of continuous-field compositions *(figure 9.5)*. Way's work deals with process, the imposition of one system of abstract patterns over another. The space in her drawing *Shots* resembles a computer game. The drawing is made by overlaying small triangular shapes behind larger white slivers. A third system of lined rectangles provides an emphatic horizontal balance, while connecting lines seem to stitch the rectangles in place. Way's method is programmed; she says she creates rules for her drawings so she can constructively depart from them. The merging systems seem to extend in all directions; each pattern maintains its own integrity

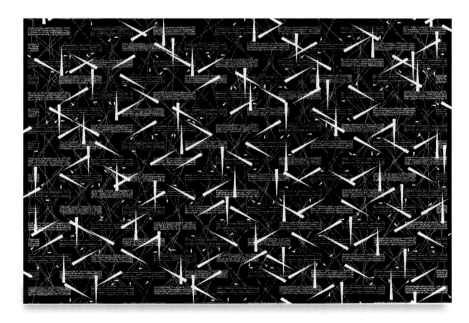

9.5. **ANDREA WAY. Shots.** 1986. Ink on paper, 3' x 4'3½" (91 cm x 1.31 m). *Collection of George T. Moran.*

9.6. **SYLVIA PLIMACK MANGOLD.** *Untitled (Wide Plank).* 1973–1974. Acrylic and pencil on paper, 2'6" x 3'4" (76 cm x 1.02 m). *Courtesy Alexander and Bonin, New York.*

within the picture plane yet relates with the others in a non-chaotic way. Each system is on its own wavelength.

Although most continuous-field drawings are abstract, some artists work with an overall articulation using recognizable subject matter. Vija Celmins maps the night skies. Her work with its black field and white stars is difficult to reproduce. Celmins's night skies are exactly duplicated at a given time from a particular geographic location. The Postminimalist artist Sylvia Plimack Mangold has created a continuous field in the drawing of the wooden planks of her studio floor *(figure 9.6).*

PROBLEM 9.3

Continuous-Field Compositions

Make a drawing that extends the limits of the picture plane. Choose for your subject a continuous field, such as water or grass. Create an overall surface so that no segment of the drawing has precedence over another. There should be no dominant center of interest.

Arrangement of Images on the Picture Plane

The Abstract Expressionists introduced continuous-field compositions, but in the 1960s Pop artists were influential in adding new compositional options by introducing commercial design techniques into fine art. Included in their innovative approach were compositions using extreme close-ups of details or fragments; isolation of forms (such as a centralized image in an empty field); schematic simplification, eliminating modeling or shadows; stark contrasts and limited color range; color and texture applied by commercial means (silkscreen and benday dots); silhouetted forms; and serial compositions. Modernist preferences for the grid, along with concerns with the flatness of the picture plane, continue to present options for contemporary artists.

The decade 1965 to 1975 is recognized as a time when the picture plane itself was the primary concern, so much so that its status as object superseded the images on it. Drawing became a favored medium and has maintained its position since.

The importance of the relationship between positive and negative space has been emphasized throughout the book. In dealing with the demands of the picture plane, positioning of positive and negative shapes is of the utmost importance in asserting or denying the limitations of the picture plane. Placement of an image calls attention to the shape and size of the plane on which it is placed. A small shape can be dwarfed by a vast amount of negative space, a large shape can crowd out negative space, and a centralized image can stabilize the space. Pat Steir's *Chrysanthemum* *(figure 9.7)* illustrates these three points.

Center, top, bottom, and sides are of equal importance until the image is placed; then priority is given to a specific area. Centralizing an image results in maximum balance and symmetry, and if that centralized image is stated frontally (that is, not viewed from an oblique angle), the horizontal and vertical axes of the picture plane will be further reinforced, as in the drawing of a monumental environment by Robert Stackhouse *(figure 9.8)*. Stackhouse's image has been described as "an over-lapping grid composed of lines that converge, intersect and vanish on the surface of

9.7. PAT STEIR. *Chrysanthemum.* 1981. Oil on canvas, 3 panels, each 5' x 5' (1.52 m x 1.52 m). *Collection Gloria and Leonard Luria. Robert Miller Gallery, New York. Photo by D. James Dee, New York.*

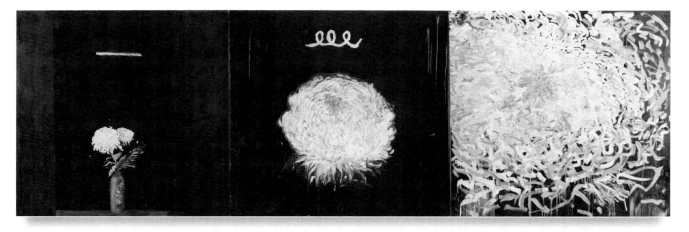

9.8. ROBERT STACKHOUSE. *Inside Shiphall.* 1985. Watercolor, charcoal, and graphite on paper, 2'5½" x 3'5½" (74.9 cm x 1.05 m). *Arkansas Arts Center Foundation Collection: Purchased with a gift from Virginia Bailey. 1987.024.002.*

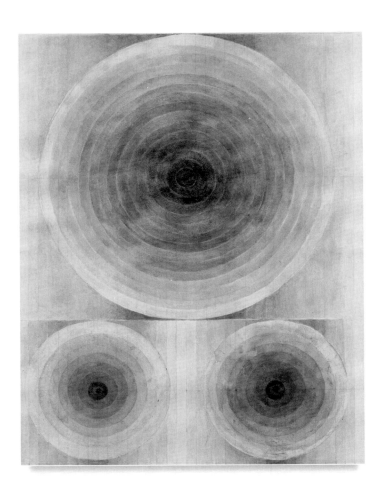

9.9. **EVA HESSE.** *Untitled.* 1966. Black ink wash and pencil on paper, 11¾" x 9¾" (cm x cm). *Collection of Tony Gail Ganz, Los Angeles. © The Estate of Eva Hesse, Hauser and Virth, Zurich, London.*

the paper [creating] a space that is both visionary and palpable" (Wolfe, *Revelations*, p. 81). Stackhouse's perspective qualifies as antiperspectival since the radiant pattern explodes outward to the edges. As if to contain the radiating beams, Stackhouse has reiterated the shape of the picture plane in a heavy graphite line. This illustration employs both a centralized image and an emphasis on the edges.

In the drawing by Eva Hesse *(figure 9.9)*, three circles are made static by their symmetrical placement. The two lower circles levitate in their space while the upper one seems to rest on top of a shelf or base line. The subject of the work is the accretion of the marks themselves.

Repeated motif is another compositional device favored by contemporary artists. In Bruce Conner's drawing *(figure 9.10)*, inkblot shapes are the repeating motif. Conner calls these inkblots "ersatz notations that might be thought of as music" (John Yau, "Folded Mirror," *Art on Paper*, May–June 1998, p. 30). Conner begins by scoring the paper in equidistant vertical lines. He then draws the inkblot shapes on the center line, moving alternately from side to side until the page is filled. Repeating geometric shapes furnish the organizing structure. Note how spatially different are the works of Stackhouse and Conner, even though both artists are using stripes and triangles.

In *Bright River (figure 9.11)*, Wayne Thiebaud has given his landscape a distinctive twist through use of a diagonally divided plane, an unusual compositional device. The composition is built up of a series of triangular and rectilinear units. The river that flows at an angle through the middle of the picture plane divides foreground from background. The larger geometric segments are at the bottom,

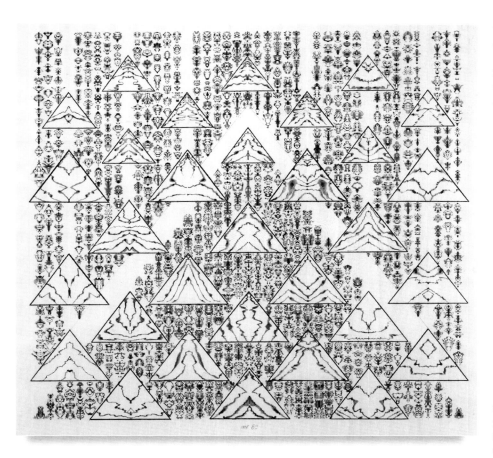

9.10. **BRUCE CONNER.** *Inkblot Drawing, 8/12/1995.* 1995. Ink and graphite pencil on paper, 1'7⅛" x 1'7" (48.6 cm x 48.3 cm); image, 1'3⅛" x 1'4³⁄₁₆" (38.4 cm x 41.1 cm). *Courtesy Michael Kohn Gallery, Los Angeles.*

9.11. **WAYNE THIEBAUD.** *Bright River.* 1996. Oil on canvas, 1'11¾" x 3' (60.3 cm x 91.4 cm). *Photo courtesy Campbell-Thiebaud, San Francisco. © Wayne Thiebaud/Licensed by VAGA, New York.*

while smaller divisions are at the top, creating a space that flips forward as it progresses from bottom to top.

Another strategy for arranging images on the picture plane, one favored especially by Postmodern artists, is overlay. In Al Souza's *Arc de Triomphe (figure 9.12)*, there are three separate overlays of images: the rocking chair, the golf players, and the landscape. The golf scene is appropriated from an older source and forms the field for the chair. The images are not integrated by color, style, or scale. Seemingly unrelated images of contradictory size, proportion, and orientation announce that the picture plane is not a place for a logical illusion of reality; rather, it is a plane that can be arranged any way the artist chooses.

Earlier in the book, we saw examples of Outsider art, work by untrained artists (see *figure 6.16*). A crowded picture plane is a favored compositional device in their work. The term *horror vacui* is often applied to artwork that leaves no empty space. The term literally means "fear of the void," and it carries psychological connotations. The Swiss artist Adolf Wölfli's incredibly complex drawings, with their compulsively filled spaces *(figure 9.13)*, are examples of *horror vacui*. A few years after Wölfli was institutionalized as a schizophrenic at age 31 in 1895, he turned to intense, compulsive, and obsessive art making, creating a massive and original body of work (including 45 text- and image-filled books). In his work shown here, ornate musical staves create an architectonic structure. Words and images crowd the negative nooks and crannies. The images expand and contract, like sounds reverberating against a resonant wall. The corners are filled with compact music patterns, while semicircular figurative images press in from the top and sides.

Jane Hammond, who has been called the quintessential paper artist of our time, mixes and matches layers of distinct and seemingly unrelated images in her work, an example of which can be seen in *figure 9.14*. She uses the space of a flatbed press, laying the images on top of each other and compressing the space.

9.12. **AL SOUZA.** *Arc de Triomphe.* 1986. Oil on canvas, 1'10½" x 3'5" (57.2 cm x 1.041 m). *Courtesy of the artist.*

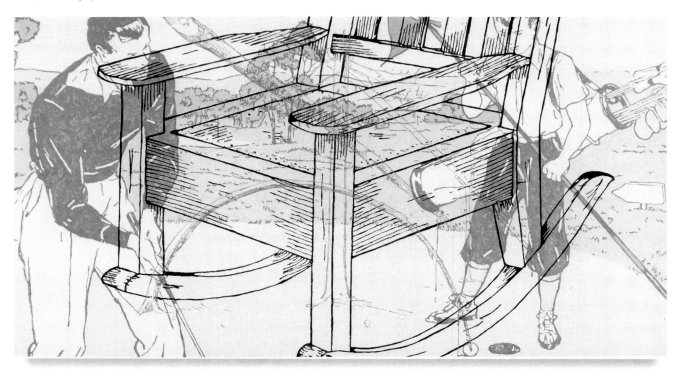

9.13. **ADOLF WÖLFLI.** *General View of the Island.* 1911. Pencil and colored pencil, 3'3²⁄₇" x 2'4" (99.8 cm x 71.2 cm). *Kunstmuseum Bern, Adolf-Wölfli-Stiftung, Bern, Switzerland.*

9.14. **JANE HAMMOND.** *Untitled (Red Frog #2).* 2000. Ink and watercolor on gampi paper, 2'5" x 2'8" (73.7 cm x 81.3 cm). *The Metropolitan Museum of Art, New York. Photo by Peter Muscato.*

Hammond's images come from a lexicon of hundreds of images that she has collected from a variety of printed sources. Hammond's obsession with images originated in her childhood. She explains, "When I was a kid I cordoned off these 50-foot square grids on our property with string, and I had notebooks, and I catalogued everything that was in there—the rocks, the trees. I mean that's the sensibility, either you have it or you don't have it." As an adult she continued her quest for images. She says she "let them associate themselves in different configurations" (Faye Hirsch, "Paper Pulse: A Conversation with Jane Hammond," *Art on Paper*, March–April 2002, p. 64).

Some of the images in Hammond's work are hand-drawn, others are printed from linoleum blocks, some are taken from rubber stamps, and others are photocopy transfers. Hammond says she has a field but not a focus. "I'm always interested in fragmented, multipartite reality. I like art with a high degree of internal contradiction, where order is wrenched out of a huge amount of chaos" (Hirsch, "Paper Pulse," p. 69). Hammond's compositional approach is indicative of two Postmodern practices: overlay and fragmentation.

PROBLEM 9.4

Placing Images on the Picture Plane

For this problem, make two drawings in which placement of images is the primary concern. In the first drawing, centralize and isolate the image; in the second, emphasize edges and corners by dropping out the center.

Use a 12-inch square of heavy rag paper for each drawing. Choose a photograph from a magazine or newspaper and use masking tape to block off an area of 6 inches by 6 inches. In the first drawing, use a solvent to transfer the photographic image to the center of the page. For the second drawing, choose a 12-inch by 12-inch photograph and mask out the center 6-inch square. Transfer this image to the second sheet to emphasize the edges and corners. Use pencil or colored pencils to enhance the transferred images.

PROBLEM 9.5

Filling the Picture Plane

In a drawing, overlay and superimpose images. For each layer choose a different medium, using a diffused pale value for the first layer; darken the value or change colors with each succeeding layer. Draw the final layer in a more decisive manner. The images should be unrelated. You can combine images from various historical periods, or from catalogs or old books.

Division of the Picture Plane

Just as superimposing images is the signature compositional approach of the Postmodernists, the grid is the identifying format of the Modernists. In addition to reiterating the flatness of the picture plane, grids introduce the element of sequence, which in turn brings up the idea of time. Most traditional art is viewed synchronically; that is, the composition is seen all at once in its entirety. Grids, on the other hand, are viewed both synchronically and linearly. The entire grid is registered at a first glance, but in a more sustained look, the composition demands to be read sequentially, segment by segment.

Pat Steir's composition *(figure 9.15)* is divided by intersecting lines in the upper two-thirds and by horizontal lines in the lower third. The grid alternately advances and recedes in different segments of the painting. Pronounced rectangular shapes call attention to the horizontal and vertical axes. The irregular line that divides the two major segments can be read either as the horizon or as a fluctuating graph line. The idea of sequence and of time is reinforced by the title, *Three Green Days.*

Lynda Benglis uses an implied, irregular grid in her mixed-media collage *(figure 9.16).* The grid seems bent out of shape; it is loosely divided into a four-part structure with units of various sizes and shapes. The interplay of organic shapes with their overlap creates a complex spatial tension. If each segment of the work

9.15. PAT STEIR. *Three Green Days.* 1972. Oil, crayon, pencil, and ink on canvas, 6' x 9' (1.83 m x 2.74 m). *Collection Mrs. Anthony J. A. Bryan. Robert Miller Gallery, New York. Photo by Bevan Davies, New York.*

9.16. LYNDA BENGLIS. *Patang Fossil Papers, Drawing No. 6.* 1979. Cloth, foil collage, thread, tissue on handmade paper, 2'2" x 2'10" (66 cm x 86.4 cm). *Lent by Douglas Baxter. Paula Cooper Gallery, New York. © Lynda Benglis/Licensed by VAGA, New York.*

were reassembled in a strictly horizontal and vertical format, the newly constructed composition would be larger than the original one.

The grid can be stated in a sequential pattern to suggest a stopped-frame, or cinematic, structure. Although grids can be read in a number of ways—horizontally, diagonally, or vertically—in cinematic structure each frame logically follows the other. There is a definite sense of time lapse and movement.

Jody Mussoff uses a segmented picture plane related to a stopped-frame composition—gridded at the top, with one large segment at the bottom—for her drawing *Atlas (figure 9.17)*. Conceptually, the divided picture plane is appropriate for the content. Close-ups of the girl's face fill the top units. The kneeling figure is peering from behind the screen of faces; in another view, she seems to be the supporting actor. Although the subject may deal with vulnerability and the pose may portray a tentative position, Mussoff's line quality is strong and assured; it builds a powerful structure on which to hang a world of meaning.

Most stopped-frame compositions use a regular geometric division, but a sequential reading can be achieved by omitting the lines that divide the units. (See *figure 1.1* in which the artist Yooah Park has eliminated the frames. A sense of movement is enhanced since there is no disruption in the sequence.)

Related to both cinematic structure and the divided picture plane is the comic strip. In recent decades, a group of artists began working in a cartoon format in a more serious vein. The term *graphic novel* has emerged to describe their work. *Figure 9.18* is a page from one such work by Chris Ware. In the graphic novel, when text is used, it is disjointed or broken up across several frames. A shorthand convention deletes connective frames that would give the reader-viewer clues to what is going on. Ware's drawing here is a "record of nothing happening: eating, waiting, being disappointed," an indictment of our times.

Loosely related to the divided picture plane is the composition with an inset. An *inset* creates an opposition between itself and the primary subject and sets up a

9.17. **JODY MUSSOFF.** *Atlas.* 1986. Colored pencil on paper, 4'½" x 5' (1.232 m x 1.524 m). *Collection of Mr. and Mrs. Irving Tofsky. Courtesy of the artist.*

9.18. **CHRIS WARE.** A page from the graphic novel *Jimmy Corrigan, the Smartest Kid on Earth.* © *2000 Chris Ware.*

feeling of discontinuity between the two images, as we saw in Barbara Kruger's work (see *figure 6.19*). Kruger, you remember, overlays photographic images with terse statements meant to reveal or expose hidden or underlying biases.

In Don Suggs's landscape *(figure 9.19)*, a painted image of Mount Shasta is blocked by an inset of intrusive vertical stripes. Suggs appropriates his images from photographs in books. These secondhand images (like postcards) stand between us and the real experience of nature in the same way that Suggs's vertical stripes "bar" us from the painted image. The striped inset blocks a perspective view of the mountain; the viewer's focus is abruptly brought back to the space of the picture plane. By means of a bold compositional device, the inset, Suggs has rearranged the visual and emotional focus of the work.

PROBLEM 9.6

Composing with a Grid

Make three drawings in which you use a grid. In the first drawing, establish a grid with each unit the same size. Papers with various sizes of printed grids are readily

9.19. **DON SUGGS.** *Proprietary View (Mount Shasta).* 1985. Oil and alkyd on panel, 1'9¾" x 3'3¾" (55.2 cm x 1.009 m). *L. A. Louver Gallery, Venice, Calif.*

available; it might be interesting to use multiple grids in the same composition—grids within grids, while maintaining a master grid of the same size.

In the second drawing, lightly establish the grid; then use value, texture, line, or a combination to negate or cross over the regular divisions.

In the third drawing, use a grid of irregular units. Cut or tear up old drawings and reassemble them by jumbling the pieces to create a loose grid. (See Benglis's collage, which follows this process, *figure 9.16.*)

PROBLEM 9.7

Dividing the Picture Plane

Divide a picture plane into two equal segments. Make a diptych with an image in one half totally unrelated to the image in the other half. This is not as easy to do as it sounds, since we attempt to relate any two images seen simultaneously. For the first image choose a visual cliché, an icon such as the Statue of Liberty. Pair it with a second image that is totally unrelated by form, media, technique, scale, or meaning. The result should be unsettling to the viewer.

PROBLEM 9.8

Using Inset Images

Make a drawing that employs an inset. Attach a postcard to the center of the picture plane; by drawing, extend the images at the edges of the card out onto the white space of the picture plane. In extending the images, change scale, size, and medium. For example, if you have chosen a black-and-white postcard, use colored media for the extended drawing, or use black ink with a colored postcard. Consider the dichotomies Suggs sets up in his landscape (see *figure 9.19*).

PROBLEM 9.9

Using Linear Sequence

For this problem, use a cartoon style and format to take an imaginary character through a catastrophic day. Tell the story graphically using no words.

THE WALL AS PICTURE PLANE

Pictorial images have escaped even the confines of the picture plane to appear on walls of galleries and museums. Kara Walker uses silhouette tableaux as elements in her narrative art derived from African-American history. She subverts the clichés concerning the slavery era to tell a starker black history *(figure 9.20)*. Her large cutouts are arranged directly on the wall, as seen in the installation at the Guggenheim Museum. "Silhouette looks so clear-cut, so crisp, it operates just as derogatory stereotypes do, making a reduction out of a real person" (Elizabeth Hayt, "Simple, Austere, an Old Genre Is Daringly New," *New York Times*, November 16, 1997, AR 51).

Monumental wall-sized drawings are a defining mark of drawings in the twenty-first century. Throughout this book, we have called attention to size, noting the enormous scale of many contemporary drawings. A third development in the wall-as-picture-plane is wall compositions comprised of accumulated drawings. A third development in the wall-as-picture-plane is wall compositions comprised of accumulated drawings and objects. Annette Messager's wall-sized installations are amalgamations of drawings, fabrics, and objects. *The Pikes (figure 9.21)* refers to the impaled heads paraded through the streets during the French Revolution. Messager challenges heirarchies—here the heirarchy is art itself.

9.20. **KARA WALKER. Installation view of *Insurrection (Our Tools were Rudimentary, Yet We Pressed On)*. 2000.** Cut paper silhouettes and light projections, dimensions vary with installation. *Solomon R. Guggenheim Museum, New York. Purchased with funds contributed by the International Director's Council and Executive Committee Members, 2000.68. Photographed by Ellen Labenski © The Solomon R. Guggenheim Foundation, New York.*

9.21. **ANNETTE MESSAGER.** *The Pikes (les Piques).* 1991–1993. Installation view, Musée National d'Art Moderne, Centre Georges Pompidou, Paris, 1993. Detail as shown. Parts of dolls, fabric, nylon, colored pencils, colored pencil on paper under glass and metal poles.
Courtesy Annette Messager and Marian Goodman Gallery, New York/Paris © 2007 Artists Rights Society (ARS), New York/ ADAGP, Paris.

CONCLUSION

We have seen many choices that contemporary artists have at their disposal to deal with the demands of the picture plane. The list is by no means comprehensive, for each time artists are confronted with the clean, unblemished surface of the picture plane, new options arise. Out of the artist's personal experience come solutions. For some artists the response to the demands of the picture plane is made on a conscious level; for others the response is more intuitive. The organization of the picture plane not only is a response to formal concerns but also reinforces the content in a work.

In your own work, whatever approach you take, the solution should not be turned into formula, for there are no pat answers to any problem in art. Familiarity with the concerns and styles of other artists offers you expansive choices in your own work.

SKETCHBOOK PROJECTS

Over a period of a week make a collection of drawings, filling a single page of your sketchbook with multiple drawings before you move on to the next page.

PROJECT 1

Crowding the Picture Plane

This will be a composition in which you crowd the surface with a great number of images (see *figure 8.2*). They can be totally unrelated, recognizable, abstract, and nonobjective. Overlap and overlay images; turn your paper from time to time so the orientation of the drawing is not always the same. Try not to think in terms of top, bottom, or sides.

After you have crowded the page with drawings, impose some minimal order by use of value or by connecting lines and shapes. Make several of these composite compositions in your sketchbook. When you fill one page, proceed to the next. Think of these drawings as visual diaries; the imagery and thoughts contained in them could be taken from your hour-to-hour experiences.

PROJECT 2

Attention to the Edge

Choose one page of the drawings done in the preceding exercise and using some correction fluid (like Liquid Paper or Wite-Out), gesso, white acrylic, or tracing paper, cover the center part of the page, leaving the images showing around the edges. Apply the transparent paper or white paint so that faint images from the original drawing show through. Integrate the center with the edges.

PROJECT 3

Divided Picture Plane

Use masking tape to block out a grid of four or six equal segments or a linear division of three or more units. Leave the masking tape intact and proceed as in Project 1, filling the page with drawings done over several drawing sessions. Do not confine the drawings to the delineated segments; draw over the full page, over the masking tape and paper. When an interesting texture develops, remove the masking tape to reveal the underlying white negative lines of the grid.

COMPUTER PROJECT

PROJECT 1

Using Superimposed, Layered Images

Overlaying and superimposing images is a technique that is easily done on the computer. Create three or four different compositions of linear images on the computer; use different subjects and different sizes for each composition. Print the compositions, overlaying them on the same sheet of paper; that is, run the same sheet of paper through the printer for each different composition. Use light ink for the first printing and a different color, value, and texture for the second printing. Continue to print layer after layer until you have achieved a satisfactory solution.

Printing on transparencies (using the same procedure as described above) is another way of trying out ideas for superimposed images. Print several pages of images on transparencies (check what transparencies your printer requires). Overlay the printed sheets of acetate on a piece of white paper to see the results. You can juggle the layers for different effects. Try placing the darkest images on the lower level, the lightest on top; then reverse the procedure. Scan and print several of the most successful arrangements. Hand-color some of the images with felt-tip pen. Even with a black-and-white printer, you can make successful compositions using transparent superimposed images. Vary line quality, value, and texture for the various levels. You can add areas of wash either before or after printing the overlaid images. Print your final selections on a good quality, 100 percent cotton rag paper.

CHAPTER 10

If something is meaningful, maybe it's more meaningful said ten times. If something is absurd, it is much more exaggerated, much more absurd if it's repeated. —EVA HESSE

Thematic Development

DEVELOPING A BODY OF RELATED WORK

The emphasis in a thematic series is on process rather than product: Thematic drawings present options. Since they are an open-ended body of work, they provide a way to express more ideas and variations than is possible in a single drawing. Nothing can better illustrate the number of compositional and stylistic variations on a given subject than a set of connected drawings.

Thematic drawings have the power to point out similarities and differences. They reveal the artistic process at work, they expose patterns, and they explore creative thought. A thematic series allows you to go into your own work with more involvement and greater concentration, and you learn to work more independently, setting your own pace.

A first step toward developing thematic drawings is to look at the way other artists have handled a theme in their works. This chapter discusses three themes: word and image; the figure/body art/portraiture; and appropriation.

WORD AND IMAGE

A thematic thread that weaves through art is the relationship between word and image. The drawn image, of course, preceded the written word, but as soon as writing developed, image and word were solidly united, each serving to amplify the other. Even this tradition has been undermined by contemporary artists such as Richard Prince in his appropriation of existing images and texts *(figure 10.1)*. Prince uses jokes from the 1950s and 1960s as captions to accompany found images from the period. The words and image misfire and malfunction, each subverting the other.

The most basic connection between the pairing of words and images is found in the role a title plays in a work of art; traditionally the title gives a reference point for the understanding of the work. Sol LeWitt points out the dissolving boundaries between title and image and between art and design in his work *(figure 10.2)*. His

What a kid I was. I remember practicing the violin in front of a roaring fire. My old man walked in. He was furious. We didn't have a fireplace.

10.1. **RICHARD PRINCE.** *What a Kid I Was.* 1989. Acrylic and silkscreen on canvas, 68" x 48" (172.7 cm x 121.9 cm). © *Richard Prince. Courtesy Gladstone Gallery, New York, RP603.*

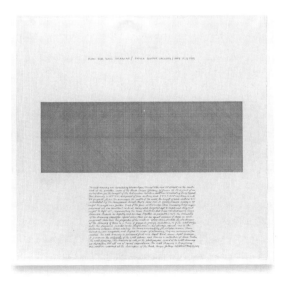

10.2. **SOL LEWITT.** *Plan for Wall Drawing.* 1969. Pen and ink, and pencil on paper. 20⅞" x 20¾". *D.S. and R.H. Gottsman Foundation, The Museum of Modern Art. Photo Credit: Digital Image © The Museum of Modern Art/Licensed by SCALA/Art Resource, NY.*

plan for a wall drawing includes title and drawing as well as instructions for making the drawing, all on the same picture plane. LeWitt's work deals with process and product, both of which are fully explicit in this multi-layered drawing.

In the 1970s and 1980s, the relationship between word and image underwent explosive changes. Conceptual artists led the way in asserting the primacy of words and written documents as stand-ins for the actual art objects. Joseph Kosuth's title (used for more than one work) *Art as Idea as Idea* accompanied an enlargement of the dictionary definition of the word *idea*. In *figure 10.3*, he presents three ways of perceiving and conceiving an object: An actual suitcase is placed in front of a photograph of a suitcase and a dictionary definition of a suitcase.

Neither the isolated text nor the isolated object nor the copy of the image provides the ultimate meaning; it is the combination (or disjunction) of the three that generates new and different meanings.

In Surrealism, the subconscious furnishes irrational associations for the artist. Tom Sale disrupts rational thinking by presenting the viewer with visual/verbal paradoxes. In his *Self-Study Primer (figure 10.4)*, images are juxtaposed with words that give clues to interpret the drawing. In one drawing, a fishing lure with an eyehook is combined with a centralized image of teeth; the single word written in a style akin to that in a handwriting manual reads "pacify." The second panel in the triptych includes a rocket, a fingertip bone, a pencil, and the words "distal phalanx."

From the title, *Self-Study Primer*, we know that these drawings are lessons, a symbolic self-portrait. Two of the boards contain images that refer to seeing: the

10.3. JOSEPH KOSUTH. *One and Three Valises.* 1965. Photograph, actual wooden valise, dictionary definition. *Courtesy Sean Kelly Gallery, New York.*

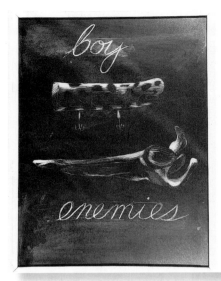

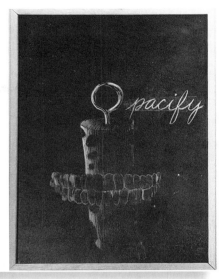

eyehook on the fishing lure (two visual/verbal puns). In the third drawing, a face is made of objects: rocket-eyes, bone-nose, pencil-mouth. Pointers direct where to look, lures intrigue, eyehooks grab, rockets destroy, pencils create, teeth bite lures. We see the makings of a story in these incongruent images and words.

Ed Ruscha uses the word itself as image. In *figure 10.5*, the word *chop* has been turned into an illusionistically three-dimensional object; the word seems to be constructed from a streamer of paper folding and turning in perspectival space. After intense concentration on the word, we finally begin to lose the sense of its meaning, and see it as an object.

A second drawing by Ruscha will extend our understanding of his strategy. This time word and image work together to create a visual and verbal double entendre *(figure 10.6)*. The words are negative to the ghostly image behind them. The statement "Brave Men Run in My Family" can be taken on at least two levels: The men are either brave or they run away. The ship supports both interpretations, but it is an impossibility to hold both in mind simultaneously. A third level presents the ghostly Ship of Romanticism fading in the fog.

10.6. EDWARD RUSCHA. *Brave Men Run in My Family.* 1988. Dry pigment on paper, 5' x 3'4" (1.524 m x 1.022 m). *Collection Richard Salmon, London. © Paul Ruscha.*

Some postmodern artists work in a more clearly defined narrative mode. Dotty Attie insinuates messages beneath the surfaces of old masters' paintings. Her goal is to unveil secrets through recombining segments of the work with invented stories *(figure 10.7)*. By focusing on details that are secondary in the actual work (such as hands, feet, and glances), Attie subverts the original meaning and implies through her texts that the old masters themselves are involved in secret schemes and cover-ups. She generally works in small, six-inch-square units arranged sequentially, either horizontally or in grids. She painstakingly and convincingly copies not only the image but also the original brush strokes.

10.7. DOTTY ATTIE. *Barred from the Studio.* 1987. Oil on canvas, 11" x 2'10" (28 cm x 86 cm) overall. *P.P.O.W., New York.*

   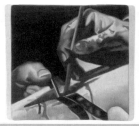 

Combining details from two different paintings by the nineteenth-century American artist Thomas Eakins, Attie insinuates a disreputable story. We are aware of the art history context from which the images are taken; the artist creates a disjunction by removing them from that frame of reference and offering us another view.

The text in the initial frame reads: "Barred from the studio while male models were posing, female art students were placed in a corridor where a small window provided a distant view of the sitter's back." This is a fact of the actual practice of art schools of the time, but the following two narrative fragments leave viewers to draw their own conclusions concerning exactly what Eakins did that was so shocking in trying to rectify the situation. The second and fourth squares are bloody details taken from Eakins's painting *The Gross Clinic*; these, combined with the famous image of Eakins's oarsman, leave us in a quandary. The figure's central position and his intent gaze offer some clues to the underlying message. Looking, gazing, seeing, close inspection, close-up views, being barred from looking—these activities are either explicitly or implicitly stated in verbal and visual images throughout the six-part narrative. We can surmise that voyeurism itself is the subject of the work. Voyeurism operates on several levels in the images: The oarsman returns the viewer's gaze; the viewer is implicated by looking at the gory details; both artists, Eakins and Attie, are involved in the voyeuristic activity of making art.

The handmade artist book bridges the categories of the machine-produced book and contemporary art (see Dottie Love, *figure 6.7*). In 2005, Susan Marie Dopp created 52 handmade books, a page a day, for a year *(figure 10.8)*. It is clear from her project that the thematic aspect is in the process of daily artmaking. Related to one-of-a-kind artist books are altered and manipulated books, an example of which is the collaborative effort of several artists—Marshall Weber, Mark Wagner, and Amy Mees. In their found album titled *Souvenir (figure 10.9)*, images are manipulated and faces are blocked out and replaced by words.

10.8. **SUSAN MARIE DOPP.** *Every Day Books.* 2005. 52 handmade books, various dimensions, one page made every day in 2005. *Courtesy Hosfelt Gallery.*

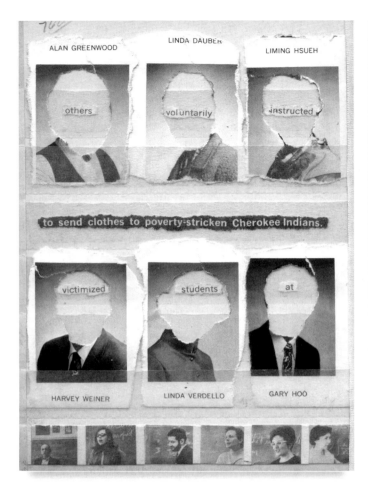

10.9. MARSHALL WEBER. *Souvenir.*
2003. 28 pages on Mohawk Vellum paper and other archival papers and clothes. 8" x 6" (20.5 cm x 15 cm). *Brooklyn Artists Alliance.*

A final example of the word and image theme is the drawing by the conceptual artist Bruce Nauman *(figure 10.10)*. The two words "Face" and "Mask" seem to be hinged together so the mask can flip over and hide the face. Actually, if you view the drawing in a mirror, a reversal takes place: "Face" is properly oriented, and "Mask" is reversed. Nauman presents complex conceptual ideas by minimal means. Like Jasper Johns, Nauman treats the letters as objects themselves' he uses mixed media to make the letters look as if they were chiseled in wood or stone.

In our look at word as image, we have seen that modes differ from artist to artist, but the cross-circuitry between language and images provides a spark for viewer and maker alike. The contemporary issue is not to make illustrative art where picture and text function in tandem to the same ends, but to create combinations that produce resonances between the verbal and the visual that are lacking in each separately.

PROBLEM 10.1

Word and Image

In this problem dealing with word and image, unify a group of thematic drawings by media, technique, and idea. Take your compositional cues from the section called Division of the Picture Plane in Chapter 9.

Create the effect of blackboard and chalk for this series of drawings. Blackboard paint can be purchased in a hardware store or you can use a flat black or dark green

10.10. **BRUCE NAUMAN.** *Face Mask.* 1981. Synthetic polymer paint, charcoal, and pencil on paper, 52¼" x 70⅞". *Acquired with matching funds from The Lauder Foundation and the National Endowment for the Arts. The Museum of Modern Art, New York, New York. © The Museum of Modern Art/Licensed by SCALA, Art Resource, New York. © 2007 Bruce Nauman/Artists Rights Society (ARS), New York.*

latex paint in imitation of a blackboard. Cover a panel (wood or cardboard) with the paint and let it dry overnight before drawing with chalk or pastels. Be sure to use a spray fixative on the final drawings since chalk and pastels erase easily.

Pair a word with an image in each panel; present a visual/verbal paradox using irrational associations. An example of this bizarre pairing is René Magritte's *The Key of Dreams (figure 10.11)*, in which he names a hat "the snow," a shoe "the moon," and a glass "the storm."

PROBLEM 10.2

Frames of Reference

For this problem, select five or six postcards with reproductions of paintings or drawings from art history.

For captions, use found words or fragments of texts, no more than three or four lines each. They can be random sentences from any book on hand. It is your job to create a sequence. Form a narrative or story from the words and images by combining captions and pictures.

Place the postcards face down on the table and let chance determine which text goes with which image. Alter the images with paint or collage, or cut the cards into grids and rearrange the parts. Arrange the text to be a part of the composition. Stencils or rub-on letters are options.

10.11. **RENÉ MAGRITTE.** *The Key of Dreams.* 1930. Oil on canvas, 2'7⅞" x 1'11⅝" (81 cm x 60 cm). *Private collection. Photo Credit: Banque d'Images, ADAGP/Art Resource, NY. © 2007 C. Herscovici, Brussels/Artists Rights Society (ARS), New York.*

PROBLEM 10.3

Pages from an Altered Book

Using a discarded book, manipulate and alter the cover and several double pages, keeping a single theme throughout the project. You can draw, fold, cut, add, or block out images. (See Judy Pfaff's manipulated pages, *figure 6.21.*)

THE FIGURE/BODY ART/PORTRAITURE

The figure (or the body, as it is known in art parlance) has held center stage for artists throughout the 1990s and into the twenty-first century. Contemporary artists employ a number of representational strategies in dealing with the figure. Some artists work directly from life, as did Don Bachardy in the series he made of his dying friend, Christopher Isherwood (see *figure 5.20*). Some portraits are mediated through photography (see Chuck Close *figure II.15*). Close's monumental "heads," as he calls them, of himself, his family, and friends are fixed by the camera. Although verisimilitude to the Polaroid photograph is important to Close, his work is detached and process-driven. His technique is to grid the picture plane by charting each square like a topographical map of the terrain of the sitter's face. Individually, each square is a mini-abstraction.

Alex Katz's work deals with simplification, yet the result is a portrait that remains recognizable both as an individual and as a representative of a privileged class *(figure 10.12)*. In close-up views, Katz uses unmodulated color to create shapes that could easily be cut out and reassembled. Katz works thematically; over the years he has made innumerable portraits of friends and of his wife Ada.

Women artists took the lead in redefining and revalidating the body as subject matter in the 1980s. Male-dominated mainstream traditions of how women's bodies have been depicted have been challenged through women's body art. The Iranian filmmaker Shirin Neshat presents the tensions facing Muslim women in her portrait *Speechless (figure 10.13)*. The silent woman's face is covered with written words in Arabic calligraphy.

Marlene Dumas's interest in portraiture has a social and political purpose. Using a camera to record individual expressions, she then transforms them into universal statements. Her work is a catalog of emotion rather than a mapping of physical likeness. Dumas sees serialization and repetition *(figure 10.14)* as a route to exploring relationships within a group.

Leslie Dill takes an alternative approach to the self-portrait. Her interest in literature carries over into her art. The title *The Soul Has Bandaged Moments . . . (figure 10.15)* is a line from an Emily Dickinson poem. The bandage Dickinson speaks of becomes the skin of the figure; the words are literally made flesh. In an artist's statement Dill writes, "Sometimes I feel skinless. How right to slip inside

10.12. **ALEX KATZ. *Homage to Frank O'Hara: William Dumas.*** 1972. Lithograph, 2'9¼" x 2'1½" (84 cm x 65 cm). *Edition of 90. Courtesy Brooke Alexander Editions, New York. © Alex Katz/Licensed by VAGA, New York/ Marlborough Gallery, New York.*

10.13. **SHIRIN NESHAT.** *Speechless.*
1996. RC print, 3'10¾" x 2'9⅞"
(1.187 m x 86 cm). *© 1996 Shirin
Neshat. Photo taken by Larry Barns. Courtesy
Barbara Gladstone Gallery, New York.*

words, the meaning and the shape of some emotion you're feeling, and go out
into life." She adds, "Maybe we do have words on us, invisible texts we all wear"
(Wolfe and Pasquine, *Large Drawings and Objects*, p. 94). The direct frontal
stance of the figure in this dark, mysterious, life-size drawing suggests vulnerability.
The head disappears into the black charcoal background, leaving the body to
speak for itself.

Through his self-portraits, Francisco Clemente deals with introspection and
mystical intimations. For Clemente, doubleness is a form of unity; *Codice 1* is taken
from a group of pastel studies of 11 double portraits which include objects or
animals (see *figure 1.20*).

The figure, body art, and portraiture are informed by our experiences, beliefs,
and cultural conditioning.

PROBLEM 10.4

Alternate Self-Portrait

Everyday objects can be stand-ins for the self. Common objects present themselves
as familiar companions capable of being transformed. Find one such object that has
special significance for you. Let it be a mirror of yourself. Transform the object with
elements of your own features to create an anthropomorphic image.

PROBLEM 10.5

Self-Portrait in Different Styles

Using a photograph of your head and face, depict yourself in three different styles
on the same picture plane. Find styles from an art history book. You might make a
transparent overlay of a head from the Cubist period or from Pop art; place it over
your photograph and draw the composite face. Use three distinct styles in the final

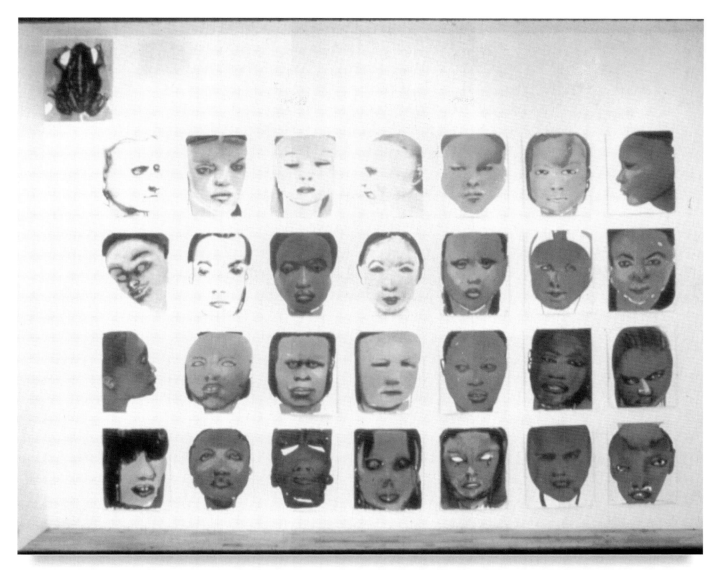

work, actual images by specific artists. Do not concoct a style. Keep your references identifiable.

10.14. **MARLENE DUMAS.** *Betrayal.* 1994. 29 drawings. Ink on paper, 2' x 1'7¾" (61 cm x 50.2 cm) each. Installation view. *Courtesy Jack Tilton/Anna Kustera Gallery, New York.*

PROBLEM 10.6

A Psychological Portrait

Make a double self-portrait, a diptych, in which you present yourself in two different modes, in two states of being.

You will find that in making self-portraits you are presented with a chance to look in two directions at once as you depict your external world as well as your internal self.

Paint, pastels, or watercolor are appropriate for this drawing.

APPROPRIATED IMAGES

A third thematic thread that runs through contemporary art is appropriation. In appropropriation, artists take preexisting images of earlier art and give the image

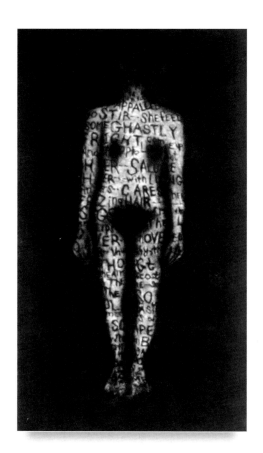

10.15. **LESLIE DILL.** *Untitled (The Soul Has Bandaged Moments)*. 1994. Charcoal on paper, 73 in. x 48 in. *Arkansas Arts Center Foundation Collection: Purchase, Tabriz Fund. 1995.008.*

new meaning. Appropriation of images as a dominant strategy entered the art scene in the 1980s and is still alive and strong today. Artists appropriate images not only from art history but also from mass media.

Andy Warhol meets Leonardo da Vinci in Josef Levi's two Lizs *(figure 10.16)*. Mona Lisa's face harks back to her origins in the Italian Renaissance with its

10.16. **JOSEF LEVI.** *Still Life with Warhol and Leonardo.* 1993. Acrylic and graphic on canvas, 3'1" x 4' (94 cm x 1.22 m). *O.K. Harris Works of Art, New York.*

chiaroscuro, idealized features, and smooth brush strokes. Levi even imitates the aged cracked surface of the painting. The second Liz is a pop icon from the 1960s. The style suggests commercial techniques. Disjunction and disorientation, appropriation and irony, criticism and humor are found in these two clashing symbols.

Other artists who make use of appropriation are Baechler, Hammond, Hurson, and Souza (see the index to find their work shown in this book). They are among many artists who have taken subjects from earlier art and given them new meaning. Paul Giovanopoulos presents an art history exam in his 25 units of apple conversions *(figure 10.17)*. How many artists and styles can you identify?

PROBLEM 10.7

Appropriation—An Art History Homage

Choose as your subject a work from art history. Make a series of sketches with the work as a point of departure. Use a contemporary compositional format taken from Chapter 9.

Change the meaning of your appropriated image by transforming it into a scientific, secular, or religious context. The use of grids and other contemporary devices, such as collage or photomontage, will give your subject a contemporary look.

You might crop the original image and blow up a detail of the work. In keeping with the postmodern technique of overlaid images, you might use this strategy in your work. In any case, keep the source of your subject apparent to the viewer.

10.17. **PAUL GIOVANOPOULOS.** *Apple-Léger.* 1985. Mixed media on canvas, 5' x 3'4" (1.524 m x 1.016 m).
Louis K. Meisel Gallery, New York. Photo by Steve Lopez.

A Series of Opposites

We have seen how contemporary artists frequently create a feeling of disjunction by placing together two dissimilar objects. In this series you are to choose one object that will appear in each drawing. With that recurring image, juxtapose another object that will either amplify or cancel the first object's meaning or function.

In Gael Crimmins's *Spout (figure 10.18)*, the source of the painting within the painting is Piero della Francesca's fifteenth-century portrait of the Duke of Urbino. The small portrait is combined with a milk carton that is analogous to the duke's profile. This pairing points to the richness of the old contrasted to a consumer world with its habits of use and discard.

SUMMARY

Sometimes an artist works with an idea in different media and in different styles, yet the theme is constant. In other artists' work, the theme is the result of a stylistic consistency, and the imagery is changed from piece to piece.

Here are some variables to help you in structuring your thematic series:

- subject matter, imagery, or motif
- media or material
- technique
- style
- organization of the picture plane
- use of space (determined by how you use line, shape, color, texture, and value)
- scale

This chapter presented thematic drawings and how artists develop and handle a theme in their work. The three themes presented were word and image, the figure/body art/portraiture, and appropriation. Before you begin developing and incorporating themes into your work, find a theme that is important to you. Each

10.18. GAEL CRIMMINS. *Spout (after Piero della Francesca, Duke of Urbino).* 1983. Oil on paper, 1'10" x 1'10½" (56 cm x 57 cm). *Private collection, Los Angeles. Photo by Susan Einstein/Hunsaker-Schlesinger Gallery, Los Angeles.*

drawing should suggest new ideas for succeeding drawings. An artist must observe, distinguish, and relate; these three steps are essential in developing thematic work.

Review these actions in making a series:

- Build
- Reshape
- Mediate
- Manipulate
- Edit
- Arrange
- Select
- Modify
- Change
- Reflect
- Correct
- Reinvent
- Look
- Think
- Concentrate
- Transform
- Abstract
- Describe
- Focus

Once you have reviewed and considered these actions, consider yourself one step closer to developing your own unique theme.

SKETCHBOOK PROJECTS

Collecting ideas is a continuing process for the artist. Thematic series can evolve from simple sources.

PROJECT **1**

Visual and Verbal Descriptions

Over a two-week period set yourself the task of drawing single, individual objects. You are to draw from life. After you have made the first drawing of the object, look at it again. You no doubt have a different perception of it now than before you drew the first study.

Next, you are to write about the object. Your writing should be as descriptive as possible. After writing an accurate description, introduce metaphors and allusions. What is the object like? What does it remind you of? How does it make you feel? What associations with other objects, memories, or events does it evoke?

A personal, unedited response is valuable in doing this project. If you want to make lists of words or use sentence fragments or try your hand at poetry, do not feel intimidated. You are trying to construct a personal, comprehensive, perceptual, and conceptual response to the object. The goal is to expand the way you look at and interpret the world. A fresh, open-ended, unexpected response is what you are after.

After drawing and writing about the object, make a second drawing of it. Compare the first and second drawings. How has the graphic concept changed? How did writing about the object inform and affect your second drawing?

Juxtaposition of Word and Image

Reverse the order of the preceding exercise. Begin with a written description, follow with a drawing, and conclude with a second written response.

Words can alter the way we perceive an image and, reciprocally, images can change the meaning of words. Juxtapositions of words and images can produce resonances between them that can jolt our perceptions. This exercise can result in a reinvestment of meaning in the most common of objects.

Reduce your verbal description and responses to a single word. Pair that word with a drawn object. Word and image may or may not derive from the same object. Note the influence the single word has on the object. Try for multiple effects by changing the word but retaining the same drawn object.

COMPUTER PROJECT

PROJECT 1

Transformation Using Computer-Generated Images

The process of drawing with a computer is closely related to design; however, the distinction between drawing and design is that in design there are stated problems to solve and goals to be met. In this drawing you are to respond to what you see on the computer screen, allowing the image to govern what happens next. Do not let preconceptions interfere with the process.

Use a program that allows input from a digital camera or scanner to capture the image; alter it, converting the image to lines, dots, or value shapes. Make a concentrated search for interesting images. Old science textbooks or magazines might be a good source. A grid can be manipulated to create interesting backgrounds. Stretch, distort, enlarge, and crop your chosen image on the computer. Include words in your composition. Various typefaces also come with computer programs; these, too, can be manipulated, altered, enlarged, and cropped. Even isolated letters or numbers can be used as images.

Print the computer-generated drawings; then photocopy them, enlarging or reducing the composition to an appropriate scale. Consider making the drawings some size other than the standard 8 by 11 inches. A square or long, narrow, vertical, or horizontal format might be more interesting since it is not the expected computer printout size. In addition, working with different-shaped picture planes is more challenging and will sharpen your computer skills.

Take a page out of Danielle Fagan's book *(figure 10.19)* and make a book out of your computer designs. Artists' books do not follow the traditional format of printed books—they can have a limited number of pages, each page can be on different paper, and the ink can be any color. You can dispense with a title page and end sheets, although these conventional book parts offer space for real creative manipulation. The book can be bound using a spiral binding or a plastic slip-on binding, both of which are sold in copy shops. The pages can be stapled or sewn together or they can be placed in a handmade box. You can even recycle a cover from an old book. There are dozens of options for presentation.

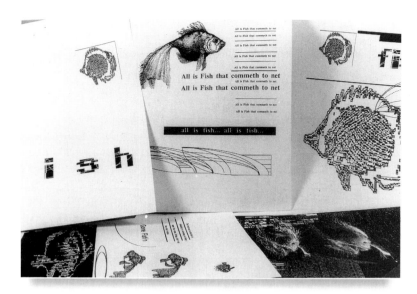

10.19. **DANIELLE FAGAN.** *Fish Book.*
1990. Computer-generated book, 8½"
x 11" (21.6 cm x 28 cm). *Collection of
the artist. Photo by Dottie Love.*

Fish Book was produced entirely on a computer following the steps outlined above. Fagan manipulated an image of a fish by stretching, compressing, enlarging, deleting, compiling, and combining with some found texts referring to fish. She altered a grid to become a net, which she printed in red ink on clear acetate. The gridded net image is dispersed throughout the book as if to catch the fish on the pages that lie beneath the acetate. Blue paper is used for some of the pages, an obvious reference to water.

Fagan says the fish is a metaphor for the artist who might "fall prey to the fishermen or be trapped on the outer isles." She recommends a metaphorical summer as a good time to go fishing—fishing for new ideas, images, questions, and answers.

One final comment: Computers can be helpful tools for artists, especially for beginning students because more sophisticated images can be used at an early stage of a student's career. Frequently, beginning students want to produce more involved work than their hand skills permit. Many variations can quickly be made on the computer; you do not have to imagine what an image or a composition would look like if, for example, it were bigger, blue, moved to the left, doubled, or turned sideways. The computer can turn your "what ifs" into concrete form. Computers are experimental tools; they can be freeing; images can be discarded and retrieved easily. But computer art does have a "sneaky" aesthetic and process all its own. It is important not to buy into it completely. In the hands of an artist with a good foundation in art, computers can be helpful aids, and the resulting drawings can be exciting, creative, and personal.

CHAPTER 11

Do not define today. Define backward and forward, spatial and many-sided. A defined today is over and done for. —PAUL KLEE

A Look at Drawing Today

WHAT'S NEW IN THE TWENTY-FIRST CENTURY

More inclusive than any other art form, drawing is the most dynamic category in the twenty-first century. Throughout this book, we have pointed to drawing's elemental character as well as to its conceptual and theoretical role. In contemporary art, drawing serves multiple functions. Drawing is valued as an image generator, as a means of improvising, and as a register of social, political, and cultural commentary. Drawing is capable of mapping both the visible and invisible worlds, of recording intensely private moments, of conveying ideas of time and space, and of telling stories. And drawing can be done anywhere; neither studio nor expensive tools are required.

Artists in the 1960s and 1970s laid the groundwork for a less restricted approach to drawing. The 1980s and 1990s were even more receptive to the role that drawing played in the discourse of contemporary art. As the critic, curator, and editor Emma Dexter has written, "The current resurgence in drawing in recent years is perhaps the first moment in history when artists can opt for drawing as their principal medium, confident in the knowledge it will

240

not suffer in status as a result" (Emma Dexter, *Vitamin D: New Perspectives in Drawing*, 2005, p. 8). Dexter marks the mid-1990s as the time when artists began expanding the boundaries of drawing and taking it in new directions, when drawing became "a primary mode of expression for the more inventive and influential artists of the time" (Dexter, p. 8).

Over the past decade, drawing has taken a prominent place in the ever-growing number of international and biennial exhibits (currently there are over 200 such biennials worldwide). Particularly among the younger generation of artists, drawing is a primary medium. Deborah Singer, one of the curators of the 2004 Whitney Biennial, states, "Following a period of slick, high-performance art-making, artists are returning to more direct and immediate modes of working" ("Whitney Biennial," *Art on Paper*, March–April 2004, p. 14).

In a time of political, economic, and social instability, when no single stylistic or aesthetic mode holds claim over another, it comes as no surprise that artists respond by employing images and strategies that are also in flux. An acquaintance with current issues will increase your knowledge of art and provide a reservoir that will strengthen your work.

CONTEMPORARY TRENDS IN DRAWING

In previous chapters we have discussed new approaches to drawing, so you are already familiar with many current developments and techniques. We will now look at some categories that cover the terrain of drawing in the twenty-first century. Some artists appear in more than one category. These groupings are not meant to limit, but to offer a way to begin to sort through the many directions drawing is taking at the moment.

Influence of Outsider Art

The critic Lyle Rexer, writing about outsider art (works done by untrained artists), claims that "the art forms [that] challenge the very definitions of Western art, not to mention mainstream taste, [have] become part of the wallpaper of contemporary visual culture" (Rexer, *How to Look at Outsider Art*, 2005, p. 166). Outsider art is definitely insider art when it comes to popularity with artists and collectors. Through their contact with outsider art, many artists have experienced a profound effect on their work. Obsessive linear drawing and repeated patterning, so characteristic of outsider art, has found its way into much contemporary art.

James Siena's drawings are related to outsider work in their elaboration of detail. Siena's small-scale drawings are constructed of a repeated motif resulting in an abstract pattern *(figure 11.1)*. *Double Recursive Combs (Red and Black)* is subtly activated by a sagging and warping of the forms to create a spatial illusion. In outsider art, this multiple elaboration is called "obsessive-compulsive"; in contemporary art it is referred to as "spatial sequencing." Siena's drawings, like outsider art, devote equal attention to each element; the apparent sameness of treatment binds the work together and becomes a meditative focus.

Many artists, such as Jockum Nordström *(figure 11.2)* and Jean-Michel Basquiat (see *figure 1.14*), imitate the naïveté of outsider art, mining it for its expressive, raw look. Idiosyncratic subjects are another shared link between self-taught artists and contemporary artists.

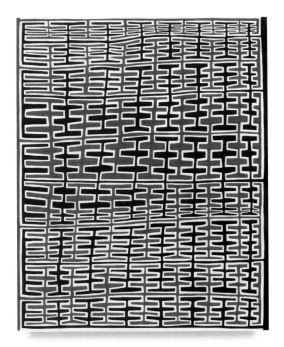

11.1. **JAMES SIENA.** *Double Recursive Combs (Red and Black).* 2004–2005. Gouache on paper, 11" x 8½" (28 cm x 22 cm). © *James Siena, courtesy Pace Wildenstein, New York. Photo by: Kerry Ryan McFate, courtesy Pace Wildenstein, New York +M288.*

11.2. **JOCKUM NORDSTRÖM.** *The Four Cardinal Points.* 2001. Mixed media and collage, 48⅝" x 34¼" (123.5 cm x 87 cm). *Zwirner Gallery, New York. © 2007 Artists Rights Society (ARS), New York/BUS, Stockholm.*

Illustration-Based Narrative Drawing

Narrative tendencies continue their stronghold on today's art with a return to more expressive themes. Myth, storytelling, folklore, and fantasy provide resident forms for artists such as Nordström, an illustrator of children's books and a maker of animated films. Nordic folktales from his native Sweden fuel his work, but the strange spatial composition is Nordström's own invention. His collage can be oriented to any of the four cardinal points; the center seems to collapse in on itself. Nordström's faux-naïve style supports his view of the world, culturally conditioned but personally expressive.

Kara Walker uses silhouettes as elements in her narrative tableaux derived from antebellum slave sources from African-American history (see *figure 9.20*). The paper cutouts subvert the clichés concerning the slave era and retell a starker history. "Silhouette looks so clear-cut, so crisp, it operates just as derogatory stereotypes do, making a reduction out of a real person" (Elizabeth Hayt, "Simple, Austere, an Old Genre Is Daringly New," *New York Times*, November 16, 1997. AR 51).

Ornamental Embellishment

Pattern and decoration artists of the 1970s led the way in making a style of ornamental embellishment.

Chris Ofili employs a repeated pattern of dots to create a stylized portrait of a regal African woman *(figure 11.3)*. The simple design harks back to Art Deco and Art Nouveau; underlying the decidedly contemporary figure are delicately drawn leaves and flowers. Ofili's self-stated goal is to break down hierarchical looking and making.

11.3. **CHRIS OFILI.** *Untitled (Woman).* 2000. Pencil on paper, 30" x 22" (76 cm x 56 cm). *Courtesy Chris Ofili-Afroco & Victoria Miro Gallery.*

11.4. **AMY CUTLER.** *Octavia.* 2005. *Leslie Tonkonow Art Works and Projects, 535 West 22nd St. New York City.*

Neo-Romantic Drawing

The drawings by Amy Cutler are like visual fairy tales. In Cutler's allegories, women are thwarted by unwelcome intrusions, such as stitching up sleeping tigers, making camping tents from their long dresses, and bearing exotic burdens *(figure 11.4)*. With their delicate patterning and their eighteenth-century fashions, Cutler's drawings also qualify for the Ornamental Embellishment category. It is a surprise to learn that Cutler's scenes don't strictly adhere to eighteenth-century themes. Viewers will find references to current events such as the hunt for Saddam Hussein and reality-based television programs in her work.

Shahzia Sikander (see *color plate 7.3*), like Cutler, updates traditional conventions in her contemporary versions of Persian miniatures. East meets West, classical bumps into postmodern in Sikander's jewel-like versions. Again, Sikander's work fits into the Ornamental Embellishment category. Artists like Cutler and Sikander propose a new way of looking at old techniques.

Abstraction

The idea that the essence of art is abstract still holds with artists such as Richard Tuttle, who makes objects that combine drawing, sculpture, and painting *(figure 11.5)*. His quiet, tender works made from mundane materials—Styrofoam, cord, wire, sticks, and lined notebook paper—are childlike yet sophisticated. For Tuttle, drawing is integral to all his work. He effects transformations with a delicate touch and a sure eye; the results are elegant, refined, and minimal.

Daniel Zeller's intricate drawings (see *color plate 7.13*) are of "imaginary places and systems that don't actually exist" (John Yau, "Intricate Worlds," *Art on Paper*, March–April 2004, p. 40). Zeller says he derives his images from "satellite images, electron micrographs, topographical maps, anatomical and schematic diagrams— representations which might be generally categorized as two dimensional translations of the three dimensional world" (Yau, p. 40).

We are nearly as involved in looking at Zeller's work as he is in making it.

11.5. **RICHARD TUTTLE.** *Space-is-Concrete, (19).* 2005. Acrylic and graphite on spun plastic with metal thumbtacks, 36" x 20" (91.4 cm x 60 cm). *Private Collection. Courtesy Sperone Westwater, New York.*

Alternative Worlds

As the poet and art critic Barry Schwabsky has noted, "Rational planning and utopian fantasy have always been surprisingly difficult to disentangle. Both take form, above all, in drawing" (Barry Schwabsky, "Drawing on the New Town: Chad McCail and Paul Noble," *Art on Paper*, July–August 2000, p. 34). This quote describes the subject matter of many contemporary artists whose work deals with alternative worlds. Their drawings represent imaginary, other-worldly architectural spaces (see *figure 8.21*). They challenge the traditional boundaries of drawing in their looming, massively-scaled work. In *figure 11.6*, Noble combines ancient ruins with science-fiction structures. Julie Mehretu, in building her alternative worlds, incorporates computer images with architectural plans and elevations. Her sources are wide ranging; fragments and details of both historical and contemporary structures weave in and out of an explosion of textures suggesting meteorological diagrams of storms, rain, clouds, fire, and smoke (see *figure 1.2*).

In contrast to the utopian stance of Noble and Mehretu is Trenton Doyle Hancock's dystopian view, with its perspectival frenzy and anthropomorphic creatures *(figure 11.7)*. The leaking universe with its conic accretions and knobby body parts is one we would hesitate to enter. Hancock's art illustrates a convoluted, mind-bending narrative full of densely congested images, an escape into pure fantasy.

Subcultures into Art

Vernacular illustrations from the subcultures responsible for graffiti art, comic strips, tattoo catalogs, and the like have crossed over into the mainstream of art.

11.6. **PAUL NOBLE.** *Ye Olde Ruin.* 2003–04. Pencil on paper, 426 cm x 732 cm. *Courtesy Maureen Paley, London.*

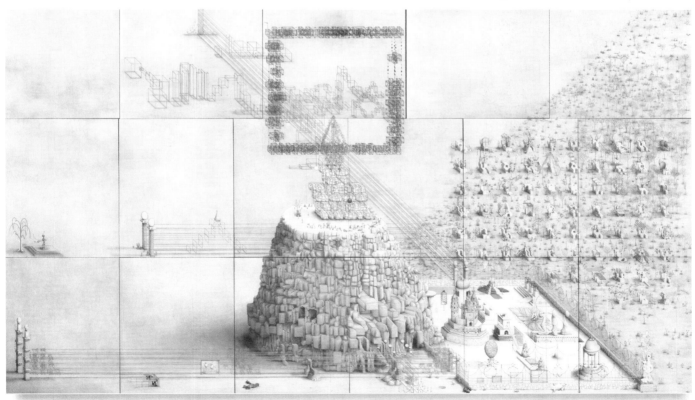

11.7. **TRENTON DOYLE HANCOCK.** *In the Blestian Room.* 2005. Mixed Media, 90" x 108" x 6". *James Cohan Gallery, New York.*

Since the 1950s, artists have been playing with the possibility of comic strip imagery and technique. Popular comics and advertisements were Pop Art's aesthetic forbearers. Raymond Pettibon (see *figure 8.3*), one of today's preeminent draftsmen, led the charge in the 1970s in breaking the barriers between so-called high and low art.

Incongruous as it seems, Mehretu is an artist who incorporates popular imagery into her drawings. Some of her sources are skateboarder magazines, computer games, game plans for the National Football League, and tattoo designs.

Japanese animated cartoons, called *anime*, have been particularly influential on art and design worldwide. Yoshitomo Nara is an artist whose imagery derives from this popular subculture.

Nostalgia

Many artists today, like Mary Snowden, establish a mood of nostalgia in their work. Snowden satirizes a woman's role as homemaker while using recollected images, products, and fashions from the 1940s and 1950s. In *figure 11.9*, Little Orphan Annie is burdened with dishes. She stands in sharp contrast to the apprehensive group on the right. Snowden's jig-saw puzzle shapes together fragments from the past to reproduce the look of old magazines. Snowden's characters, like Orphan Annie and Little Lulu, use their feminine skills to emerge as victors.

D-L Alvarez's nostalgic theme takes a different course. Alvarez makes drawings from archival photographs *(figure 11.10)*, drawings that depict the collapse of cultural ideals. The drawing shown here deals with the "Manson family" murders of

11.8. **YOSHITOMO NARA.** *OH! MY GOD! I MISS YOU.* 2001. Synthetic polymer paint and pencil on printed paper, 20" x 14". *© The Museum of Modern Art/ Licensed by SCALA/Art Resource, New York.*

11.9. **MARY SNOWDEN.** *Annie's Chores.* 2000. Five-color lithograph, $^{15}/_{15}$, 21" x 37$^{3}/_{8}$". *Mildred Lane Kemper Art Museum, Washington University in St. Louis. University purchase, St. Louis Printmarket Fund, 2001.*

11.10. **D-L ALVAREZ.** © \. 2003. Pencil on paper, 38¾" x 27½". *Fund for the Twenty-First Century, NY, USA. Digital Image © The Museum of Modern Art/Licensed by SCALA/Art Resource.*

the late 1960s. Alvarez pictures one of the Manson family members just before the murders take place to highlight the moment when the nation's innocence turns to tragedy. The grid format conveys the idea of breakup; nostalgia itself is caught in the act of disappearing.

Drawings with Social and Political Themes

Chrissie Iles, a curator for both the 2004 and 2006 Whitney Biennial, observed, "There's quite an apocalyptic mood at the moment. . . . I think in the last Biennial [2004], there was a sense of escapism, introspection, and grief. This time it's very different" (Calvin Tomkins, "How American Is It?," *The New Yorker*, March 13, 2006, p. 54).

Drawing provides a voice for dissent, as seen in the ongoing wall installation by Emily Prince *(figure 11.11)*. Prince's drawing, *All the American Servicemen and Women Who Have Died in Iraq, But Not Including the Wounded Nor the Iraqis*, is made up of more than 2,000 thumbnail drawings of American service soldiers killed in Iraq. These small portraits are attached to a map of the United States locating the hometowns of the soldiers.

The impact of violence and war is less geographically specific in Steve DiBenedetto's drawing, which describes a scene of disaster with a brutally entangled helicopter and Ferris wheel *(figure 11.12)*. Since 2000, DiBenedetto has retained the same motifs that have in common rotating elements—helicopters, carousels, and octopi. They are all on a collision course with their whirring, centrifugally spinning blades and arms. In other works, background details, such as palm trees and minarets, provide clues that the artist is referring to the war in the Middle East.

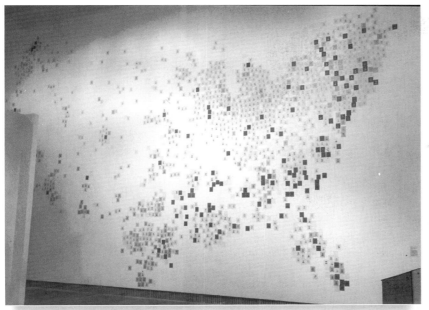

11.11. EMILY PRINCE. *All the American Servicemen and Women Who Have Died in Iraq, But Not Including the Wounded, Nor the Iraqis.* 2005. 1,894 drawings on paper, each 4" x 3½" (10 cm x 9 cm). *Original photo from www.militarycity.com.*

Hand-Drawn Animation

A March 2006 show at the Drawing Center in New York exhibited work by 18 artists who make films in which the movement is hand-drawn frame by frame. The technique of the South African filmmaker William Kentridge involves the labor-intensive making of thousands of drawings photographed in stop-action after each modification *(figure 11.13)*. His charcoal and pastel drawings are always in a state of change; every drawing contains a residual memory of the previous drawing and becomes a palimpsest for subsequent drawings. Kentridge calls his films a portrait of Johannesburg, the landscape and social background for his political and social narratives. His subject is the lasting scars of apartheid.

11.12. STEVE DIBENEDETTO. *Hover and Crash.* 2005. Charcoal pencil on paper, 19¾" x 27¾" (50 cm x 70.5 cm).

11.13. **WILLIAM KENTRIDGE.** *Drawing from Stereoscope.* 1999. Charcoal and pastel on paper, 3'11¼" x 5'3" (1.20 m x 1.60 m). *Courtesy Goodman Gallery, Johannesburg, South Africa.*

Drawings Made from Direct Observation

Postmodern art was characterized as being art about pictures, images derived from photographs, with appropriation as the prevailing mode. And its dominant mood is irony. For postmodern artists, recontextualization is the ruling strategy. Contemporary artists such as Ugo Rondinone (see *figure 4.25*) have made a decisive return to drawing directly from nature. Rondinone's mural-sized drawings are enlargements made from on-site sketches. Painstaking observation is required for his complex black-and-white drawings. While Rondinone revives old-master techniques, the results, which resemble photographic negatives, are a twenty-first-century *tour de force.*

Joan Linder also draws from life, making finished ink "tree portraits" on-site *(figure 11.14)*. The nature of her medium requires a sureness of touch and a concentration of vision. Some of her drawings nearly match the height, up to 17 feet, of the tree itself. Linder allows insects and other material that happen to fall on the paper to remain as part of the work. In another series of on-site works, she depicted the contents of her grandmother's apartment, drawing every day for two months.

CONCLUSION

We have seen how drawing is a mirror of the artist's actions, how it is a means of self-exploration and concentration, how it hones perception, and how it encompasses our daily lives. Drawing is open for artists to make of it what they choose.

Literacy is the ability to decode words. *Visual literacy* is the ability to decode images—the capacity to discover in them meaning and knowledge about ourselves and our world.

11.14. **JOAN LINDER.** *Untitled (Orange Tree).* 2004. Ink on paper, 86½" x 24" (2.20 m x 61 cm). *Mixed Greens Gallery.*

In his novel *The Captive*, Marcel Proust writes, "The only true voyage of discovery, the only really rejuvenating experience would not be to visit strange lands, but to possess other eyes, to see the universe through the eyes of another, of a hundred others, to see the hundred universes that each of them sees." Art offers that voyage of discovery.

USEFUL WEBSITES

Listed below are websites of major art museums. These are helpful in keeping abreast of contemporary developments in art. You can access these collections by theme, name of art objects, and name of artist. This provides a research library in your home. You can explore collections or take a virtual tour at some of these sites. Further, you can Google any contemporary artist for additional information.

- The Tate Galleries, www.tate.org.uk
- The Louvre, www.louvre.fr
- Los Angeles Museum of Contemporary Art, www.moca.org
- Museo Nacional del Prado, Madrid, http://museoprado.mcu.es
- The Rijks Museum, Amsterdam, www.rijksmuseum.nl
- Centre Pompidou, Paris, www.centrepompidou.fr
- San Francisco Museum of Modern Art, www.sfmoma.org
- The Getty Museum, www.getty.edu
- The Metropolitan Museum of Art, New York, www.metmuseum.org
- The Museum of Modern Art, New York, www.moma.org
- The Drawing Center, New York, www.drawingcenter.org

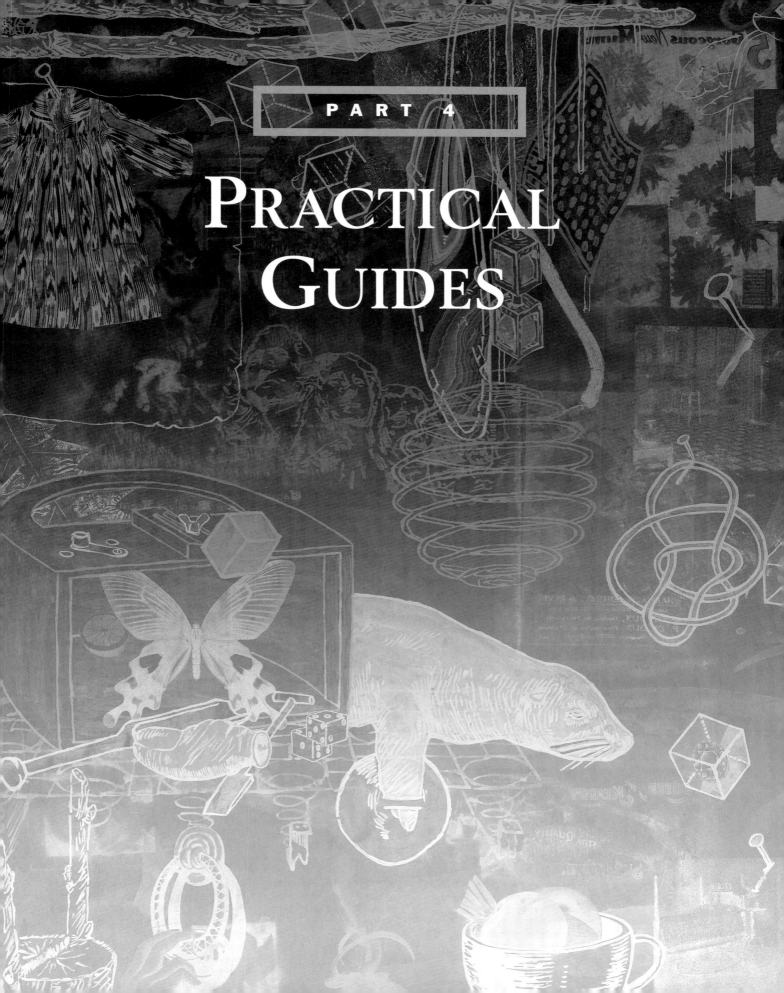

PART 4

PRACTICAL GUIDES

Materials

THE IMPORTANCE OF MATERIALS

Media, the materials for making art, are pure potentiality waiting for the artist to give them a chance. Marcel Duchamp said that a drawing could be nothing more than a breath of air on glass. Ann Hamilton covered 100,000 pennies in honey and let a film of dust develop over them. Richard Long creates drawings of mud on paper. Each medium speaks of its origins. Drawing carries memories of substances and surfaces; watercolor washes carry the memory of water. A large part of the meaning of a drawing derives from its basic material—what kind of medium is used on what kind of surface. Qualities such as wet or dry, brittle or supple, hard or soft, strong or fragile—all register at a glance. The materials from which drawings are made are so integral to the work that we fail to give them credit for the primary role they play.

The relationships among form, content, subject matter, materials, and techniques are the very basis for art, so it is essential that the artist develop a sensitivity to materials—to their possibilities and limitations. The problems in this book call for an array of drawing materials, some traditional, some unconventional. The supplies discussed in this chapter are all that are needed to complete the problems.

> **WARNING:** Since many materials used in the manufacture of art supplies are toxic, you should carefully read the labels and follow directions. Always work in a well-ventilated room.

PAPER

To list all the papers available to an artist would be impossible—the variety is endless. The importance of the surface on which you draw should not be minimized. The paper you choose, of course, affects the drawing.

Because the problems in this book require the use of a large amount of paper, and the emphasis is on process rather than product, expensive papers are not recommended for the beginning student. Various types of papers, ranging from newsprint to wrapping paper, nevertheless are serviceable and inexpensive. Experimentation with papers, however, is encouraged—you may wish to treat yourself to better-quality paper occasionally.

Newsprint and *bond paper* are readily available, inexpensive, and practical. Both come in bulk form—in pads of 100 sheets. Buying paper in bulk is much more economical than purchasing single sheets. Newsprint comes either rough or smooth; the rough is more useful. Newsprint is good for warm-up exercises. Charcoal and other dry media can be used on newsprint; it is, however, too absorbent for wet media. Bond paper, a smooth, middleweight paper, is satisfactory for most media.

Ideally, *charcoal paper* is recommended for charcoal drawing, since the paper has a tooth—a raised texture—that collects and holds the powdery medium. Charcoal paper is more expensive than bond paper and is recommended for only a few problems, those in which extensive rubbing or tonal blending is emphasized.

A few sheets of black *construction paper* are a good investment. Using white media on black paper makes you more aware of line quality and of the reversal of values. A few pieces of toned charcoal paper would likewise furnish variety. Only the neutral tones of gray or tan are recommended.

A serviceable size for drawing paper is 18 inches by 24 inches (46 cm by 61 cm). If you draw on a smaller format, you can cut the paper to size.

An inexpensive way to buy paper is to purchase it in rolls. End rolls of newsprint can be bought from newspaper offices at a discount. Photographic backdrop paper is another inexpensive rolled paper. It comes in 36-foot (10.98-m) lengths and 10-foot (3.05-m) widths. The paper must be cut to size, but the savings may be worth the inconvenience. The advantage to buying rolls of paper is that you can make oversize drawings at minimal cost. Brown wrapping paper also comes in rolls and is a suitable surface, especially for gesture drawings.

Another inexpensive source of paper is scrap paper from printing companies. The quality of the paper varies, as do the size and color, but it would be worthwhile to visit a local printing firm and see what is available. Office supply stores are a good source of inexpensive papers; look at their inventory of photocopy paper, index cards, gridded papers, lined papers, notebooks, and ledgers.

Shopping for drawing papers can be a real treat. You need to examine the paper for its color, texture, thickness, and surface quality—whether it is grainy or smooth. In addition to these characteristics, you need to know how stable the paper will be. Paper is, of course, affected by the materials from which it is made, by temperature, and by humidity. Paper that has a high acid or a high alkaline content is less stable than a paper made from unbleached rag or cotton; acidic or alkaline papers are not lightfast, for example. The selected papers in the following list are more expensive than the newsprint, bond, and charcoal paper that are recommended for most of the exercises in this text. Remember to select a paper that seems to you to be right for a given project. Becoming acquainted with various papers and learning their inherent qualities are among the joys of drawing.

Selected Papers for Drawing (high rag content)

Many of the papers listed below come in various weights. Arches, a hot press paper, absorbs ink well, and Arches 140-lb weight is good for colored pencils. Fabriano is suitable for graphite, ballpoint, and colored pencil. Lanaquarelle is a very heavy, smooth paper, good for washes. All papers below (except index) are appropriate for any art media, including wash. Index is a slick paper and is good for pen-and-ink drawing. Rives BFK and Italia are especially good for transfer drawings made with a solvent. Stonehenge is a very serviceable strong paper that will stand up to abrasive actions. Strathmore paper has a heavy weight and a tooth; it will not leave blotches from wet media. Tracing paper and vellum, a stiff translucent paper that breaks easily when bent, are good for transferring or tracing images. They also can be used in collages, especially when layering is used, when it is important to see through to another level. Clay-coated papers, such as Karma, are used for silverpoint or watercolors. Their surfaces are gessoed and finely sanded; the texture is like a photographic paper, and they do not bleed.

Oriental papers frequently have recognizable fibers such as pieces of bark or leaves. They are more texturally assertive than the other papers listed here.

Arches (hot and cold press)	22" × 30"; 25" × 40"	(56 cm × 76 cm; 64 cm × 102 cm)
Copperplate Deluxe	30" × 42"	(76 cm × 107 cm)
Fabriano Book	19" × 26"	(49 cm × 66 cm)
Fabriano Cover	20" × 26"; 26" × 40"	(51 cm × 66 cm; 66 cm × 102 cm)
German Etching	31½" × 42½"	(80 cm × 105 cm)
Index	26" × 40"	(66 cm × 102 cm)
Italia	20" × 28"; 28" × 40"	(51 cm × 71 cm; 71 cm × 102 cm)
Karma (made by Potlatch), a clay-coated paper		
Lanaquarelle 400 lb (very heavy)		
Murillo	27" × 39"	(69 cm × 100 cm)
Rives BFK	22" × 30"; 29" × 41"	(57 cm × 76 cm; 74 cm × 105 cm)
Manila paper	Various sizes	
Strathmore Artists	Various sizes	
Strathmore 500 series bristol	Various sizes	
Stonehenge	Various sizes	

Stonehenge and Somerset satin come in rolls, as do other papers mentioned above.

Some Suggested Oriental Papers (plant fiber content)

Chiri	paper contains traces of bark	
Hosho	16" × 22"	(41 cm × 56 cm)
Kochi	20" × 26"	(51 cm × 66 cm)
Moriki 1009 (white)	25" × 36"	(64 cm × 92 cm)
Mulberry	24" × 33"	(61 cm × 84 cm)
Okawara	3' × 6'	(92 cm × 1.83 m)
Suzuki	3' × 6'	(92 cm × 1.83 m)

Specialty Papers

French marbleized papers
Indian handmade papers
Other handmade papers (available in some specialty art supply stores)

Sketchbooks

The size of a sketchbook is personal—they come in various sizes so choose one that is comfortable to carry. Some are hardbound, others are spiral-leaf. You can easily make a sketchbook of unbound papers that are kept in a rigid folder. This method allows you to include a variety of papers. For ease of handling and to protect the edges, they should all be cut to the same size. You can use a plastic slip-on binder for a small number of pages. The advantage to loose-leaf papers is that you can prepare surfaces ahead of time and keep them ready for use in the folder. You can tone the papers with ink or acrylic washes, or with charcoal. Be sure to spray-fix the charcoal papers before placing them in the folder.

An easily portable size is usually no larger than 11 inches by 14 inches (28 cm by 36 cm).

CHARCOAL, CRAYONS, AND CHALKS

Charcoal is produced in three forms: vine charcoal, compressed charcoal, and charcoal pencil.

Vine charcoal, as its name indicates, is made from processed vine. It is the least permanent of the three forms. It is recommended for use in quick gestures since you can remove the marks with a chamois skin and reuse the paper. The highly correctable quality of vine charcoal makes it a good choice for use early in the drawing, when you are establishing the organizational pattern. If vine charcoal is used on charcoal paper for a longer, more permanent drawing, it must be carefully sprayed several times with fixative.

Compressed charcoal comes in stick form and a block shape. With compressed charcoal you can achieve a full value range rather easily. You can draw with both the broad side and the edge, creating both mass and line.

Charcoal pencil is a wooden pencil encasing a slender cylinder of compressed charcoal. It can be sharpened into a point and will produce a much finer, more incisive line than a stick or block of compressed charcoal.

Charcoal is easily smudged; it can be erased, blurred, or smeared with a chamois skin or kneaded eraser. All charcoal comes in soft, medium, and hard grades. Soft charcoal is recommended for the problems in this book.

Conté crayons, too, can produce both line and tone. They are available in soft, medium, and hard grades. A conté crayon comes in both stick and pencil form. It has a clay base and is made of compressed pigments. Conté crayon is available in white, black, sanguine, and sepia.

Water or turpentine will dissolve charcoal or conté crayon if a wash effect is desired.

Colored chalks, or *pastels*, can be used to layer colors. These are manufactured either with or without an oil base.

Another medium in stick and pencil form is the *lithographic crayon* or *lithographic pencil*. Lithographic crayons have a grease base and are soluble in turpentine. They too can be smudged, smeared, or blurred and are effective tools for establishing both line and tone. The line produced by a lithographic crayon or pencil is grainy; lithographic prints are readily identified by the grainy quality of the marks. (Lithographic crayons and pencils are specially made for drawing on lithographic stone, a type of limestone.) Lithographic crayons are produced in varying degrees of softness. Again, you should experiment to find the degree of softness or hardness you prefer.

China markers, like lithographic pencils, have a grease base and are readily smudged. Their advantage is that they are manufactured in a variety of colors.

Colored oil sticks are an inexpensive color medium that can be dissolved in turpentine to create wash effects.

PENCILS AND GRAPHITE STICKS

Pencils and *graphite sticks* come in varying degrees of hardness, from 9H, the hardest, to 7B, the softest. Keep the following in mind: The harder the graphite, the lighter the line; conversely, the softer the graphite, the darker the tone. 2B, 4B, and 6B pencils and a soft graphite stick are recommended. Graphite sticks produce tonal quality easily and are a time-saver for establishing broad areas of value. Pencil and graphite marks can be smudged, smeared, erased, or dissolved by a turpentine wash. A good investment for long-term use is the Mars Lumograph pencil.

Colored pencils are made in a wide range of colors, and water-soluble pencils can be combined with water for wash effects.

ERASERS

Erasers are, of course, a correctional tool, but they are highly recommended as a drawing tool. There are four basic types of erasers. The *kneaded eraser* is pliable and can be kneaded like clay into a point or shape; it is self-cleaning when it has been kneaded. *Gum erasers* are soft and do not damage the paper. A *pink rubber pencil eraser* is recommended for use with graphite pencils or sticks; it is more abrasive than the gum eraser. A *white plastic eraser* is less abrasive than the pink eraser and works well with graphite. A *barrel refillable eraser* feeds the eraser down a tube. It provides more control than a slab eraser.

Although a *chamois skin* is not technically an eraser, it is included here because it can be used to smudge marks made by vine charcoal and to tone paper. It also can be used on charcoal and conté to lighten values or to blend tones. As its name indicates, it is made of leather. The chamois skin can be cleaned by washing it in warm, soapy water; after it dries you should rub it vigorously to soften it and restore it to its original pliable condition. A blackened chamois skin can be used to tone paper.

INKS AND PENS

Any good drawing ink is suitable for the problems in this book. Perhaps the most widely known is black *India ink*. It is waterproof and is used in wash drawings to build layers of value. Both black and sepia ink are useful as well.

Pen points come in a wide range of sizes and shapes. Again, experimentation is the only way to find the ones that best suit you. A crow-quill pen, a very delicate, inexpensive pen that makes a fine line, is recommended. More expensive than disposable pens is the Rapidograph technical pen (Rotring cartridge type).

Felt-tip markers come with either felt or nylon tips. They are produced with both waterproof and water-soluble ink. Water-soluble ink is recommended; washed areas can be created with brush and water applied over the drawn line. Invest in both broad and fine tips. Discarded markers can be dipped in ink and used to produce interesting line quality.

PAINT AND BRUSHES

A water-soluble *acrylic paint* is useful. You should keep tubes of white and black acrylic in your drawing kit. You might wish to supplement these two tubes with an accent color and with some earth colors—for example, burnt umber, raw umber, or yellow ochre.

Brushes are important drawing tools. For the problems in this book, you need a 1-inch (2.5-cm) and a 2-inch (5-cm) varnish brush, which you can purchase at the hardware store; a number 8 nylon bristle brush with a flat end; and a number 6 Japanese bamboo brush, an inexpensive reed-handled brush. As your skill and confidence increase, add more brushes to your supply kit. Experiment with various sizes and shapes (square tips and tapered tips), and with natural and nylon bristles.

OTHER MATERIALS

A small can or jar of *turpentine* should be kept in your supply box. Turpentine is a solvent that can be used with a number of media—charcoal, graphite, conté, and grease crayons. Other solvents are alcohol, for photocopy transfers, and gasoline or Nazdar thinner, for transfer of magazine images.

Rubber cement and *white glue* are useful, especially when working on collage. Rubber cement is practical, since it does not set immediately and you can shift your collage pieces without damage to the paper. However, rubber cement discolors with age and becomes brittle. White glue dries transparent, it is long lasting, and it does not discolor. An acid-free paste is available and is highly recommended for use in collage or in attaching a drawing to a backing. This paste is used in book-binding; it does not discolor and because it is not liquid it also does not shrink or wrinkle the paper. Acid-free spray adhesive is a good choice for affixing paper, such as photographs or other paper products, to a paper or cardboard surface.

Sponges are convenient. They can be used to dampen paper, apply washes, and create interesting texture. They are also useful for cleaning up your work area.

Workable fixative protects against smearing and helps prevent powdery media from dusting off. Fixative comes in a spray can. It deposits a uniform mist on the paper surface, and a light coating is sufficient. The term *workable* means that drawing can continue without interference from the hard surface left by some fixatives.

A Masonite *drawing board* is strongly recommended. It should be larger than your largest drawing pad. (If you are using a 24-by-36-inch pad, the board should be 30 by 42 inches.) The pad or individual sheets of paper can be clipped to the board with large metal clips. The board will furnish a stable surface; it will keep paper unwrinkled and prevent it from falling off the easel. If you are drawing on individual sheets of paper, be sure to pad them with several sheets of newsprint to ensure an unmarred drawing surface.

Also keep in your supply box masking tape, gummed paper tape, a mat knife and blades, single-edge razor blades, scissors, several sheets of fine sandpaper (for keeping your pencil point sharp), and several metal or plastic containers for washes.

NONART IMPLEMENTS

Throughout the book, experimentation with different tools and media has been recommended. This is not experimentation just for experimentation's sake. A new tool does not necessarily result in a good drawing. But frequently a new tool will help you break old habits; it will force you to use your hands differently or to approach the drawing from a different way than you might have with more predictable and familiar drawing media. Sticks, vegetables (potatoes or carrots, for example), pieces of foam rubber or Styrofoam, a piece of crushed paper, pipe cleaners, sponges, and cotton-tipped sticks are implements that can be found easily and used to good effect. The artist Mark Tansey makes his own tools by combining found implements.

In today's art world, many artists intentionally use ephemeral art materials to make art that fades, wears out, dissolves, or disappears. Although Ed Ruscha's carrot, berry, and lettuce juice drawings may cause conservators nightmares, they are still being shown and collected.

Keep your supply box well stocked. Add to it newly found materials and drawing tools. Keep alert to the assets and liabilities of the materials you use. Experiment and enjoy old materials used in new ways, and new materials used in traditional ways—they can give a lift to your art making.

> **WARNING:** Remember to read all warning labels on all products and to work in a well-ventilated room!

"I was constantly drawing, which in turn makes you look harder, see more, remember more. And I realized, this is fun!" —**DAVID HOCKNEY**

Keeping a Sketchbook

David Hockney's observation captures the enthusiasm of and the reason for keeping a sketchbook.

At the end of chapters 2 through 10 are sections called "Sketchbook Projects," which propose exercises designed to help you solve formal and conceptual problems encountered in the text. This guide will amplify the role of a sketchbook as an essential extension of studio activity.

The sketchbook takes art out of the studio and brings it into daily life. Through the sketchbook, actual experience is introduced into the making of art. This is a vital cycle, infusing your work with direct experience and at the same time incorporating newly acquired abilities learned in the studio.

The first consideration in choosing a sketchbook is that it be portable, a comfortable size to carry. A good alternative to a sketchbook is a spring binder with a firm backing to hold loose-leaf papers securely. This device will allow you to use a variety of papers, permitting you to remove individual sheets to post in your studio as a source of ideas, and it will provide a means for grouping drawings out of sequence. In a folder, you can collect collage material that easily can be removed and stored. Loose-leaf pages can be filed and cataloged to suit your needs. If you choose to use a spring binder in lieu of a bound sketchbook, it is advisable also to carry a small notebook in which you can jot down both written and drawn notes.

Any medium is appropriate for a sketchbook, but a small portable drawing kit should be outfitted to accompany the sketchbook. Some useful contents would be crayons, water-soluble felt-tip markers, pencils, pen and ink, a glue stick, a roll of masking tape, and a 6-inch (15-cm) straightedge, along with a variety of erasers, found implements, a small plastic container with a lid, a couple of large clips for holding paper in place, and a small, efficient pencil sharpener or several sharp single-edged razor blades.

Although it may seem artificial and awkward in the beginning, you should use your sketchbook daily—365 days a year. You will soon develop a reliance on it that will prove profitable. The sketchbook will become a dependable outlet for your creativity. In it you can experiment freely; your sensitivity and abilities will become keener with every page.

WHY KEEP A SKETCHBOOK?

Two of the most valuable assets for an artist are a retentive memory and the ability to tap into the unconscious. Memory and the unconscious are both generators of imagery and ideas for the artist. By developing your memory and recording your dreams, you have a built-in image-making source. Keeping records of your dreams and events in your life can jolt your memory, reminding you of important information you might otherwise have forgotten.

Jonathan Borofsky is only one of the many artists who use dream images to bring important insights to their work *(figure PG.B1)*. Shakespeare summed up these observations succinctly: "We are such stuff as dreams are made on."

In the sketchbook, germs of potential images or ideas take hold. Quick notations, like Francis Bacon's *Bending Figure (figure PG.B2)*, can be like storyboards recording nonverbal, non-narrative concepts, worksheets on which ideas can be amplified,

PG.B1. **JONATHAN BOROFSKY.** *I Dreamed a Dog Was Walking a Tightrope . . . at 2,445,667 & 2,544,044.* 1978. Ink and pencil on paper, 1' x 1'1" (30 cm x 33 cm). *Private collection, New York. Paula Cooper Gallery.*

PG.B2. **FRANCIS BACON.** *Bending Figure No. 2.* ca. 1957–1961. Ballpoint pen and oil on paper, 13" x 11" (34 cm x 27 cm). *Purchased with assistance from the National Lottery through the Heritage Lottery Fund, the National Art Collections Fund and a group of anonymous donors in memory of Mario Tazzoli, 1998. Photo credit: Tate Gallery, London/Art Resource, NY. Tate Gallery, London, Great Britain.* © 2007 *The Estate of Francis Bacon/ARS, New York/DACS, London.*

transformed, multiplied, enlarged, and extended. It would be impossible for us to carry out all our ideas. The sketchbook is the ideal place to record ideas for selection and development at a later time. Over the years, sketchbooks become a valuable repository. Your growth as an artist can be traced through these records.

An example of how a faithful commitment to keeping a sketchbook can pay off is seen in a work by William Anastasi in which he has photocopied pages from his sketchbooks and journals kept for over 20 years to use as collage on large canvases *(figure PG.B3)*. He has amplified and extended the journals' visual themes by the addition of colored pencil, crayon, and ink.

PG.B3. **WILLIAM ANASTASI.** *The Invention of Romance.* 1982. Collage, 5'8" x 4'8" (1.73 m x 1.42 m). *Collection of Drs. Barry and Cheryl Goldberg. Courtesy of the artist.*

In the long run, sketchbooks are time-savers. Quickly conceived ideas are often the most valid ones. Having a place to jot down notations is important. A quick oil sketch on paper by Vincent Desiderio *(figure PG.B4)* shows the first stages of an idea which will result in a painting. The artist has blocked out large general shapes, omitting details. He has established a range of values to reflect backlighting. Rectangular forms organize the picture plane. The sketch remains flexible for further adjustments in composition and detail. A powerful idea, the allegory of painting, takes shape through a series of studies.

Preliminary ideas for Robert Smithson's earthwork *The Spiral Jetty* (constructed on the Great Salt Lake in Utah) were rapidly stated in notational, schematic drawings. The written notes are minimal and the drawing style is hasty, yet the finished earthwork demanded exacting technical and mechanical facility to construct *(figure PG.B5)*. Great ideas have modest beginnings.

The sketchbook can function as both a written and visual journal. It serves as a memory bank for elusive feelings and information. It is an appropriate place to record critical and personal comments on what you have read, seen, and experienced. Written and visual analogies can be quickly noted for possible use later on.

Claes Oldenburg's many notebooks record his ingenious visual analogical thinking. In his two-part sketch of *London Knees (figure PG.B6)*, Oldenburg shows how the process takes form. By focusing on scale, he creates a sense of colossal objects in a landscape. The crushed cigarettes in the bottom drawing form a mountainous

PG.B4. **VINCENT DESIDERIO. *Studies for an Allegory of Painting.*** 1992. Ink and pencil on paper, each sketchbook page 6" x 3.75" (15.2 cm x 9 cm). © *Vincent Desiderio, courtesy Marlborough Gallery, New York, NY.*

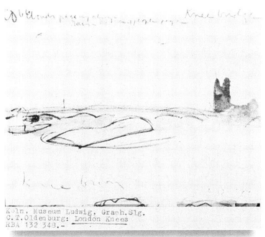

PG.B5. **ROBERT SMITHSON.** *The Spiral Jetty.* 1970. Pencil, 11⅞" x 9" (30 cm x 23 cm). *© Estate of Robert Smithson/ Licensed by VAGA, New York.*

PG.B6. (left) **CLAES OLDENBURG.** *London Knees.* 1966. *Folge, Kötn, Museum Ludwig, Cologne, Germany.*

PG.B7. (right) **CLAES OLDENBURG.** *London Knees.* 1966. *Folge, Kötn, Museum Ludwig, Cologne, Germany.*

expanse of space. Eventually the cigarette/knee transforms into a flattened bridge over the Thames River *(figure PG.B7)*.

Quick thinking, responsive drawing, sensitivity to visual stimuli, heightened analytical abilities, enhanced memory, and immediacy of response—these are only a few of the many benefits of daily sketchbook practice. In Eugene Leroy's gesture studies (see *figure 2.13*), we see how skills acquired in the studio can be translated to the sketchbook.

Many times the way artists revitalize their work after a period of inactivity is to use the sketchbook as a place of new beginnings. Even an old sketchbook when reviewed after a while offers fresh new ideas. Seeds of ideas take longer than we think to germinate. It is exciting to trace our preferences for certain forms and relationships over an extended period. There is no place better to find those embedded thoughts than in the sketchbook.

APPROPRIATE SUBJECTS FOR A SKETCHBOOK

We could make a one-word entry under the heading of what is appropriate subject matter for sketchbooks: everything. Every experience in your life, your musings about them, all have a place in your sketchbook. Fill it up with your life. Friends, family *(figure PG.B8)*, and even animals *(figure PG.B9)* are accessible subjects.

Sketchbook activity should not be strictly confined to making marks in a notebook. Idea gathering on a wider scale is really the goal. There are limitless methods of finding subjects and infusing them with ideas.

Art history, as we have seen throughout this text, is a never-ending source for new ideas or old ideas reworked with fresh insights (see *figures 1.25* and *10.18*).

Self-portraits present us with the chance to look in two directions at once as we depict our external as well as our internal selves. Everyday objects can even be stand-ins for the self. Common objects present themselves as familiar companions capable of being transformed, as in Clemente's small—6 by 3 inches—pastels *(figure PG.B10)*.

Geographic locales, both familiar and exotic, can provide a world of subject matter. You could, like Red Grooms *(figure PG.B11)*, record your travels in memory pictures in your sketchbook. Grooms has compressed time in his rodeo scene so that everything is happening at once. This large composite drawing is made up of

PG.B8. **ALBERTO GIACOMETTI.** *Portrait of Annette in Bed.* 1949. Graphite, India rubber, sketchbook page, 11½" x 8¾" (291 mm x 223 mm). *The Royal Museum of Fine Arts, Copenhagen. © 2007 Artists Rights Society (ARS), New York/ADAGP, Paris.*

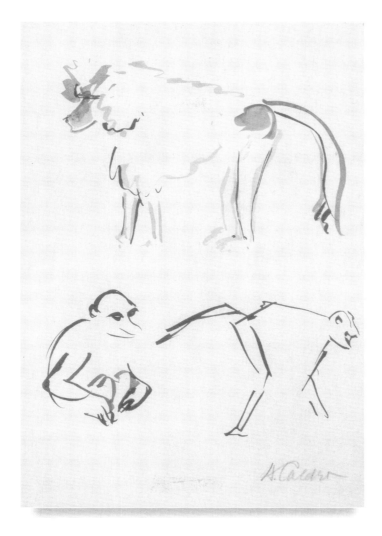

PG.B9. **ALEXANDER CALDER.** *Baboon and Two Lesser Monkeys.* Ink and water-color on paper c. 1924, 15⅛" x 10⅛". *© ARS, NY. Art Resource, New York. Private collection.*

17 sheets of paper, each of which could have been taken from a sketch pad. Grooms has used a shorthand approach to indicate the crowds seated in the arena. His cursory, cartoon style reflects his artist-as-trickster personality. Quick contours and a sketchy cast of characters add up to a droll account of a Wild West ruckus. Not only is the drawing fun to look at, but it also must have been fun to make.

Travel not only affords graphic insights, it also provides memorabilia, such as ticket stubs and stamps, that can find a home in your sketchbook in the form of collage. Printed bits and scraps of papers seem to spark the artist's urge to scavenge and salvage.

The artist Ellsworth Kelly has made collections of fragments and doodles that he has accumulated over a period of 25 years. He kept his finds in loose groupings in drawers into which he occasionally dipped for ideas. When the art historian Yves-Alain Bois saw the trove of material, he suggested a show of the then-unorganized material. Bois recognized that the boxes of collected material formed a window into Kelly's idea-gathering process of turning randomness into order. For an exhibition of the material, Kelly arranged the fragments on 200 pieces of large white paper, grouping the scraps and doodles according to his own special visual cataloging system *(figure PG.B12)*. *Tablet,* a suite of 200 collages, shows how the most ordinary, discarded scraps can spark ideas.

Every object and image has the potentiality of being transformed into art. The objects that we choose to live with are revelatory on many levels. You might make a series of sketchbook drawings that are based on contents—contents of

PG.B10. **FRANCESCO CLEMENTE.** *From Near and from Afar.* 1979. 20 pastels on paper, 6⅜" x 3½" (16.2 cm x 9 cm) to 1'1" x 1'1¾" (33 cm x 35 cm).
Anthony d'Offay Gallery, London.

billfolds, purses, medicine cabinets, closets, tool chests, refrigerators, or pantries, for example. Andy Warhol's iconic soup cans had their beginnings in a quick sketch *(figure PG.B13)*.

Alexis Rockman reinvigorates the now-faded tradition of the "studio-in-the-wild" and shows us how an update of this convention can be an effective sketch-book project. For Rockman, paintings are done in the studio, drawings are done on-site. His subjects include flora, fauna, and fossils. Whether he is in the Amazon basin or at the La Brea tar pits, Rockman uses the materials of the site; for the La Brea series his medium was tar, and the drawings were made with brushes and sticks. For the drawings shown here *(figure PG.B14)*, Rockman drew with *leachate*, a liquid that drains from garbage landfills. In your own work, making descriptive drawings of flora and fauna will enhance your ability to inspect forms intently and to analyze relationships. Insects, twigs, birds, feathers, leaves, and flowers can be added attractions in the sketchbook's reservoir.

PG.B11. **RED GROOMS.** *Rodeo Arena.*
1975–1976. Colored felt-tip pens on
17 sheets of paper, 3'11" x 6'8⅜"
(1.19 m x 2.03 m). *Collection of the
Modern Art Museum of Fort Worth, Museum
Purchase and Commission with funds from the
National Endowment for the Arts and the
Benjamin J. Tillar Memorial Trust. Acc. no.
1976.1.PS. © 2007 Red Grooms/Artists
Rights Society (ARS), New York.*

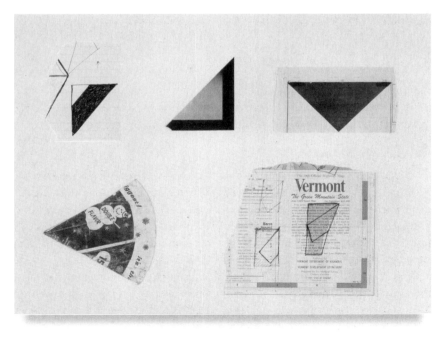

PG.B12. **ELLSWORTH KELLY.** *Tablet # 34 -*
Five sketches, 1950s, 1960s. Ink on
paper. 15½ X 21 inches (39.4 X 53.3
cm.) *The Menil Collection © Ellsworth Kelly.*

PG.B13. ANDY WARHOL. *Big Tom Campbell's Soup Can (Pepper Pot).* 1962. Synthetic polymer paint on canvas, 71¾" x 51¾". *© 2007 The Andy Warhol Foundation for the Visual Arts/Artists Rights Society (ARS), New York.*

PG.B14. ALEXIS ROCKMAN. *German Cockroaches and Little Brown Bat.* 2001. Leachate and acrylic polymer on paper, 1' x 9" (30.5 cm x 22.9 cm) each. *Courtesy Gorney Bravin & Lee, New York. © 2007 Alexis Rockman/Artists Rights Society (ARS), New York.*

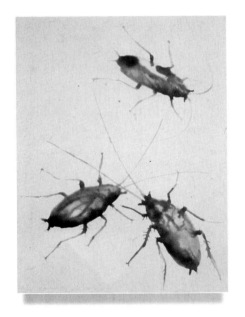

Subjects for your sketchbook need not be limited to the natural world. You can use your own or others' writing and respond to the written words by marks or shapes that connect you to the work. You can use imagined, conceptual subjects or invented, abstracted, or nonobjective forms. Explorations of pure form are ideal sketchbook endeavors.

The sketchbook's best companion, however, may be music. Draw while listening to music. Let the music, the drawing implement, and your feelings control your decisions. Strange and wondrous forms can evolve.

Some suggestions for sketchbook drawings:

1. Experiment with form and variations.
2. Note quick visual and written ideas.
3. Experiment with different techniques, tools, or media.
4. Develop an object or an idea through several pages of sketches.
5. Experiment with different compositions; place objects and shapes in different juxtapositions.
6. Record objects through sustained observation.
7. Investigate. Make preparatory drawings.
8. Use your sketchbook as a diary or journal, recording your interests and activities.
9. Make comments on artwork (your own or others').
10. Attach clippings that interest you.
11. Draw from memory.
12. Draw your feelings.
13. Draw from nature.
14. Record your dreams, both visually and in writing.
15. Experiment with new and playful imagery.

SUMMARY

Sketchbook practice promotes freshness of vision and intensity of seeing—of seeing something as if for the first time. Each page of your sketchbook can become a site of departure for another view, another work. Sketchbooks are filled with new beginnings. When you make several drawings on the same subject, the content level of the drawings increases.

Sketchbooks are a locus of memories; a glance through old sketchbooks can trigger memories of images and ideas from the past. An image from the past can project ideas into the future.

The important thing to keep in mind about a sketchbook is that you are keeping it for yourself; it is as personal as a diary. Both process and progress are the rewards of dedication to keeping a sketchbook.

Looking back through your daily drawings can give you direction when you are stuck, providing a source of ideas for new work. Germs of potential forms and ideas are embedded in sketchbooks. When you use an idea from the sketchbook, you have the advantage of having chosen an idea that has some continuity to it; you have already done some work with that idea. A new viewpoint adds yet another dimension. The sketchbook is a place where your art communicates with itself. It is a book of possibilities.

Breaking Artistic Blocks and Making Critical Assessments

There are two times when artists are susceptible to artistic blocks: while working on a problem drawing, one that has somehow gone wrong; and when getting started at all seems impossible. These are common problems that all artists, even the most experienced, must face and learn to move quickly to correct.

CORRECTING THE PROBLEM DRAWING

What can you do with a drawing you cannot seem to complete? The initial step in the corrective process is to separate yourself, physically and mentally, from the drawing in order to look at it objectively. You, the artist-maker, must become the critic-viewer. This transformation is essential to assess your work. The original act of drawing was probably on the intuitive level; now you begin the process of critical analysis. You are going to learn to bring into consciousness what has been intuitively stated.

Turn away from your work for a few minutes. Occupy your mind with some simple task such as straightening equipment or sharpening pencils. Then pin the drawing on the wall, upside down or sideways. Have a mirror handy through which to view the drawing. The mirror's reversal of the image and the new perspective of placement will give you a new orientation so that you can see the drawing with fresh eyes. This fresh viewpoint allows you to be more aware of the drawing's formal qualities, regardless of the subject you have chosen.

When you can see how the formal elements of line, value, shape, volume, texture, and color are used, you are not so tied to the subject matter. Frequently the problem area will jump out at you. The drawing itself tells you what it needs. Be sensitive to the communication that now exists between you and your work. Before, you were in command of the drawing; now it is directing you to look at it in a new way. At this stage you are not required to pass judgment on the drawing. You simply need to ask yourself some nonjudgmental questions about the piece. The time for critical judgment comes later. What you need to discover now is strictly some information about the drawing.

Questions Dealing with Form

Here are some beginning questions dealing with form to ask yourself.

1. What is the subject being drawn?
2. Which media are used and on what surface?
3. How is the composition related to the page? Is it a small drawing on a large page? A large drawing on a small page? Is there a lot of negative space? Does the image fill the page? What kind of space is being used in the drawing? Where is the primary focus? Is there a secondary one? What is the connection between the two? How are the edges and corners treated? Where does the viewer "enter" the drawing—top, bottom, sides, corners, middle? By what means are the viewer's eyes led through the picture plane? Is one area over- or underdeveloped?
4. What kinds of shapes predominate? Amoeboid? Geometric? Do the shapes exist all in the positive space, all in the negative space, or in both? Are they large or small? Are they the same size? Are there repeated shapes? How have shapes been made? By line? By value? By a combination of these two? Where is the greatest weight in the drawing? How is that weight balanced? Are there volumes in the drawing? Do the shapes define planes or the sides of a form? Are the shapes flat or volumetric?
5. Divide value into three groups: lightest light, darkest dark, and midgray. How are these values distributed throughout the drawing? Is value used in the positive space only? In the negative space only? In both? Do the values cross over objects or shapes, or are they contained within the object or shape? Is value used to indicate a single light source or multiple light sources? Does value define planes? Does it define space? Does it define mass or weight? Is it used ambiguously? Are the value transitions gradual or abrupt?
6. What is the organizational line? Is it a curve, a diagonal, a horizontal, or a vertical? What type of line is used—contour, scribble, calligraphic? Where is line concentrated? Does it create mass? Does it create value? Does it define edges? Does it restate the shape of a value? Again, note the distribution of different types of line in the drawing; ignore the other elements. What kind of line quality is used? Is there more than one kind of line employed in the drawing?
7. Is invented, simulated, or actual texture used in the drawing? Are there repeated textures, or only one kind? Is the texture created by the tool the same throughout the drawing? Have you used more than one medium? If so, does each medium remain separate from the other media? Are they integrated?

This list of questions looks long and intimidating at first glance, but you can learn quickly to make these assessments—make them almost automatically, in fact. Of course, many of these questions may not apply to each specific piece, and you may think of other questions that will help you in making this first compilation of information about your drawing.

Critical Assessment

After letting the drawing speak to you and after having asked some nonjudgmental questions about it, you are ready to make a critical assessment. It is time to ask questions that provoke judgments.

Does the drawing do what you meant it to do? Does it say something different— but perhaps equally important—from what you meant it to say? Is there confusion or a contradiction between your intent and what the drawing actually says? There may be a conflict here because the drawing has been done on an intuitive level, whereas the meaning you are trying to verbalize is on a conscious level. Might the drawing have a better message than your original intention?

Can you change the drawing to make the meaning clearer? Remember, form is the carrier of meaning. Separate the two functions of making and viewing. What is the message to you as viewer?

An important reminder: Go with your feelings. If you have any doubts about the drawing, wait until a solution strikes you; however, do not use this delay to avoid doing what you must to improve the drawing. Try something—even if the solution fails and the drawing is "ruined," you have sharpened your skills and provided yourself with new experiences. The fear of ruining what might be a good drawing can become a real block to later work.

Be alert to what accidents can offer. A large part of aesthetic intelligence consists of an awareness of accidents and a readiness to employ them to creative effect. To see possibilities in chance events is a talent that should be developed. Be assertive; experiment; do not be afraid to fail. A work of art is a series of discoveries, not of preplanned ideas. The best ideas come when you least expect them.

Extraordinary things can happen very quickly. Be attentive to them.

Problems in an individual piece tend to fall within these five categories:

- inconsistency of style, idea, or feeling
- failure to determine basic structure
- tendency to ignore negative space
- inability to develop value range and transitions
- failure to observe accurately

Let's take a closer look at each of these factors in turn.

Inconsistency of Style, Idea, or Feeling

Inconsistency here refers to the awkward combination of various styles, ideas, or feelings within a single work. A number of techniques and several types of line may be employed within a single drawing, but the techniques and elements must be compatible with one another and with the overall idea of the drawing. Frequently an artist will unintentionally use unrelated styles in the same drawing. For example, a figure drawing may begin in a loose and gestural manner; suddenly, however, when details are stated, the artist tightens up and begins to conceptualize areas such as the face and hands. The style of the drawing changes—the free-flowing lines give way to a tighter, more constricted approach. As conceptualization takes the place of observation, the smooth, almost intuitive interrelationship of the elements is lost. The moment of panic is a signal for you to stop, look, analyze, and relax before continuing.

Failure to Determine Basic Structure

A frequent problem encountered in drawing is the *failure to determine basic structure*, to distinguish between major and minor themes. For example, dark geometric shapes may dominate a drawing, while light amoeboid shapes are subordinate. Although it is not necessary for every drawing to have a major and minor theme, in which some parts dominate and others are subordinate, it is important for the artist to consider such distinctions in light of the subject and intent of a particular drawing. Details should overshadow the basic structure of a drawing only if the artist intends it. The organization of a drawing is not necessarily predetermined; however, at some point in its development, you should give consideration to the drawing's basic structure.

Tendency to Ignore Negative Space

Humans are object-oriented and have a *tendency to ignore negative space*. We focus our attention on objects. A problem arises for the artist when the space around the object is ignored and becomes merely leftover space. It takes conscious effort to consider positive and negative space simultaneously. Sometimes it is necessary to train ourselves by first looking at and drawing the negative space. When we draw the negative space first, or when positive and negative space are dealt with simultaneously, there is an adjustment in both. In other words, the positive and negative shapes are altered to create interrelationships. There are times when only one object is drawn on an empty page. In these instances, the placement of the drawing on the page should be determined by the relationship of the negative space to the object.

Inability to Develop Value Range and Transitions

One way to organize a drawing is by the distribution of values. Problems arise when students are *unable to develop value range and transitions*. For many students, developing a value range and gradual value transitions is difficult. The problem sometimes is a lack of ability to see value as differentiated from hue. At other times, it is a failure to consider the range of value distribution most appropriate for the idea of the drawing. Too wide a range can result in a confusing complexity or a fractured, spotty drawing. Too narrow a range can result in an uninteresting sameness.

Failure to Observe Accurately

The final problem, *failure to observe accurately*, involves lack of concentration on the subject and commitment to the drawing. If you are not interested in your subject or if you are not committed to the drawing you are making, this will be apparent in the work.

Once you have pinpointed the problem area, think of three or more solutions. If you are still afraid of ruining the drawing, do three drawings exactly like the problem drawing and employ a different solution for each. This should lead to an entirely new series of drawings, triggering dozens of ideas.

The failure to deal with this first category of problems—being unable to correct an individual drawing—can lead to an even greater problem—not being able to get started at all.

GETTING STARTED

A second type of artistic blockage, in some ways more serious than the first, is when you cannot seem to get started at all. There are a number of possible solutions to this problem. You should spread out all the drawings you did over the period of a month and analyze them. It is likely that you are repeating yourself by using the same medium, employing the same scale, or using the same size paper. In other words, your work has become predictable.

When you break a habit and introduce change into the work, you will find that you are more interested in executing the drawing. The resulting piece reflects your new interest. A valid cure for being stuck is to adopt a playful attitude.

An artist, being sensitive to materials, responds to new materials, new media. This is a good time to come up with some inventive, new, nonart drawing tools. Frequently you are under too much pressure, usually self-imposed, to produce "art," and you need to rid yourself of this stifling condition. Set yourself the task of producing 100 drawings over a 48-hour period. Be playful. Employ the "what if" approach. Use any size paper, any medium, any approach—and before you get started, promise yourself to throw them all away. This will ease the pressure of producing a finished product and will furnish many new directions for even more drawings. It may also assist you in getting over the feeling that every drawing is precious.

All techniques and judgments you have been learning are pushed back in your mind while your conscious self thinks of solutions to the directions. Your intuitive self, having been conditioned by some good solid drawing problems, has the resource of past drawing experience to fall back on. Art is constantly a play between what you already know and the introduction of something new, between old and new experience, the conscious and the intuitive, the objective and the subjective.

Art does not exist in a vacuum, and although it is true that art comes from art, more to the point is that art comes from everything. If you immerse yourself totally in doing, thinking, and seeing art, the wellsprings soon dry up and you run out of new ideas. Exhausting physical exercise is an excellent remedy, as is reading a good novel, a scientific journal, or a weekly news magazine. A visit to a natural history museum, a science library, a construction site, a zoo, a cemetery, a concert, a political rally—these will all provide grist for the art mill sooner or later. Relax, "invite your soul." Contact with the physical world will result in fresh experiences from which to extract ideas, not only to improve your art but also to sharpen your knowledge of yourself and your relation to the world.

Keep a journal—a visual and written one—in which you place notes and sketches relating to ideas, quotes, or whatever occupies your mind. After a week reread the journal and see how you spend your time. How does the way you spend your time relate to your artistic block?

Lack of authentic experience is damning. Doing anything, just existing in our complex society, is risky. Art is especially risky. What do we as artists risk? We risk confronting things unknown to us; we risk failure. Making art is painful because the artist must constantly challenge old ideas and experiences. Out of this conflict comes the power that feeds the work.

An artistic block is not necessarily negative. It generally means that you are having growing pains. You are questioning yourself and are dissatisfied with your previous work. The blockage may be a sign of good things to come. It is probably an indication that you are ready to begin on a new level of commitment or concentration, or that you are ready to begin a new tack entirely. When you realize this, your fear—the fear of failure, which is what caused the artistic block in the first place—is reduced, converted, and put to use in constructive new work. Rigid expectations result in petrified perceptions. Loosen up, draw; draw for the fun of it! Don't put up fences between you and your art.

The richness of art is that it offers great potential for self-growth and increased awareness. It presents us with a route to self-discovery; and when we think we have come to a dead end, it surprises us with new pathways.

Presentation

SOME CONTEMPORARY MODES OF PRESENTATION

Since contemporary artists have questioned every aspect of art making, it is no surprise that the way a work is presented has also been under review. Does putting a frame around a work of art indicate that it is important or that its value is increased? Modernism's stripped-down framing aesthetic is definitely being challenged by postmodern framing tactics. Greg Constantine presents *The World's Greatest Hits*, snippets of well-known paintings along with fragments of their historically appropriate frames *(figure PG.D1)*.

Some contemporary works on paper are attached directly to the wall by pushpins or clips, such as Kiki Smith's mural-size drawing, *Lucy's Daughters (figure PG.D2)*. Smith allows the folded creases of the paper to be an element of the work. Jayashree Chakravarty's exhibition of scrolls is made of layered, glue-stiffened paper, which twists and turns down from the ceiling and onto the floor *(figure PG.D3)*. Chakravarty's drawings are patterned after Bengali folk scrolls—their surfaces are crumpled and worn, showing the signs of much work and handling. In spite of their monumental size, they can easily be rolled up for storage.

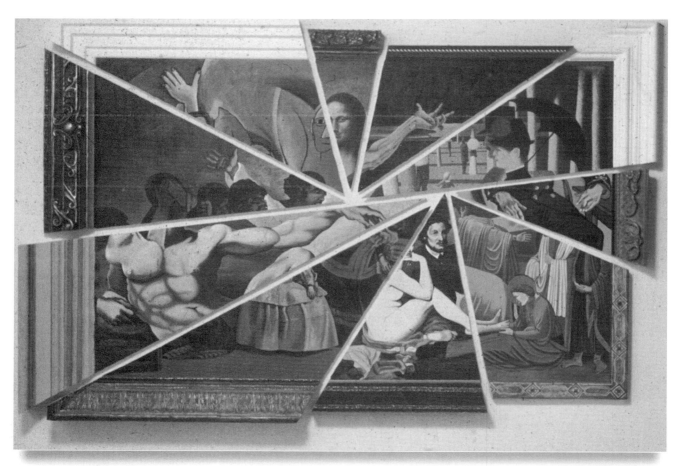

PG.D1. **GREG CONSTANTINE.** *The World's Greatest Hits.* 1989. Acrylic on canvas and wood, 7'5" x 11'3" x 8" (2.26 m x 3.43 m x 20.3 cm). *OK Harris Works of Art, New York.*

Some works are placed in frames that become an integral, inseparable part of the artwork, like Jess's intimately scaled collage in its reclaimed, bás-relief frame *(figure PG.D4)*.

Some works are installations drawn on the wall itself, as in Julie Mehretu's room drawing, *Implosion/Explosion* (see *figure 1.2*).

Richard Tuttle "frames" his drawings with a thin pencil line that is drawn directly onto the wall. Many contemporary artists show their work unframed as a sort of humbling gesture, whereas others use nontraditional, exaggerated framing devices such as those we have just seen.

Thematically related drawings are usually presented in the same style of frames and mats. Look at the arrangement of Francesco Clemente's 20 pastels (see *figure PG.B10*).

The selection of drawings to represent your work is an important undertaking. Your portfolio should show a range of techniques and abilities. The four most important criteria to keep in mind are accuracy of observation, an understanding of the formal elements of drawing, media variety and exploration, and expressive content.

After you have chosen the pieces that best incorporate these considerations, your next concern is how to present them. The presentation, in addition to being portable, must keep the works clean and intact, free from being torn or bent. Since framing stands in the way of portability, and since framing is dependent on the work being shown, that option will not be discussed here.

Possible ways to present your work are backing and covering with acetate, stitching in clear plastic envelopes, laminating, dry mounting, and matting. Each method of presentation has its advantages and disadvantages.

PG.D2. **KIKI SMITH.** *Lucy's Daughters.*
1996. Ink on paper with string,
8' x 14'10" (2.44 m x 4.52 m).
Collection Rose Art Museum, Brandeis University, Waltham, Mass. Hays Acquisition Fund, 1992. Photo: Ellen Page Wilson, © Kiki Smith.

PG.D3. **JAYASHREE CHAKRAVARTY.** *Untitled.*
1997. Glue-stiffened layered paper.
Photo by Cathy Carver/The Drawing Center.

PG.D4. **JESS.** *Echo's Wake: Part I.* 1960–1966. Paste-up, 9' x 12' x 3'6" (2.74 m x 3.66 m x 1.07 m). *Photo by Ben Blackwell. Odyssia Gallery, New York. © 2007 Artists Rights Society (ARS), New York/Beeldrecht, Amsterdam.*

ACETATE

A simple method of presenting work is to apply a firm backing to the drawing and then cover both drawing and backing with a layer of acetate, a clear thin plastic that holds the drawing and backing together. More important, the covering provides protection against scuffing, tearing, and soiling. (Matted drawings can also be covered with acetate.) Backing is a good option if a work is too large for matting or if the composition extends to the edge and you cannot afford to lose any of the drawing behind a mat. The backing can be made from foam core or mat board. An acid-free foam core is available. If you use a backing that is not acid-free, a barrier paper should be placed between the drawing and the backing to ensure that the acid content of the backing does not leach onto the paper.

Another option is to attach the drawing with gummed linen tape to a larger piece of paper and cover it with acetate. The drawing then has a border of paper around it and can retain its edges. The drawing lies on top; it is loose, not pinned back by a mat. The size of the backing paper is an important consideration. The drawing might need a border of an inch (2.5 cm); it might need one several inches wide. Experiment with border sizes before cutting the backing paper and attaching it to the drawing.

Paper is available in more varieties and neutral colors than mat board. The choice of paper is important. The drawing and the paper it is done on should be compatible with the texture, weight, value, and color of the backing paper. Backing paper should not dominate the drawing.

A disadvantage to acetate as a protective cover is its shiny surface. This interferes with the texture of the drawing and with subtleties within the drawing.

PLASTIC ENVELOPES

If flexibility or the idea of looseness is important to the drawing, another simple means of presentation is to stitch the drawing in an envelope of clear plastic. For a drawing of irregular shape—for example, one that does not have square corners—a plastic envelope might be an appropriate choice. A plastic casing would allow a drawing done on fabric to retain its looseness and support the idea of flexibility.

A disadvantage to clear plastic is its watery appearance and highly reflective surface, which distort the drawing. The greatest advantage to this method of presentation is that large drawings can be rolled, shipped, and stored easily.

LAMINATION

Lamination is midway in stiffness between drawing paper and a loosely stitched plastic envelope. You are familiar with laminated drivers' licenses and credit cards.

Laminating must be done commercially. It is inexpensive, but cost should not be the most important consideration. The means of presentation must be suited to the concept in the drawing. Laminating is a highly limiting way to present work—once sealed, the drawing cannot be reworked in any way.

DRY MOUNTING

If the likelihood of soiling and scuffing is minimal, you might want to *dry mount* the drawing. You do this in exactly the same way as you dry mount a photograph, sealing the drawing to a rigid backing and leaving the surface uncovered. Dry-mount tissue is placed between drawing and backing. Heat is then applied by means of an electric dry-mount press, or if done at home, by a warm iron. Dry-mount tissue comes in a variety of sizes; rolled tissue can be found for large drawings. This tissue must be the same size as the drawing. Wrinkling can occur, and since a drawing sealed to backing is not easily removed, extreme care should be taken in the process. Carefully read and follow the instructions on the dry-mount tissue package before you start.

Since dry mounting is done with heat, it is important that the medium used in the drawing not run or melt when it comes in contact with heat. Greasy media such as china markers, lithographic sticks, or wax crayons should not be put under the dry press for mounting.

For mounting drawings made with greasy media, you can use a spray fixative to adhere the drawing to its backing. Acid-free spray-mount should be used to protect the drawing from discoloration.

MATTING

Matting is the most popular and traditional choice for presentation. The mat separates the drawing from the wall on which it is hung and provides an interval of rest before the eye reaches the drawing. Second, a mat gives the drawing room to "breathe." Like a rest in music, it offers a stop between the drawing and the environment; it allows for uncluttered viewing of the drawing. And, finally, the mat furnishes space between the drawing and the glass when framed so that the drawing does not come into direct contact with the glass, since changes in temperature can cause moisture-related problems, such as wrinkling and discoloration.

Mats should not be the focus of attention nor detract from the drawing. A colored mat that screams for attention diminishes a drawing's impact. White or off-white mats are recommended at this stage, especially since most of the problems in this book do not use color. An additional argument for white mats is that art is usually displayed on white or neutrally colored walls, and the mat furnishes a gradual transition from the wall to the drawing. Most competitive shows call for works on paper to be matted in white mats.

Materials for Matting

The materials needed for matting are:

- a mat knife with a sharp blade
- 100 percent cotton rag mounting board
- gummed linen tape or acid-free paper tape
- a 36-inch-long (96-cm-long) metal straightedge
- a pencil
- a gum or vinyl eraser
- a heavy piece of cardboard to be used for a cutting surface

Change or sharpen the blade in your knife often. A ragged edge is often the result of a dull blade. A continuous stroke will produce the cleanest edge. Mat blades should not be used for cutting more than one mat before being discarded.

The expense of a blade is minimal in comparison with the cost of mat board, so be generous in your use of new, sharp blades.

Do not use illustration board or other kinds of board for your mat. Cheaper varieties of backing material, since they are made from wood pulp, contain acid and will harm the drawing by staining the fibers of the paper and making them brittle. Use white or off-white, all-rag mat board, sometimes called museum board, unless special circumstances dictate otherwise. A heavyweight, hot-pressed watercolor paper can be used as a substitute for rag board.

Masking tape, clear tape, gummed tape, and rubber cement will likewise discolor the paper and should be avoided. They will lose their adhesive quality within a year or so. Use gummed linen or all-rag paper tape, both of which are acid free.

Instructions for Matting

Use the following procedure for matting. Work on a clean surface. Wash your hands before you begin.

1. Carefully measure the drawing to be matted. The edges of the mat's opening will overlap the drawing by 3/8 inch (1 cm) on all sides.
2. For an 18-by-24-inch (46-by-61-cm) drawing, the mat should have a 4-inch (10-cm) width on top and sides and a 5-inch (13-cm) width at the bottom. Note that the bottom border is slightly wider—by up to 20 percent—than the top and sides.
3. On the front surface of the mat board, mark lightly with a pencil the opening to be cut. You can erase later.
4. Place a straightedge on the mat just inside the penciled line toward the opening and cut. Hold down both ends of the straightedge. You may have to use your knee. Better still, enlist a friend's help. If the blade slips, the error will be on the part that is to be discarded and can, therefore, be corrected. Cut the entire line in one continuous movement. Do not start and stop. Make several single passes from top to bottom; do not try to cut through completely on your first stroke *(figure PG.D5)*.
5. Cut a rigid backing 1/8 inch (.3 cm) smaller on all sides than the mat.
6. Lay the mat face down and align the backing so that the two tops are adjoining. Cut four or five short pieces of linen tape, and at the top, hinge the backing to the mat *(figures PG.D6, PG.D7)*.

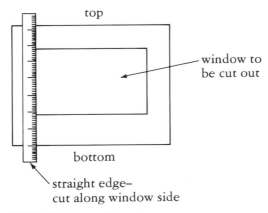

PG.D5. Cutting mat board.

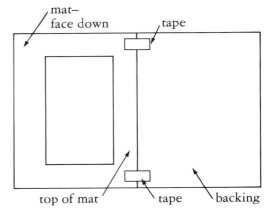

PG.D6. Hinging the mat.

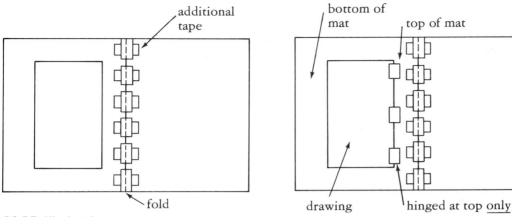

PG.D7. Hinging the mat.

PG.D8. Hinging drawing at the top.

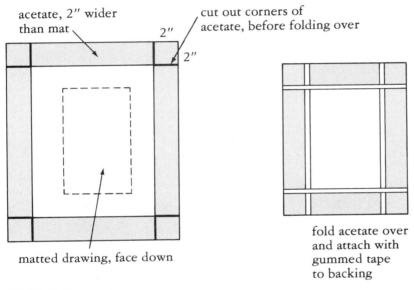

PG.D9. Cutting acetate.

7. Minor ragged edges of the mat can be corrected with fine sandpaper rubbed lightly along the edge of the cut surface.

8. Erase the pencil line and other smudges on the mat with a gum or vinyl eraser.

9. Hinge the drawing to the backing at the top only. This allows the paper to stretch and contract with changes in humidity *(figure PG.D8)*.

10. You may cover the matted drawing with acetate, which will protect both the drawing and mat. Place the backed, matted drawing face down on a sheet of acetate 2 inches (5 cm) wider on all sides than the mat. Cut 2-inch (5-cm) squares from each corner of the acetate *(figure PG.D9)*. Fold the acetate over, pulling lightly and evenly on all sides. Attach the acetate to the backing with tape.

CONCLUSION

In making your decision about the most suitable presentation, you should first try to visualize the piece in a variety of ways. If you are attentive, the work itself will probably suggest an appropriate presentation. Matting is generally the safest. Stitching in plastic and lamination should be reserved for those pieces that absolutely demand that type of presentation. Whatever your choice, remember that compatibility between drawing and method of presentation is essential.

If the manner of presentation is not clear to you, experiment with the piece. Place it in a discarded mat, or use some L-frames to crop the composition exactly right. Assess the drawing without a mat. Lay it on a larger piece of paper. Does the drawing go to the edge? Can you afford to lose half an inch (1 cm) on the borders? Is the idea of looseness or flexibility important to the drawing? Would a reflective covering detract from or enhance the drawing? What kind of surface and media are used in the drawing? What kind of backing would best complement the piece? What size mat or paper backing is the most appropriate? Does a cool white, a warm white, an off-white, a neutral, or a gray look best with the drawing? Does the size of the drawing present a problem?

Contemporary drawings are frequently attached directly to the wall. Extra care must be taken because of the fragility of the paper and the wear and tear on the edges. Linen tape can be attached to the edges to reinforce them, but this additional weight may change the way the drawing "falls." Large drawings can be rolled and stored in cylinders.

The care and storage of individual drawings is a major professional concern. Minimal good care is simple. You should spray-fix your drawings as soon as they are finished. Remove any smudges by erasure, and store the drawings in a flat, rigid container slightly larger than the largest drawing. Metal drawing files are ideal. A large portfolio with handles is a good investment for transporting your drawings. This ensures that the drawings will not become dog-eared, soiled, bent, or smudged. You should place a clean piece of barrier paper between drawings so that the medium from one does not transfer onto another. It is interesting to note that when the artist Paul Klee died in 1940, he left 10,000 paintings, drawings, and prints, along with 4,000 pages of analytical texts. Good conservation pays off in the long run.

Your attitude toward your work influences others' attitudes. A bad drawing can be improved by good presentation, whereas a good drawing can be destroyed by poor presentation. Proper care and handling of your work are good habits to establish early in your career.

Glossary

Italicized terms within the definitions are themselves defined in the glossary.

abstraction   An alteration of *forms*, derived from observation or experience, in such a way as to present essential rather than particular qualities.

achromatic   Relating to light and dark, the absence of *color*, as opposed to *chromatic* (relating to color).

actual texture   The *tactile* quality of a surface, including the mark made by a tool, the surface on which it is made, and any foreign material added to the surface. See also *invented texture*, *simulated texture*.

aerial perspective   The means by which atmospheric illusion is created.

aggressive line   An emphatically stated *line*.

ambiguity   An image or statement that can have two or more meanings; both interpretations cannot be mutually held.

ambiguous space   Space that is neither clearly flat nor clearly volumetric, containing a combination of both two- and *three-dimensional* elements.

amoeboid shape   See *organic shape*.

analogous colors   Colors adjacent to one another on the *color wheel*.

analytical line   A probing *line* that penetrates space, locating objects in relation to one another and to the space they occupy.

anthropomorphic image   An image in which an object or nonhuman form has been transformed by ascribing human forms or attributes.

antiperspective   Various challenges to linear *perspective* by artists who intentionally subvert its traditional conventions.

ant's-eye view   Objects seen from below.

appropriated image   An image taken from another source and used in a different context than the original.

appropriation   A process used by Postmodern artists employing ready-made ideas or images from high and low culture as subject matter in their own works.

arbitrary value   *Value* that does not necessarily conform to the actual appearance of an object; the use of value based on intuitive responses or the need to comply with compositional demands.

assemblage   A work of art composed of fragments of objects or *three-dimensional* materials originally intended for other purposes; the art of making such a work.

automatic drawing   A drawing in which the hand moves so quickly that conscious thought does not intervene.

axonometric view   A perspectival system in which an object's horizontal and vertical axes are drawn to scale, but its curved and diagonal lines are distorted.

background   See *negative space*.

baseline   The imaginary line on which an object or group of objects sits.

biomorphic shape   See *organic shape*.

bird's-eye view   Objects seen from above.

blind contour   A contour exercise in which the artist never looks at the paper.

blurred line   Smudged, erased, or destroyed *line*.

bricolage   A French term for something made or put together using whatever materials happen to be available.

cadavre exquis   French for exquisite corpse, a drawing technique devised by the Surrealists in which a group of artists work on the same drawing, each unaware of what the others have drawn.

calligraphic line   Free-flowing *line* that resembles handwriting, making use of gradual and graceful transitions.

caricature   A representation in which a subject's distinctive features are exaggerated for comic effect.

cast shadow   One of the six categories of *light*.

chiaroscuro   *Modeling*, the gradual blending of light to dark to create a *three-dimensional* illusion.

chromatic   Relating to *color*, as opposed to *achromatic* (relating to light and dark).

collage   Any flat material, such as newspapers, cloth, or wallpaper, pasted on the *picture plane*.

color   Visual assessment of the quality of *light* that is determined by its spectral composition.

color wheel   See *Munsell color wheel*.

complementary colors   Contrasting colors that lie opposite to each other on the *color wheel*.

composite shape   Two or more combined objects that create a unified, single *shape*.

composition   The organization or arrangement of the *elements of art* in a given work.

conceptual drawing   A drawing that in its essential *form* is conceived in the artist's mind, rather than derived from immediate visual stimuli.

cone of vision   Angle of sight.

constricted line   A *crabbed*, angular, tense *line*, frequently aggressively stated.

content   The subject matter of a work of art, including itsemotional, intellectual, symbolic, thematic, and narrative connotations, which together give the work its total meaning.

continuous-line drawing   A drawing in which the implement remains in uninterrupted contact with the *picture plane*, creating enclosed shapes.

continuous-field composition   A composition created such that if the *picture plane* were extended in any direction the composition would not change; it too would extend with the picture plane.

contour line   *Line* that delineates both the outside edge of an object and the edges of *planes*, as opposed to *outline*, which delineates only the outside edge of an object.

contour-line drawing   A drawing that emphasizes single, clean, incisive lines that define edges.

conventionalized space   The symbolic depiction of objects in space, which has become accepted from long use.

conventional texture   Abstracted texture that represents real texture. See *invented texture*.

cool colors   Blues, greens, and violets.

core of shadow   One of the six categories of *light*.

crabbed line   See *constricted line*.

cross-contour line   *Line* that describes an object's horizontal or cross contours rather than its vertical contours. Cross-contour line emphasizes the volumetric aspects of an object.

crosshatching   Creating value with sets of parallel lines that cross each other.

cursive line   A line related to handwriting.

décollage   A French term for unpasting, an offshoot of *collage*.

decorative texture   See *invented texture*.

density   A build-up of marks creating volume, mass, or weight.

diagrammatic drawing   A type of working drawing, demonstrating a visual form of shorthand, used widely in designs for buildings and city planning.

diptych   A work in two parts.

directional line   See *organizational line*.

elements of art   The principal graphic and *plastic* devices by which an artist composes a physical work of art. The elements are *color, line, shape, texture, value,* and *volume*.

emotive space   A psychological space that produces an emotional response in the viewer.

empty space   See *negative space*.

expressive   Dealing with feelings and emotions, as opposed to *objective* and *subjective*.

eye level   An imaginary horizontal *line* parallel to the viewer's eyes.

facture   The hand made quality in a one-of-a-kind drawing.

field   See *negative space*.

figure/field   See *positive shape*.

figure/ground   See *positive shape*.

flat space   A space having height and width but limited or no depth.

foreground/background   See *positive shape*.

foreshortening   A technique for producing the illusion of an object's extension into space by contracting its *form*.

form   In its broadest sense, the total structure of a work of art—that is, the relation of the *elements of art* and the distinctive character of the work. In a narrower sense, the *shape*, configuration, or substance of an object.

formal elements The art elements of *line, value, shape, texture,* and *color.*

free form See *organic shape.*

frottage A French term for *textural* transfer technique; the process of making rubbings with graphite or crayon on paper laid over a textured surface.

fumage A French term for *textural* technique that uses smoke as a medium.

geometric shape *Shape* created by mathematical laws and measurements, such as a circle or a square.

gestural approach A quick, all-encompassing statement of *forms.* In gesture, the hand duplicates the movement of the eyes, quickly defining the subject's general characteristics—movement, weight, *shape,* tension, *scale,* and *proportion.* See *mass gesture, line gesture, mass and line gesture,* and *sustained gesture.*

graphic novel Fictional works in cartoon format.

grattage A French term for *textural* technique that incises or scratches marks into the surface of the *picture plane* prepared with a coating, for example, gesso.

ground See *negative space.*

group theme Development of related works by members of the same schools and movements of art who share common philosophical, formal, stylistic, and subject interests.

hierarchical space A spatial system that depicts persons or things according to rank, class, or status.

highlight One of the six categories of *light.*

homage A work of art in the style of another artist to show respect to the creator of the original work.

horror vacui Latin for "fear of the void," a term with psychological connotations that is often applied to artwork that leaves no *empty space.*

hue The characteristic of a *color* that causes it to be classified as red, green, blue, or another color.

icon An image regarded with special veneration.

iconography The study of symbols used in art.

illusionistic space In the graphic arts, a representation of *three-dimensional space.*

implied line A *line* that stops and starts again; the viewer's eye completes the movement that the line suggests.

implied shape A suggested or incomplete *shape* that is mentally filled in by the viewer.

incised line A *line* that appears cut into a surface with a sharp implement.

indicative line See *organizational line.*

informational drawing A category of objective drawing, including *diagrammatic,* architectural, and mechanical drawing. Informational drawing clarifies concepts and ideas that may not be actually visible, such as a chemist's drawings of molecular structure.

inset A composition within a composition, set off by a drawn frame or by *empty space.*

installation A hybrid form of art that uses impermanent objects in a temporary space offering the viewer a temporal and spatial experience.

intensity The saturation, strength, or purity of a *color.*

interspace See *negative space.*

interstice An interval between objects or positive shapes. See *negative space.*

invented texture An invented, nonrepresentational, stylized patterning that may derive from *actual texture* but does not imitate it.

kinetic marks Marks that convey a sense of motion.

light In the graphic arts, the relationship of light and dark patterns on a *form,* determined by the actual appearance of an object and by the type and direction of light falling on it. There are six categories of light as it falls over a form: *highlight, light tone, shadow, core of shadow, reflected light,* and *cast shadow.*

light tone One of the six categories of *light.*

line A mark made by an implement as it is drawn across a surface. See also *aggressive, analytical, blurred, calligraphic, constricted, contour, crabbed, implied, lyrical, mechanical,* and *organizational* line.

line gesture A type of gesture drawing that describes interior forms, utilizing *line* rather than *mass.* See *gestural approach.*

linear perspective See *perspective.*

local color The known *color* of an object regardless of the amount or quality of *light* on it.

lyrical line A *subjective* line that is gracefully ornate and decorative.

mass In the graphic arts, the illusion of weight or density.

mass and line gesture A type of gesture drawing that combines broad value shapes with thick and thin lines. See *gestural approach.*

mass gesture A type of gesture drawing in which the drawing medium is used to make broad marks to create *mass* rather than *line.* See *gestural approach.*

mechanical line An *objective* line that maintains its width unvaryingly along its full length.

medium The category of a work of art as determined by its material or method of production. The plural of medium is **media,** the materials used in making art.

modeling The change from light to dark across a surface; a technique for creating spatial illusion.

monochromatic A color scheme using only one *color* with its various *hues* and *intensities.*

montage A French term for a technique that uses pictures to create a composition.

motif A recurring thematic image, a repeated figure or design.

multiple perspectives Different *eye levels* and perspectives used in the same drawing.

Munsell color wheel   A standard scale used in specifying *color*, named after its inventor, Albert H. Munsell.

naturalistic space   See *illusionistic space.*

negative space   The space surrounding a *positive shape*; sometimes referred to as *ground, empty space, interspace, field,* or *void.*

nonobjective   In the visual arts, work that intends no reference to concrete objects or persons, unlike *abstraction,* in which observed forms are sometimes altered to seem nonobjective.

object   A contemporary genre of art.

objective   Free from personal feelings; the emphasis is on the descriptive and factual rather than the *expressive* or *subjective.*

one-point perspective   A system for depicting *three-dimensional* depth on a *two-dimensional* surface, dependent upon the illusion that all parallel lines that recede into space converge at a single point on the horizon, called the *vanishing point.*

optical color   Perceived *color* modified by the quality of *light* on it.

organic shape   Free-form, irregular *shape.* Also called *biomorphic* or *amoeboid shape.*

organizational line   The *line* that provides the structure and basic organization for a drawing. Also called *indicative* or *directional line.*

organizational-line drawing   Drawing that uses grouped, directional lines to provide a structural, analytical framework.

origami   The Japanese technique of folding paper to create *three-dimensional* shapes.

outline   *Line* that delineates only the outside edge of an object, unlike *contour line,* which also delineates the edges of *planes.*

Outsider art   Art made by untrained, nonprofessional, self-taught artists.

papier collé   The French term for pasted paper; a technique consisting of pasting and gluing paper materials to the *picture plane.*

pastiche   A combination of several imitated styles in one work.

pentimento, *plural* **pentimenti**   The Italian term for the revealing of a part of a work that has been drawn or covered over, a correction that remains visible.

perceived color   See *optical color.*

perception   The awareness of objects through the medium of the senses.

perspective   A technique for giving an illusion of space to a flat surface.

photomontage   A technique that uses photographs to create a composition.

pictorial space   In the graphic arts, the illusion of space. It may be relatively flat or *two-dimensional,* illusionistically *three-dimensional,* or *ambiguous space.*

picture plane   The *two-dimensional* surface on which the artist works.

plan drawing   A drawing that makes use of a code or key that gives essential data contained in the drawing, such as information concerning materials and scale.

planar analysis   An approach in which *shape* functions as *plane,* as a component of *volume.*

plane   A *two-dimensional,* continuous surface with only one direction. See also *picture plane.*

plastic   The appearance of *volume* and space in a *two-dimensional* painting or drawing.

pochade   A French term for a quick sketch.

positive shape   The *shape* of an object that serves as the subject for a drawing. The relationship between positive shape and *negative space* is sometimes called *figure/field, figure/ground, foreground/background,* or *solid/void* relationship.

primary colors   Red, blue, and yellow.

private theme   Development by an individual artist of a personal, sustained, related series of works.

proportion   Comparative relationship between parts of a whole and between the parts and the whole.

realistic space   See *illusionistic space.*

reflected light   One of the six categories of *light.*

rubbing   A means of transferring texture from an actual tactile surface to a flat surface.

saturation   See *intensity.*

scale   Size and weight relationships between *forms.*

schematic drawing   A drawing derived from a mental construct as opposed to visual information.

scratchboard   A clay-coated paper whose surface is made to be scratched into.

scribbled line gesture   A type of gesture drawing using a tight network of tangled *line.* See *gestural approach.*

secondary colors   Colors achieved by mixing *primary colors*; green, orange, and violet.

shadow   One of the six categories of *light.*

shallow space   See *flat space.*

shape   A *two-dimensional,* closed, or implicitly closed configuration. The two categories of shape are *organic* and *geometric shape.*

shared theme   Thematic work in which the same images or subjects are used by different artists over a long period of time.

sighting   The visual measurements of objects and spaces between objects.

silhouette   Any dark *two-dimensional* shape seen against a light background.

simulated texture   The imitation of the *tactile* quality of a surface; can range from a suggested imitation to a highly illusionistic duplication of the subject's texture. See also *actual texture* and *invented texture*.

simultaneity   Multiple, overlapping views of an object.

solid/void   See *positive shape* and *negative space*.

stacked perspective   See *stacked space*.

stacked space   The use of stacked parallel *baselines* in the same composition.

stippling   A drawing or painting technique that uses dots or short strokes.

structural line   *Line* that helps locate objects in relation to other objects and to the space they occupy. Structural lines follow the direction of the *planes* they locate.

stylistic eclecticism   The use side by side of varying philosophies, styles, techniques, materials, and subjects.

subjective   Emphasizing the artist's emotions or personal viewpoint rather than informational content; compare *objective*.

sustained gesture   A type of gesture drawing that begins with a quick notation of the subject and extends into a longer analysis and correction. See *gestural approach*.

symbol   A *form* or image that stands for something more than its obvious, immediate meaning.

symbolic space   See *conventionalized space*.

symbolic texture   An invented textural pattern that represents or symbolizes textures in the real world. See *invented texture*.

tactile   Having to do with the sense of touch. In the graphic arts, the representation of *texture*.

tenebrism   Extreme contrast of light and dark.

tertiary colors   Colors that result when a *primary* and a *secondary color* are mixed.

texture   The *tactile* quality of a surface or its representation. The three basic types of texture are *actual*, *simulated*, and *invented texture*.

theme   The development of a sustained series of works that are related by subject, that have an idea or image in common. See *private theme*, *group theme*, and *shared theme*.

three-dimensional   Having height, width, and depth.

three-dimensional space   In the graphic arts, the illusion of *volume* or volumetric space—that is, of space that has height, width, and depth.

three-point perspective   A system for depicting *three-dimensional* depth on a *two-dimensional* surface. In addition to lines receding to two points on the horizon, lines parallel and vertical to the ground appear to converge to a third, vertical *vanishing point*.

thumbnail sketch   A small, quick preparatory drawing.

transferred texture   Texture produced by using solvents to move a printed image to the drawing.

triptych   A work in three parts.

trompe l'œil   The French term for trick-the-eye illusionistic techniques. See also *simulated texture*.

two-dimensional   Having height and width.

two-dimensional space   Space that has height and width with little or no illusion of depth, or *three-dimensional* space.

two-point perspective   A system for depicting *three-dimensional* depth on a *two-dimensional* surface, dependent upon the illusion that all parallel lines converge at two points on the horizon.

value   The gradation of tone from light to dark, from white through gray to black.

value reversal   A technique that reverses values, as in a photographic negative.

value scale   The gradual range from white through gray to black.

vanishing point   In *one-point perspective*, the single spot on the horizon where all parallel lines converge.

visual literacy   Familiarity with art history and the ability to understand images and their meanings.

void   See *negative space*.

volume   The quality of a *form* that has height, width, and depth; the representation of this quality. See also *mass*.

warm colors   Reds, oranges, and yellows.

window into space   The Italian Renaissance concept to convey the illusion of *three-dimensional space* on a flat surface.

works on paper   A classification that includes drawings, prints, photography, book illustrations, and posters.

Suggested Readings

Suggested readings concentrate on contemporary art and artists.

Students may find the following periodicals helpful: *Artforum*, *Art in America*, *Art Journal*, *ARTnews*, *Art on Paper*, *Artweek*, *Drawing*, and *October*.

Most museums and galleries have websites (see page 251 for major listings). Internet searches using Google, Yahoo, and Artcyclopedia will lead to many art connections. Some online data bases are Artnet.com, Eyestorm.com, Britart.com, and Mixed Greens. See also Lois Jones. *Art Information and the Internet: How to Find It, How to Use It*. Westport, Conn.: Greenwood Publishing Group, 1998.

SURVEYS AND CRITICISM

Alloway, Lawrence. *American Pop Art*. New York: Macmillan, 1974.

American Abstract Drawing, 1930–1987. Little Rock: Arkansas Arts Center, 1987.

Armstrong, Richard, John G. Hanhardt, Richard Marshall, and Lisa Phillips. *1989 Biennial Exhibition*. New York: Whitney Museum of American Art, 1989.

Arnason, H. H. *History of Modern Art*. 3rd ed. New York: Harry N. Abrams, 1986.

Atkins, Robert. *Artspeak: A Guide to Contemporary Ideas, Movements, and Buzzwords*. New York: Abbeville Press, 1990.

Bean, Jacob. *100 European Drawings in the Metropolitan Museum of Art*. New York: The Metropolitan Museum of Art, 1964.

Behr, Shulamith. *Women Expressionists*. New York: Abbeville Press, 1988.

Beier, Ulli. *Contemporary Art in Africa*. New York: Praeger, 1968.

Benezra, Neal, and Olga M. Viso. *Distemper: Dissonant Themes in the Art of the 1990s*. Washington, D.C.: Smithsonian Institution, 1996.

Berger, John. *The Sense of Sight*. New York: Pantheon, 1985.

——. *Ways of Seeing*. London: BBC and Penguin, 1972.

Berman, Patricia. *Modern Hieroglyphs: Gestural Drawing and the European Vanguard*. Philadelphia: University of Pennsylvania Press, 1995.

Bown, Matthew Cullerne. *Contemporary Russian Art*. New York: Philosophical Library, 1990.

Butler, Cornelia H. *Afterimage: Drawing Through Process*. Los Angeles: Museum of Contemporary Art, 1999.

Carlin, John, and Sheena Wagstaff. *The Comic Art Show.* New York: Whitney Museum of American Art, 1983.

Casslman, Bart, ed. *The Sublime Void: On the Memory of the Imagination.* New York: Ludion, 1995.

Cathcart, Linda L. *American Still Life 1945–1983.* Houston: Contemporary Arts Museum, 1983.

Celant, Germano, ed. *Biennale di Venezia* [XLVII Esposizione, 1997]. Venice: Electa, 1997.

Clay, Jean. *Modern Art, 1890 to 1990.* New York: Book Sales, 1989.

Cole, Robert. *Their Eyes Meeting the World: The Drawings and Paintings of Children.* Boston: Houghton Mifflin, 1995.

Colpitt, Frances. *Minimal Art: The Critical Perspective.* Seattle: University of Washington Press, 1993.

Constructivism and the Geometric Tradition: Selections from the McCrory Corporation Collection. New York: McCrory Corporation, 1979.

Cooper, Douglas. *The Cubist Epoch.* New York: Praeger, 1971.

Danto, Arthur C. *The Philosophical Disenfranchisement of Art.* New York: Columbia University Press, 1986.

———. *The State of the Art.* New York: Columbia University Press, 1987.

Davies, Hugh M., and Ronald J. Onorato. *Blurring the Boundaries: Installation Art 1969–1996.* San Diego: Museum of Contemporary Art, 1997.

Dennison, Lisa. *New Horizons in American Art.* New York: Solomon R. Guggenheim Museum, 1989.

Dexter, Emma. *Vitamin D: New Perspectives in Drawing.* London: Phaidon Press, 2005.

Dietrich-Boorsch, Dorothea. *German Drawings of the '60s.* New Haven, Conn.: Yale University Press, 1982.

Dowell, M., and D. Robbins. *Cubist Drawings, 1907–1929.* Houston: Janie C. Lee Gallery, 1982.

Drawings from the Permanent Collection. Fort Worth, Tex.: Modern Art Museum of Fort Worth. n.d.

Drawings: Recent Acquisitions. New York: The Museum of Modern Art, 1967.

Drawn-Out. Washington, D.C.: Corcoran Gallery of Art, 1987.

Elderfield, John. *The Modern Drawing: 100 Works on Paper from the Museum of Modern Art.* London: Thames and Hudson, 1984.

Foote, Nancy, ed. *Drawings: The Pluralist Decade.* Philadelphia: Institute of Contemporary Art, 1981.

Foster, Hal, ed. *The Anti-Aesthetic: Essays on Postmodern Culture.* Port Townsend, Wash.: Bay Press, 1983.

Fox, Howard N., Miranda McClintic, and Phyllis Roxenzweig. *Content: A Contemporary Focus 1974–1984.* Washington, D.C.: Smithsonian Institution, 1984.

Frandsen, Jan Würtz. *Drawn Toward the Avant-Garde: Nineteenth- and Twentieth-Century French Drawings from the Royal Museum of Fine Arts, Copenhagen.* Alexandria, Va.: Art Services International, 2002.

Fusco, Coco. *English Is Broken Here: Notes on Cultural Fusion in the Americas.* New York: New Press, 1995.

Gablik, Suzi. *Conversations Before the End of Time.* New York: Thames and Hudson, 1995.

Garcia, Rupert. *Aspects of Resistance.* New York: Alternative Museum, 1994.

Godfrey, Tony. *Drawing Today: Draughtsmen in the Eighties.* Oxford: Phaidon, 1990.

Golden, Thelma, et al. *Art: 21: Art in the Twenty-First Century.* New York: Harry N. Abrams, 2001.

Gottlieb, Carla. *Beyond Modern Art.* New York: Dutton, 1976.

Grynsztejn, Madeleine. *About Place: Recent Art of the Americas.* Chicago: Art Institute of Chicago, 1995.

Hoptman, Laura. *Drawing Now: Eight Propositions.* New York: The Museum of Modern Art, 2002.

Humphries, Lloyd. *Art of Our Time: The Saatchi Collection.* Vols. 1–4. New York: International Publishing, 1985.

Iles, Chrissie, and Phillippe Vergne. *Whitney Biennial 2006: Day for Night.* New York: Harry N. Abrams, 2006.

Johnson, Una E. *20th Century Drawings: Drawings of the Masters, Part II: 1940 to the Present.* New York: Shorewood Publishers, 1964.

Johnstone, Mark, and Leslie Aboud Holzman. *Epicenter: San Francisco Bay Area Art Now.* San Francisco: Chronicle Books, 2002.

Kurtz, Bruce D. *Contemporary Art, 1965–1990.* Englewood Cliffs, N.J.: Prentice-Hall, 1992.

Large-Scale Drawings from the Kramarsky Collection. Ridgefield, Conn.: Aldrich Museum of Contemporary Art, 1998.

Lee, Pamela, and Christine Mehring. *Drawing Is Another Kind of Language.* Cambridge, Mass.: Harvard University Press, 1997.

Leslie, Clare Walker. *Nature Drawing: A Tool for Learning.* New York: Simon and Schuster, 1980.

Lippard, Lucy. *From the Center.* New York: Dutton, 1976.

———. *Six Years: The Dematerialization of the Art Object from 1966 to 1972.* New York: Praeger, 1973.

Livingstone, Marco. *Jim Dine: Flowers and Plants.* New York: Harry N. Abrams, 1994.

MacGregor, John M. *The Discovery of the Art of the Insane.* Princeton, N.J.: Princeton University Press, 1989.

Maresca, Frank, and Roger Ricco. *American Self-Taught: Paintings and Drawings by Outsider Artists.* New York: Alfred A. Knopf, 1995.

Marx, Sammburg. *Beuys, Rauschenberg, Twombly, Warhol.* Munich: Prestel Verlag, 1982.

McQuiston, Liz. *Graphic Agitation: Social and Political Graphics Since the Sixties.* New York: Phaidon, 1993.

———. *Women in Design: A Contemporary View.* New York: Rizzoli, 1988.

Mitchell, W. J. T. *What Do Pictures Want? The Lives and Loves of Images.* Chicago: University of Chicago Press, 2005.

Modern Latin American Painting, Drawings and Sculpture. New York: Sotheby, 1989.

The Monumental Image. Rohnert Park, Calif.: Sonoma State University, 1987.

Morgan, Stuart, and Frances Morris. *Rites of Passage: Art for the End of the Century.* London: Tate Gallery Publications, 1995.

Morley, Simon. *Writing on the Wall: Word and Image in Modern Art.* Berkeley: University of California Press, 2003.

Moskowitz, Ira, ed. *Great Drawings of All Time, III. French 13th Century to 1919.* New York: Shorewood, 1962.

Newman, Avis, and Catherine de Zegher. *The Stage of Drawing: Gesture and Act (Selected from the Tate Collection).* New York: Tate Publishing/The Drawing Center, 2003.

Newman, Charles. *The Post-Modern Aura.* Evanston, Ill.: Northwestern University Press, 1985.

Njami, Simon, ed. *African Remix: Contemporary Art of a Continent.* Hamburg: Hatje Cantz Publishers, 2005.

Perry, Gill, et al. *Primitivism, Cubism, Abstraction: The Early Twentieth Century.* New Haven, Conn.: Yale University Press, 1993.

Pincus-Witten, Robert. *Postminimalism.* New York: Out of London Press, 1977.

Plagens, Peter. *Sunshine Muse.* New York: Praeger, 1974.

Plous, Phyllis, and Mary Looker. *Neo York.* Santa Barbara, Calif.: University Art Museum, 1989.

Ramirez, Mari Carmen, and Héctor Olea. *Inverted Utopias: Avant-Garde Art in Latin America.* Houston: Museum of Fine Arts/New Haven, Conn.: Yale University Press, 2004.

Raven, Arlene, et al., eds. *Feminist Art Criticism: An Anthology.* Ann Arbor, Mich.: UMI Research Press, 1988.

Rawson, Philip. *Drawing.* Philadelphia: University of Pennsylvania Press, 1987.

Re-Aligning Vision: Alternative Currents in South American Drawing, 1960–1990. New York: Museo del Barrio, 1997.

Rexer, Lyle. *How to Look at Outsider Art.* New York: Harry N. Abrams, 2005.

Risatti, Howard, ed. *Postmodern Perspective: Issues in Contemporary Art.* Englewood Cliffs, N.J.: Prentice-Hall, 1990.

Rogers, Ruth R. *Resonance and Response: Artists' Books from Special Collections.* Wellesley, Mass.: Wellesley College, 2005.

Rose, Barbara. *Drawing Now.* New York: The Museum of Modern Art, 1976.

Rose, Bernice. *Allegories of Modernism.* New York: The Museum of Modern Art, 1992.

Rowell, Margit. *Objects of Desire: The Modern Still Life.* New York: The Museum of Modern Art, 1997.

Rubin, William S. *Dada and Surrealist Art.* New York: Harry N. Abrams, 1969.

Sandler, Irving. *Art of the Postmodern Era from the Late 1960s to the Early 1990s.* Boulder, Colo.: Westview, 1996.

Selz, Peter. *Art in Our Times: A Pictorial History 1890–1980.* New York: Harcourt Brace Jovanovich/Harry N. Abrams, 1981.

75th American Exhibition. Chicago: Art Institute of Chicago, 1986.

Smagula, Howard. *Currents: Contemporary Directions in the Visual Arts.* Englewood Cliffs, N.J.: Prentice-Hall, 1983.

Solomon, Elke M. *American Drawings 1963–1973.* New York: Whitney Museum of American Art, 1973.

Stebbins, Theodore E. *American Master Drawings and Watercolors: A History of Works on Paper from Colonial Times to the Present.* New York: The Drawing Society, 1976.

Steinberg, Leo. *Other Criteria: Confrontations with Twentieth-Century Art.* London: Oxford University Press, 1972.

Stella, Frank. *Working Space.* Cambridge, Mass.: Harvard University Press, 1986.

Storr, Robert, et al. *Art: 21: Art in the Twenty-First Century.* New York: Harry N. Abrams, 2001.

Tansey, Richard G. *Gardner's Art Through the Ages.* Belmont, Calif: Wadsworth, 2000.

Tiberghien, Gilles A. *Land Art.* Princeton, N.J.: Princeton Architectural Press, 1995.

Tomkins, Calvin. *Post- to Neo-: The Art World of the 1980s.* New York: Henry Holt, 1989.

Tuchman, Maurice, ed. *The Spiritual in Art: Abstract Painting 1890–1985.* New York: Abbeville Press, 1986.

Tucker, Marcia. *Bad Painting in "Bad" Painting.* New York: The New Museum, 1978.

Tupitsyn, Margarita, curator. *Twenty-fourth Bienal de São Paulo.* São Paulo: Fundacão Bienal de São Paulo, 1998.

Varnedoe, Kirk, and Adam Copnick. *High and Low: Modern Art and Popular Culture.* New York: Harry N. Abrams, 1990.

Varnedoe, Kirk, and Adam Copnick, eds. *Modern Art and Popular Culture: Readings in High and Low Art.* New York: Harry N. Abrams, 1990.

Vergine, Lea. *Art on the Cutting Edge: A Guide to Contemporary Movements.* Milan: Skira, 1996.

Vogel, Sabine. *4th International Istanbul Biennial.* Istanbul Foundation of Culture and Arts, 1995.

Vogel, Susan. *Africa Explores: 20th Century African Art.* New York: Center for African Art/Munich: Prestel Verlag, 1991.

Waldman, Diane. *British Art Now: An American Perspective.* New York: Solomon R. Guggenheim Museum, 1980.

————. *Collage, Assemblage, and the Found Object.* New York: Harry N. Abrams, 1995.

————. *New Perspectives in American Art.* New York: Solomon R. Guggenheim Museum, 1983.

Wallis, Brian, ed. *Art After Modernism: Rethinking Representation*. Boston: New Museum of Contemporary Art, 1985.

Warren, Tracey, and Amelia Jones. *The Artist's Body*. London: Phaidon, 2000.

Weber, Bruce. *The Fine Line: Drawing with Silver in America*. West Palm Beach, Fla.: Norton Gallery of Art, 1985.

Whitney Museum's Biennial Catalogs. New York: Whitney Museum of American Art, from 1981 to 2001.

Wilkins, David G., and Bernard Schultz. *Art Past/Art Present*. New York: Harry N. Abrams, 1990.

Wolfe, Townsend. *The Face*. Little Rock: Arkansas Art Center, 1988.

——. *The Figure*. Little Rock: Arkansas Art Center, 1988.

——. *National Drawing Invitational*. Little Rock: Arkansas Art Center, 1994 and 1998.

——. *Objects and Drawings II: Working in Other Dimensions*. Little Rock: Arkansas Art Center, 1994.

——. *Revelations: Drawing—America*. Little Rock: Arkansas Art Center, 1988.

——. *Twentieth-Century American Drawings*. Little Rock: Arkansas Art Center, 1984.

Wolfe, Townsend, and Ruth Pasquine. *Large Drawings and Objects*. Little Rock: Arkansas Art Center, 1996.

Wye, Deborah. *Committed to Print*. New York: The Museum of Modern Art, 1988.

COLOR

Albers, Josef. *Interaction of Color*, rev. ed. New Haven, Conn.: Yale University Press, 1972.

Birren, Faber. *Principles of Color*. New York: Van Nostrand Reinhold, 1969.

Doyle, Michael E. *Color Drawing*. New York: Van Nostrand Reinhold, 1981.

Fabri, Frank. *Color: A Complete Guide for Artists*. New York: Watson-Guptill, 1967.

Itten, Johannes. *The Art of Color*. New York: Van Nostrand Reinhold, 1974.

Poling, Clark V. *Kandinsky's Teaching at the Bauhaus: Color Theory and Analytical Drawing*. New York: Rizzoli, 1986.

PERSPECTIVE

Cole, Rex Vicat. *Perspective: The Practice & Theory of Perspective as Applied to Pictures*. Philadelphia: Lippincott, 1922.

D'Amelio, Joseph. *Perspective Drawing Handbook*. New York: Leon Amiel, 1964.

Dubery, Fred, and John Willats. *Perspective and Other Drawing Systems*. London: Herbet, 1983.

Montague, John. *Basic Perspective Drawing: A Visual Approach*. New York: Van Nostrand Reinhold, 1985.

Norton, Dora M. *Freehand Perspective and Sketching*. New York: Bridgman Publishers, 1929.

Powell, William. *Perspective*. New York: W. Foster, 1989.

Walters, Nigel V., and John Bromham. *Principles of Perspective*. New York: Watson-Guptill, 1974.

WORKS ON INDIVIDUAL ARTISTS

John Baldessari

Tucker, Marcia, and Robert Pincus-Witten. *John Baldessari*. New York: The New Museum, 1981.

Van Bruggen, Coosje. *John Baldessari*. New York: Rizzoli, 1990.

Georg Baselitz

Corral, Maria, and Elvira Maluquer. *Georg Baselitz*. Madrid: Fundacion Caja de Pensiones, 1990.

Waldman, Diane. *Georg Baselitz*. New York: Guggenheim/Abrams, 1995.

Jean-Michel Basquiat

Marshall, Richard. *Jean-Michel Basquiat*. New York: Whitney/Abrams, 1995.

Romare Bearden

Romare Bearden: The Prevalence of Ritual. New York: The Museum of Modern Art, 1971.

Lynda Benglis

Lynda Benglis: 3-Dimensional Painting. Chicago: Museum of Contemporary Art, 1980.

Joseph Beuys

Adriani, Götz. *Joseph Beuys: Drawings, Objects and Prints*. Berlin: Institute for Foreign Cultural Relations and the Goethe Institute, 1995.

Schade, Werner. *Joseph Beuys: The Early Drawings*. New York: Shirmer/Mosel/Norton, 1995.

Temkin, Anne, and Bernice Rose. *Thinking Is Form: The Drawings of Joseph Beuys*. Philadelphia: Philadelphia Museum of Art/London: Thames and Hudson, 1995.

Lee Bontecou

Smith, Elizabeth A. T., and Ann Philbin. *Lee Bontecou: A Retrospective*. New York: Harry N. Abrams, 2004.

Jonathan Borofsky

Rosenthal, Mark, and Richard Marshall. *Jonathan Borofsky*. Philadelphia: Philadelphia Museum of Art/New York: Whitney Museum of American Art, 1984.

Louise Bourgeois

Bourgeois, Louise, and Lawrence Rinder. *Drawings & Observations*. New York: Bulfinch, 1996.

Paul Cézanne

Chappuis, Adrien. *The Drawings of Paul Cézanne*. Greenwich, Conn.: New York Graphic Society, 1973.

Christo

Schellmann, Jorg, and Josephine Benecke, eds. *Christo Prints and Objects*. New York: Abbeville Press, 1987.

Francesco Clemente

Percy, Ann, and Raymond Foye. *Francesco Clemente: Three Worlds*. New York: Rizzoli, 1990.

Chuck Close

Guare, John. *Chuck Close: Life and Work 1988–1995*. London: Thames and Hudson, 1995.
Yau, John. *Chuck Close: Recent Paintings*. Los Angeles: Pace Wildenstein Gallery, 1995.

Joseph Cornell

Joseph Cornell. New York: The Museum of Modern Art. 1990.
Waldman, Diane. *Joseph Cornell*. New York: Braziller, 1977.

Vincent Desiderio

Bradway, Todd, ed. *Vincent Desiderio: Paintings 1975–2005*. New York: Marlborough, 2005.

Richard Diebenkorn

Richard Diebenkorn: Paintings and Drawings, 1943–1980. Buffalo, N.Y.: Albright-Knox Art Gallery/New York: Rizzoli, 1980.

Jim Dine

Gordon, John. *Jim Dine*. New York: Praeger/Whitney Museum of American Art, 1970.
Livingstone, Marco. *Jim Dine: Flowers and Plants*. New York: Harry N. Abrams, 1994.

Jean Dubuffet

Drawings, Jean Dubuffet. New York: The Museum of Modern Art, 1968.

Marcel Duchamp

Baruchello, Gianfranco, and Henry Martin. *The Imagination of Art (How to Imagine* and *Why Duchamp; 2 vol.)*. Kingston, N.Y.: McPherson, 1986.
Marcel Duchamp. Philadelphia: The Philadelphia Museum of Art/New York: The Museum of Modern Art, 1973.

Walton Ford

Katz, Steven, and Dodie Kazanjian. *Walton Ford: Tigers of Wrath, Horses of Instruction*. New York: Harry N. Abrams, 2002.

Lucian Freud

Penny, Nicolas, and Robert Johnson. *Lucian Freud: Works on Paper*. London: Thames and Hudson, 1988.

Alberto Giacometti

Bonnefoy, Yves. *Giacometti*. New York: Abbeville Press, 1995.
Giacometti, Alberto. *Giacometti: A Sketchbook of Interpretive Drawings*. New York: Harry N. Abrams, 1967.

April Gornik

Gedeon, Lucinda H., ed. *April Gornik: Paintings and Drawings*. New York: Hudson Hills Press, 2004.

Nancy Graves

Padon, Thomas. *Nancy Graves: Excavations in Print*. New York: Harry N. Abrams, 1996.

Juan Gris

Rosenthal, Mark. *Juan Gris*. New York: Abbeville Press, 1983.

Red Grooms

Tully, Judd. *Red Grooms and Ruckus Manhattan*. New York: Braziller, 1977.

George Grosz

Grosz, George. *Love Above All and Other Drawings: 120 Works by George Grosz*. New York: Dover, 1971.

Philip Guston

Dabrowski, Magdalena. *The Drawings of Philip Guston*. New York: The Museum of Modern Art, 1988.

Jane Hammond

Snyder, Jill. *Jane Hammond: The Ashbery Collaboration*. Cleveland: Cleveland Center for Contemporary Art, 2001.

Mona Hatoum

Schneede, Uwe M., et al. *Mona Hatoum*. Hamburg: Hatje Cantz Publishers, 2004.

David Hockney

Luckhardt, Ulrich, and Paul Melia. *David Hockney: A Drawing Retrospective*. Los Angeles: Chronicle Books, 1995.
Melia, Paul, ed. *David Hockney*. New York: St. Martin's Press, 1995.
Tuchman, Maurice, and Stephanie Barron. *David Hockney: A Retrospective*. New York: The Museum of Modern Art, 1988.

Jenny Holzer

Waldman, Diane. *Jenny Holzer*. New York: Harry N. Abrams, 1990.

Robert Irwin

Weschler, Lawrence. *Seeing Is Forgetting the Name of the Thing One Sees: A Life of Contemporary Artist Robert Irwin*. Berkeley: University of California Press, 1982.

Yvonne Jacquette

Ratcliff, Carter. *Yvonne Jacquette* (catalog). New York: The Museum of Modern Art, 1990.

Neil Jenney

Rosenthal, Mark. *Neil Jenney*. Berkeley: University Art Museum, 1981.

Jess

Jess: A Grand Collage 1951–1993. Buffalo, N.Y.: Albright-Knox Art Gallery, 1993.

Jasper Johns

Castleman, Riva. *Jasper Johns: A Print Retrospective*. New York: The Museum of Modern Art, 1986.
Francis, Richard. *Jasper Johns*. New York: Abbeville Press, 1984.

Rosenthal, Mark. *Jasper Johns: Work Since 1974*. Philadelphia: Philadelphia Museum of Art, 1988.
Shapiro, David. *Jasper Johns: Drawings, 1954–1984*. New York: Harry N. Abrams, 1984.

Ilya Kabakov

Kabakov, Ilya, and Amei Wallach et al. *Ilya Kabakov: The Man Who Never Threw Anything Away*. New York: Harry N. Abrams, 1996.

Wassily Kandinsky

Grohmann, Will. *Kandinsky*. London: Thames and Hudson, 1959.

William Kentridge

Tone, Lilian. *William Kentridge*. New York: The Museum of Modern Art, 1999.

Anselm Kiefer

Rosenthal, Mark. *Anselm Kiefer*. New York: Te Neues, 1988.

Paul Klee

Grohmann, Will. *Paul Klee*. New York: Harry N. Abrams, 1945.

Barbara Kruger

Linker, Kate. *Love for Sale: The Words and Pictures of Barbara Kruger*. New York: Harry N. Abrams, 1990.

Rico Lebrun

Lebrun, Rico. *Rico Lebrun: Drawings*. Berkeley: University of California Press, 1968.

Fernand Léger

Fabre, Gladys C., Barbara Rose, and Marie-Odile Briot. *Léger and the Modern Spirit: An Avant-Garde Alternative to Non-Objective Art*. Houston: Museum of Fine Arts, 1983.

Sol LeWitt

Minimalism. Seattle: University of Washington Press, 1990.
Reynolds, Jack, and Andrea Miller-Keller. *Sol LeWitt: Twenty-Five Years of Wall Drawings, 1968–1993*. Seattle: University of Washington Press, 1995.

Roy Lichtenstein

Waldman, Diane. *Roy Lichtenstein*. New York: Solomon R. Guggenheim Museum/Rizzoli, 1993.

Richard Long

Seymour, Anne, and Hamish Fulton. *Richard Long: Walking in Circles.* New York: Braziller, 1991.

Robert Longo

Fox, Howard N. *Robert Longo.* Los Angeles: L.A. County Museum/New York: Rizzoli, 1989.

Nino Longobardi

Rose, Barbara. *Living on the Edge: The Drawings of Nino Longobardi.* Lund, Sweden: Kalejdoskop Förlag, 1987.

David Macaulay

Macaulay, David. *Great Moments of Architecture.* Boston: Houghton Mifflin, 1978.

Brice Marden

Kertess, Klaus. *Brice Marden: Paintings and Drawings.* New York: Harry N. Abrams, 1992.
Lewison, Jeremy. *Brice Marden Prints, 1961–1991.* London: Tate Gallery, 1992.

Henri Matisse

Carlson, Victor. *Matisse as a Draughtsman.* Baltimore, Md.: Baltimore Museum of Art/Greenwich, Conn.: New York Graphic Society, 1971.
Elderfield, John. *Henri Matisse: A Retrospective.* New York: The Museum of Modern Art, 1992.

Mario Merz

Eccher, Danilo. *Mario Merz.* New York: Hopeful Monster, 1995.

Annette Messager

Conkelton, Sheryl, and Carol S. Eliel. *Annette Messager.* New York: Harry N. Abrams, 1995.
Grenier, Catherine. *Annette Messager.* Paris: Flammarion, 2001.

Joan Miró

Rowell, Margit. *The Captured Imagination: Drawings by Joan Miró from the Fundacio Joan Miró, Barcelona.* New York: American Federation of the Arts, 1987.

Piet Mondrian

Hammacher, A. M. *Mondrian, De Stijl and Their Impact.* New York: Marlborough, 1964.

Mondrian, Piet. *The New Art—The New Life: The Collected Writings of Piet Mondrian.* Harry Holtzman and Martin St. James, eds. Boston: G. K. Hall, 1986.

Henry Moore

Garrould, Ann, ed. *Henry Moore Drawings.* London: Thames and Hudson, 1988.

Giorgio Morandi

Vitale, Lamberto. *Giorgio Morandi.* 2 vols. Florence, Italy: Ufizzi, 1983.

Robert Morris

Minimalism. Seattle: University of Washington Press, 1990.

Bruce Nauman

Bruce Nauman Drawings, 1965–1986. Basel: Museum für Gegenwartskunst, 1986.
Van Bruggen, Coosje. *Bruce Nauman.* New York: Rizzoli, 1987.

Alice Neel

Hills, Patricia. *Alice Neel.* New York: Harry N. Abrams, 1983.

Shirin Neshat

Dabashi, Hamid, et al. *Shirin Neshat.* Milan: Charta, 2002.

Claes Oldenburg

Baro, Gene. *Claes Oldenburg: Prints and Drawings.* London: Chelsea House, 1969.
Celant, Germano, and Mark Rosenthal. *Claes Oldenburg: An Anthology.* New York: Guggenheim/Abrams, 1995.
Haskell, Barbara. *Claes Oldenburg: Objects into Monument.* Pasadena, Calif.: Pasadena Art Museum, 1971.
Oldenburg, Claes. *Notes in Hand.* New York: Dutton, 1971.

Philip Pearlstein

Philip Pearlstein Watercolors and Drawings. New York: Alan Frumkin Gallery, n.d.

A. R. Penck

Grisebach, Lucius, ed. *A. R. Penck.* Munich: Berlin National Galerie/Prestel Verlag, 1988.
Yau, John. *A. R. Penck.* New York: Harry N. Abrams, 1995.

Judy Pfaff

Sandler, Irving. *Judy Pfaff.* New York: Hudson Hills Press, 2003.

Pablo Picasso

Picasso, Pablo, with text by Charles Feld. *Picasso: His Recent Drawings 1966–1968.* New York: Harry N. Abrams, 1969.
Rose, Bernice. *Picasso and Drawing.* New York: Pace Wildenstein, 1995.

Sigmar Polke

Sigmar Polke Drawings 1962–1988. Bonn: Kunstmuseum, 1988.

Jackson Pollock

Friedman, B. H. *Jackson Pollock: Energy Made Visible.* New York: McGraw-Hill, 1972.
O'Connor, Francis V. *Jackson Pollock.* New York: The Museum of Modern Art, 1967.

Robert Rauschenberg

Hopps, Walter, and Susan Davidson. *Robert Rauschenberg: A Retrospective.* New York: Solomon R. Guggenheim Museum, 1997.

Paula Rego

Paula Rego. London: Tate Gallery Publishing, 1997.

Gerhard Richter

Obrist, Hans Ulrich, ed. *Gerhard Richter: The Daily Practice of Painting, Writings 1962–1993.* Cambridge, Mass.: Anthony d'Offay/MIT Press, 1995.
Schwarz, Dieter. *Gerhard Richter: Drawings 1964–1999.* Düsseldorf: Kunstmuseum Winterthur/Richter Verlag, 1999.

Larry Rivers

Rivers, Larry. *Drawings and Digressions.* New York: Clarkson Potter, 1979.

Julian Schnabel

Schnabel, Julian. *Julian Schnabel: Works on Paper 1975–1988.* Munich: Prestel Verlag, 1990.

Kurt Schwitters

Elderfield, John. *Kurt Schwitters.* London: Thames and Hudson, 1985.

Sean Scully

Scully, Sean. *Sean Scully: Paintings and Works on Paper.* Kendal, Cumbria, U.K.: Abbot Hall Art Gallery, 2005.

Richard Serra

Serra, Richard. *Richard Serra: Writings/Interviews.* Chicago: University of Chicago Press, 1994.

Kiki Smith

Posner, Helaine. *Kiki Smith.* New York: Bulfinch, 1998.
Weitman, Wendy. *Kiki Smith: Prints, Books & Things.* New York: The Museum of Modern Art, 2003.

Robert Smithson

Robert Smithson: Drawings. New York: New York Cultural Center, 1974.
Tsai, Eugenie. *Robert Smithson Unearthed: Drawings, Collages, Writings.* New York: Columbia University Press, 1991.

Saul Steinberg

Rosenberg, Harold. *Saul Steinberg.* New York: Alfred A. Knopf, 1978.

Pat Steir

Arbitrary Order: Paintings by Pat Steir. Houston: Contemporary Arts Museum, 1983.
Steir, Pat. *Pat Steir.* New York: Harry N. Abrams, 1986.

Donald Sultan

Sultan, Donald. *Donald Sultan.* Chicago: Museum of Contemporary Art/New York: Harry N. Abrams, 1987.

Stephen Talasnik

Talasnik, Stephen. *Stephen Talasnik: Drawings 1990–1994.* Greensboro: University of North Carolina Press, 1995.

Mark Tansey

Freeman, Judi. *Mark Tansey.* San Francisco: Chronicle Books, 1993.
Robbe-Grillet, Alain. *Mark Tansey.* Los Angeles: L.A. County Museum, 1995.

Wayne Thiebaud

Beal, Graham W. J. *Wayne Thiebaud Painting.* Minneapolis: Walker Art Center, 1981.
Tsujimoto, Karen. *Wayne Thiebaud.* San Francisco: San Francisco Museum of Modern Art, 1985.

Wayne Thiebaud Survey 1947–1976. Phoenix, Ariz.: Phoenix Art Museum, 1976.

Jean Tinguely

Hulten, K. G. Pontus. *Jean Tinguely: Meta*. Greenwich, Conn.: New York Graphic Society, 1975.

Mark Tobey

Rathbone, Eliza E. *Mark Tobey*. Washington, D.C.: National Gallery of Art, 1986.

Richard Tuttle

The Poetry of Form: Richard Tuttle Drawings from the Vogel Collection. Amsterdam: Institute of Contemporary Art, 1992.

Cy Twombly

Bastian, Heiner, ed. *Cy Twombly: Catalogue Raisonné of the Paintings* Vol. IV 1972–1995. Berlin: Schirmer/Mosel, 1995.

Andy Warhol

McShine, Kynaston, ed. *Andy Warhol: A Retrospective*. New York: The Museum of Modern Art, 1989.

William T. Wiley

Wiley Territory. Minneapolis: Walker Art Center, 1979.

Terry Winters

Phillips, Lisa. *Terry Winters*. New York: Whitney Museum of American Art, 1991.
Plous, Phyllis. *Terry Winters, Painting and Drawing*. Santa Barbara, Calif.: University Art Museum, 1987.

Index

of picture plane, 80–81
as plane and volume, 82–89
positive, 72–73, 91
positive/negative interchange, 73–75, 77, 79, 91, 209
silhouettes, 75–76
spatial characteristics of, 90
three-dimensional, 82
Shapiro, Joel, 24–25, 69, 82
Shots (Way), 207–208
Siena, James, 241–242
Siena (Carter), 82–83
Sighting, 43
Sighting viewers, 188
Sikander, Shahzia, 168, 244
Silhouettes, 75–76
Silver Rider (Hammond), 11
Simulated texture, 150, 153, 164
Singer, Deborah, 241
Site Plan for Grand Buildings Project (Hadid), 13
Sketchbook projects, 48
automatic drawing, 50
blind contour-line drawing, 49–50
color, 174–175
continuous-line drawing, 49
gestural line drawings, 49
line, 141
organizational-line drawing, 49
perspective, 199–200
picture plane, 220–221
shapes, 90
space folder, 66
texture, 164–165
thematic development, 237–238
value, 113
Sketchbooks, 258, 263–273
choosing, 263–264
reasons for, 264–268
subjects for, 268–273
Skull, 12
Slightly Hysterical Perspective (Wiley), 199
Sloan, Jeanette Pasin, 150, 151
Smith, Kiki, 93, 94, 161, 162, 281, 283
Smithson, Robert, 266
Smoke from Chimneys, Automatic Drawing from Rue Blainville (Kelly), 116–117
Snowden, Mary, 246–247
Social commentary, 120
Social themes, 248
Soul Has Bandaged Moments, The (Dill), 231–232, 234
Souvenir (Weber, Wagner, and Mees), 227–228
Souza, Al, 212

Space. *See also* perspective
ambiguous, 59, 75
categories of, 55–59
conventionalized, 55
electronic, 63
emotive, 63–65
hierarchical, 54, 55
levels of, 34
pictorial, 53, 55
stacked, 53
symbolic, 55
value used to describe, 108–110
Space-Is-Concrete (Tuttle), 244
Spatial ambiguities, 52, 53, 59, 137
Spatial arrangements, 56–59
Spatial characteristics
of color, 174
of line, 139–141
of shape, 90
of texture, 164
of value, 112
Spatial development, twentieth-century innovations, 59–63
Spatial notation, 22
Spatial response, development of, 52–55
Speechless (Neshat), 231, 232
Spindler-Gunnell, Kristine, 68, 76
Spiral Jetty (Smithson), 266, 267
Split Infinity (Bochner), 195
Sponges, 260
Spout (Crimmins), 236
Stacked perspective, 196–197
Stacked space, 53
Stackhouse, Robert, 209–210
Staffa—Untitled (McKeever), 122
Starling (Ford), pl. 7.10
Steinberg, Leo, 62, 179
Steinberg, Saul, 14, 15
Steir, Pat, 209, 215
Stele (Rockburne), 84
Stella, Frank, 206
Stern, David, 34
Still Life (Giacometti), 42–43
Still Life (Hauptman), 94
Still Life with Warhol and Leonardo (Levi), 234–235
Stippling, 99
Stopped-frame compositions, 216
Structural analysis, 101
Structural line, 131–132
Structure, value used to describe, 101
Studies for an Allegory of Painting (Desiderio), 266
Studio dal vero (Serse), 146
Study for Falling Dog (Alÿs), 158, 160